IMAGES
of America

SOUTH PASS CITY
AND THE SWEETWATER MINES

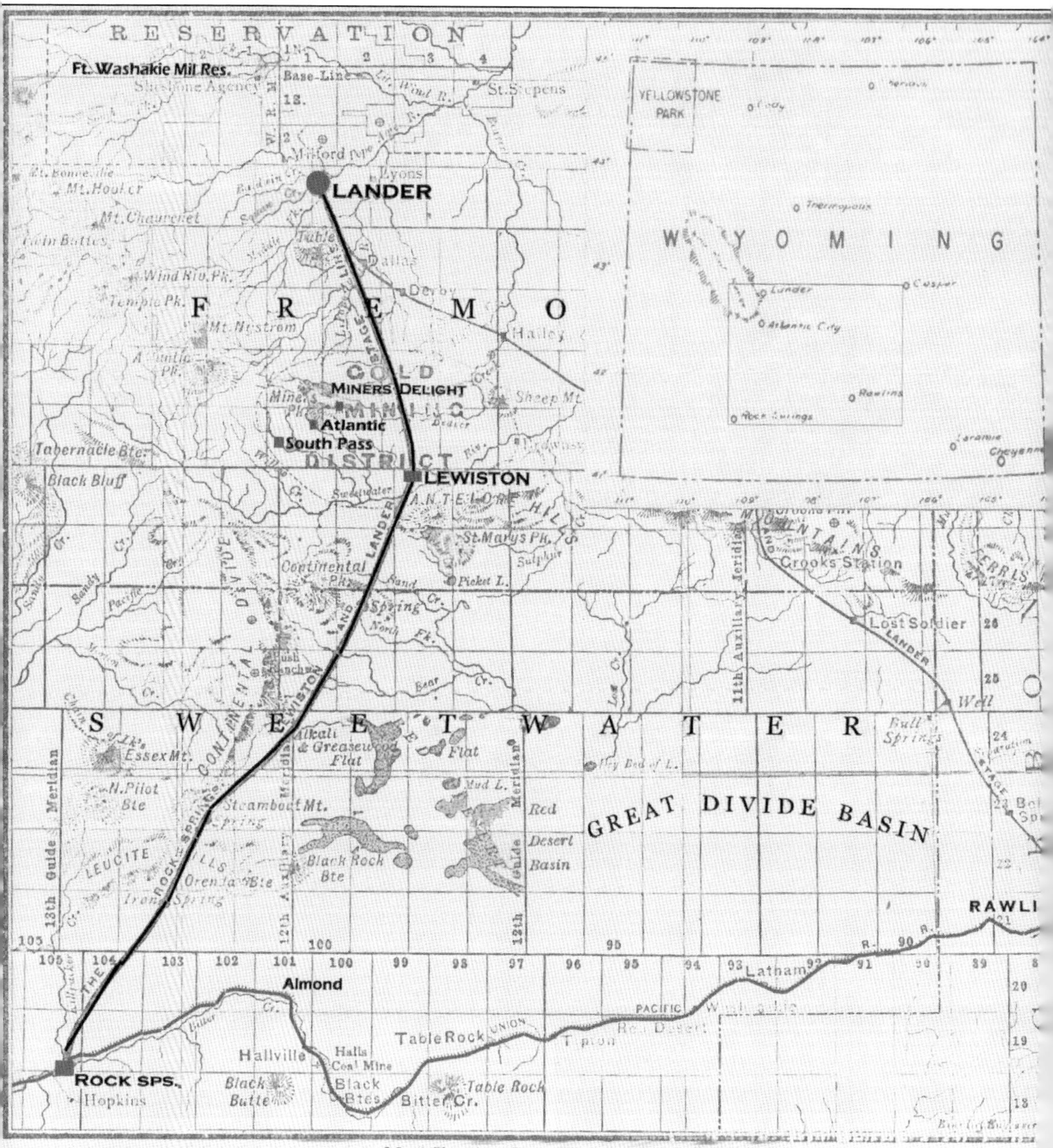

Map Showing Stage Routes and Gold Fields

The location of "South Pass City and the Sweetwater Mines" is at the foot of the Wind River Mountains. (Courtesy of South Pass City State Historic Site.)

ON THE COVER: Barney Tibbals, mine manager, and Federal Gold Mining Company Mill are pictured in 1899. (Courtesy of South Pass City State Historic Site.)

IMAGES
of America

SOUTH PASS CITY
AND THE SWEETWATER MINES

Jon Lane and Susan Layman

ARCADIA
PUBLISHING

ISBN 978-0-7385-8893-3

Published by Arcadia Publishing
Charleston, South Carolina

Printed in the United States of America

Library of Congress Control Number: 2011928293

For all general information, please contact Arcadia Publishing:
Telephone 843-853-2070
Fax 843-853-0044
E-mail sales@arcadiapublishing.com
For customer service and orders:
Toll-Free 1-888-313-2665

Visit us on the Internet at www.arcadiapublishing.com

Because of the "Hangers-on"

Contents

ACKNOWLEDGMENTS

Thank you to the Friends of South Pass for their support and Betty Pfaff and Steve Gyorvary for their input and primary documents.

All images are property of South Pass City State Historic Site, with the exceptions listed: Betty Pfaff, John Boulette, Joneta Sommers, Sweetwater County Museum, US Geological Service, Wyoming State Archives, Wyoming Pioneer Museum, Curtis Turrill, Wallace Grosvenor, Mike McClure, Edwina Anderson, North Platte Valley Museum, the Faler family, the Snowden family, Rock Springs Historical Museum, the Sherlock family, and Charles and Marian Michaelis.

INTRODUCTION

South Pass is unique. While the first overland passage across the Continental Divide in the northern Rocky Mountains was pioneered by Lewis and Clark's Corps of Discovery through Montana's Bitterroot Range, their route was too demanding to provide for the westward expansion of an entire nation. Within a handful of years, an expedition by the Pacific Fur Company crossed the Divide from west to east across a new pass far to the south. For years, however, fur trappers continued to follow the Missouri River far to the north, as had Lewis and Clark.

However, in the early 1820s, Jedediah Smith reinforced the commercial potential of the "south pass," as he quickly crossed from the Great Plains into the drainage of the Green River, and beyond to the Valley of the Great Salt Lake. Almost immediately, Capt. Benjamin Bonneville's military expedition followed, demonstrating the relative ease with which wagons could cross the South Pass. In years to come, hundreds of thousands of emigrants followed. For an entire nation, South Pass became the literal and figurative gateway to the possibilities of what lay beyond.

Rumors of earlier gold discoveries along the Sweetwater River dated to the 1840s, but the promise of greater reward involving less risk had always led gold seekers to focus elsewhere. Beginning in the 1860s, scattered handfuls of frontier military personnel were assigned to protect telegraph lines, Pony Express stations, and emigrant trails in the South Pass area. The first sizable gold excitement in the South Pass region took place when a party of men out of Fort Bridger located the Cariso Lode in June 1867. The mining region quickly came to be generally known as the Sweetwater Mines in early written accounts. The first boom only lasted a couple of seasons, but helped establish the minerals extraction industry as the foundation for Wyoming's economy from that time forward.

The initial gold rush was followed quickly by a prolonged bust as eager miners and investors were rudely acquainted with the realities of profitably working the Sweetwater Mines. Many early boomers instead sought their fortunes through agriculture on the seemingly endless tracts of nearby public ground open to homesteading. Others saw opportunity as merchants, professionals, or as government workers. Always though, there were those committed to a belief in the future of the mines. Their fidelity was rewarded as cycles of national prosperity and optimism resulted in the periodic revival of dormant mine properties. Local men obtained regular work, support industries like timber cutting and freighting surged, and the anticipation of lasting good times ahead convinced even discouraged old timers to hold on a bit longer.

While the opening and settlement of a new country, like the South Pass area, may be portrayed in some accounts as the result of a single event or discovery, the true story is usually more involved. Inevitably, events are recorded years after they occur, and usually only then by a small segment of those actually involved. Most of those present for events which, in retrospect, are considered to have been significant, simply leave no record at all. As a result, history is often incomplete, fragmented, and difficult to comprehend. Yet, just as Jedediah Smith "rediscovered" the geographic South Pass after it had been nearly forgotten, the exploration for the forgotten stories of South Pass City and the Sweetwater Mines continues.

One

THE BOOM

The gold rush of 1868 to the Sweetwater Mines was an episode of explosive growth, exploration, and development in the span of only a year or two. At the time, only two forces on the Western frontier were capable of initiating such dynamic migration—gold and the railroad. While South Pass had been the major corridor of overland emigration for three decades, it had never been a destination for settlement until the discovery of economic amounts of gold. As long as the gold remained abundant and easy to collect, the Sweetwater Mines boomed. Experienced gold rushers who had seen other Western mining booms quickly realized that the future of the district was not bright and began to move on almost immediately.

Gold rush towns cater to gold miners, providing all of the necessary mining implements, clothing, hardware, and entertainment required by a largely male workforce. Sawmills were erected to provide building materials. General merchandise stores stocked tools, explosives, foodstuffs, and even a few luxury items. Blacksmiths sharpened and tempered drill steels, fabricated parts, and shoed horses. Saloons, gaming parlors, and houses of prostitution flourished in an environment shaped by grueling physical labor, seemingly random fortune, and the limitless possibilities associated with thousands of anonymous strangers coming together for the purpose of making a fortune overnight.

The gold rush to the Sweetwater Mines ended almost as soon as it began. Many participants returned to family farms, businesses, and industry after they had "seen the elephant" in the gold rush camps of South Pass. A very few stayed in the area, convinced in the wealth hidden beneath their feet. Some moved to nearby towns based on farming and ranching. Others participated in rushes to new mining camps across the West.

When the Union Pacific Rail Road bypassed South Pass in favor of the Red Desert with its transcontinental line at nearly the same time that the gold ran out, the fate of the Sweetwater Mines seemed certain. However, other chapters remained to be written.

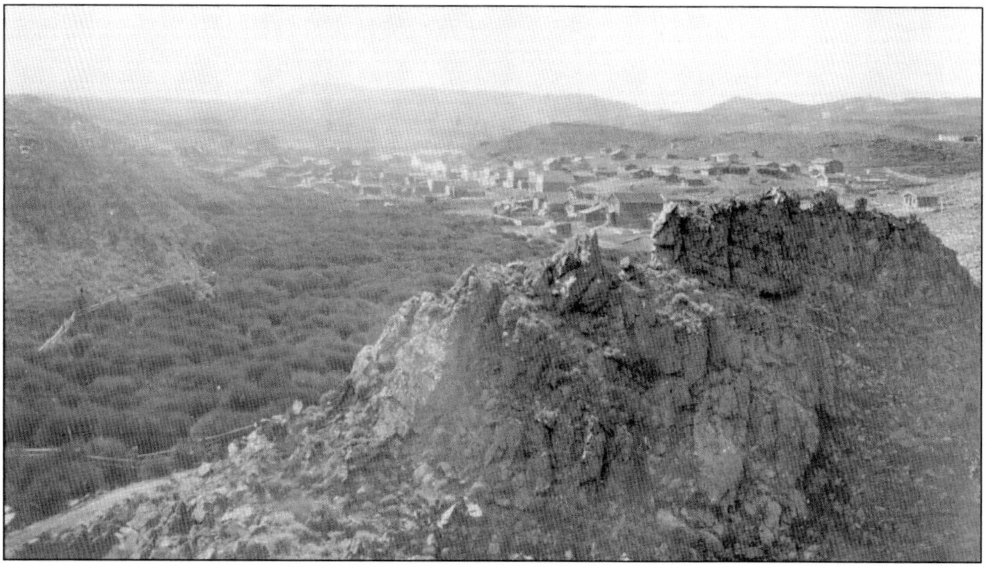

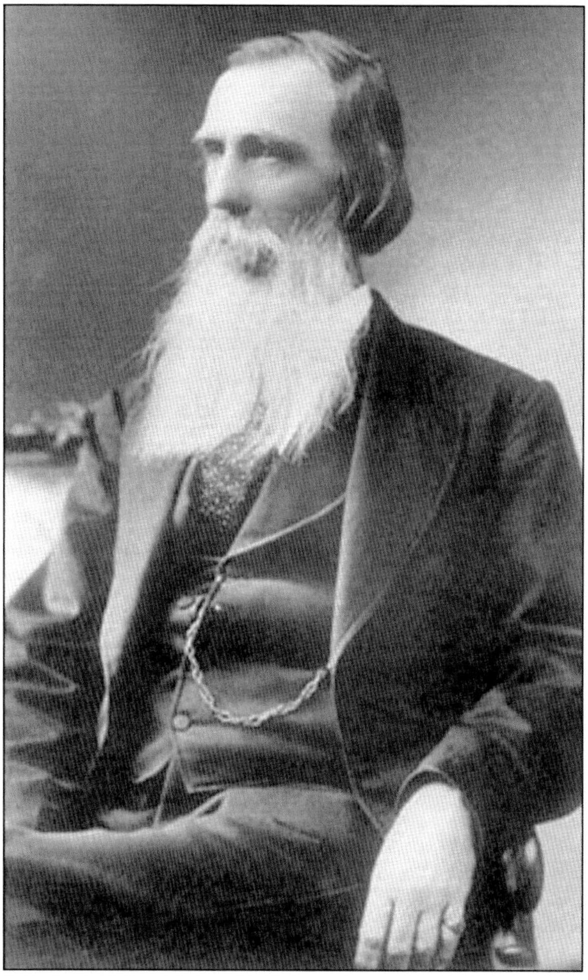

SOUTH PASS CITY. William Henry Jackson documented much of the West with his camera. His 1869 photograph of South Pass City is the only one known of a valley crowded with structures that, two years earlier, had been without a single cabin. Most new camps followed the boom and bust pattern of early fortune quickly followed by complete famine.

JUDGE WILLIAM A. CARTER. As post trader at Fort Bridger, Carter was strategically positioned at the crossroads of emigrant travel, military activity, and commerce. From surviving accounts and documents, it is apparent that Carter, also a justice of the peace, was one of the early promoters of the Sweetwater Mines. As the gold rush of 1868 swelled populations in the area, representatives petitioned Dakota Territory lawmakers in Yankton to create a new county for the benefit of the people and the governance of the remote region. Carter County, Dakota Territory, with its county seat located at South Pass City, was soon established.

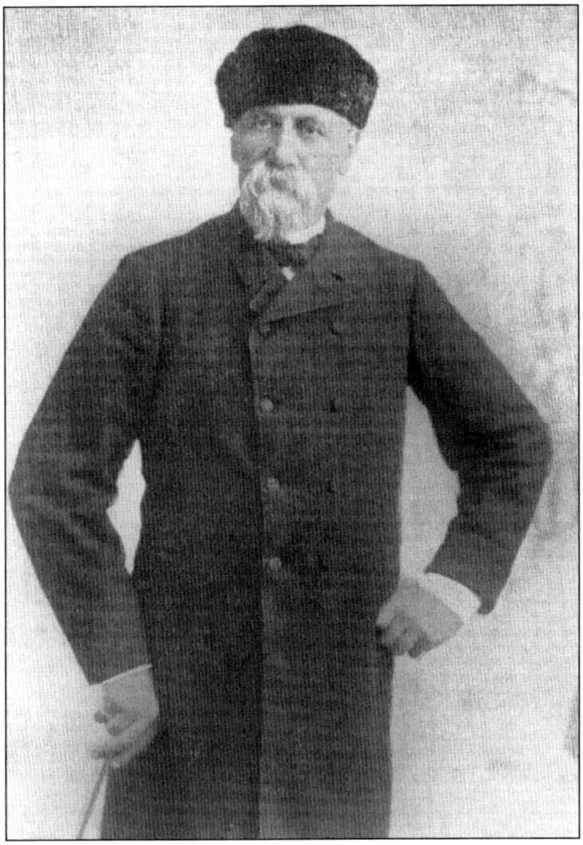

Eugene Amoretti. The Italian-born businessman arrived in South Pass City on July 4, 1868. His numerous enterprises included mining properties, a stamp mill, and several mercantile businesses. The 1870 census identifies him simply as a retail grocer. Amoretti established stores in South Pass City, Atlantic City, Miners Delight, and eventually, the budding agricultural town of Lander. He was Lander's first mayor, a member of the state legislature, and donor of the land upon which the Fremont County government buildings now stand.

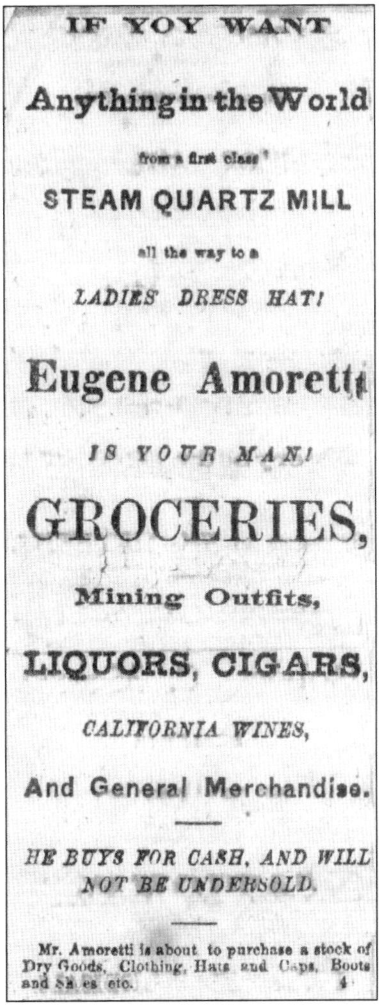

IF YOY WANT

Anything in the World

from a first class

STEAM QUARTZ MILL

all the way to a

LADIES DRESS HAT!

Eugene Amoretti

IS YOUR MAN!

GROCERIES,

Mining Outfits,

LIQUORS, CIGARS,

CALIFORNIA WINES,

And General Merchandise.

HE BUYS FOR CASH, AND WILL NOT BE UNDERSOLD.

Mr. Amoretti is about to purchase a stock of Dry Goods, Clothing, Hats and Caps, Boots and Shoes etc. 4

South Pass News, June 28, 1871. Amoretti, like other merchants in remote areas, publicly boasted of the wide variety of goods to be had at his establishment.

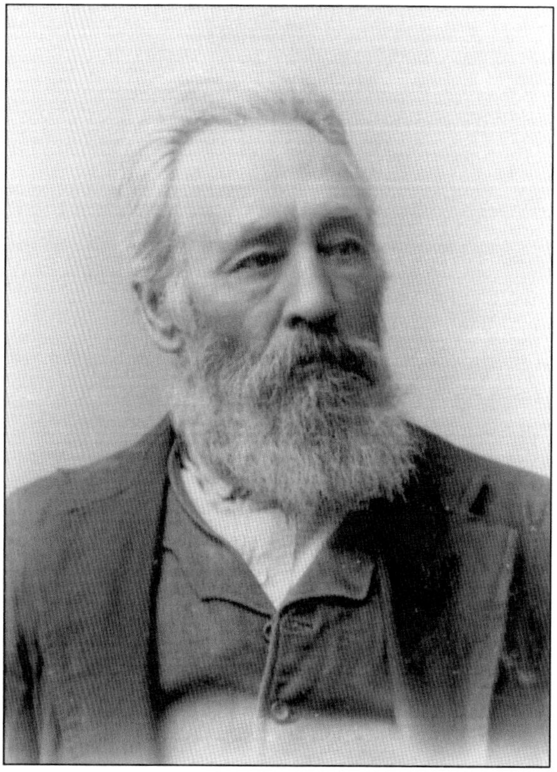

William "Boss" Tweed. Tweed, who was born in England, was the first to bring his family to South Pass City. His wife, Sarah, and children arrived with him in the early spring of 1868. In August of that year, Tweed was wounded in an Indian attack on freight wagons making their way to the mining camps with provisions. Tweed survived, and spent another season or two in South Pass City before moving to nearby Red Canyon to establish a successful farm and ranch.

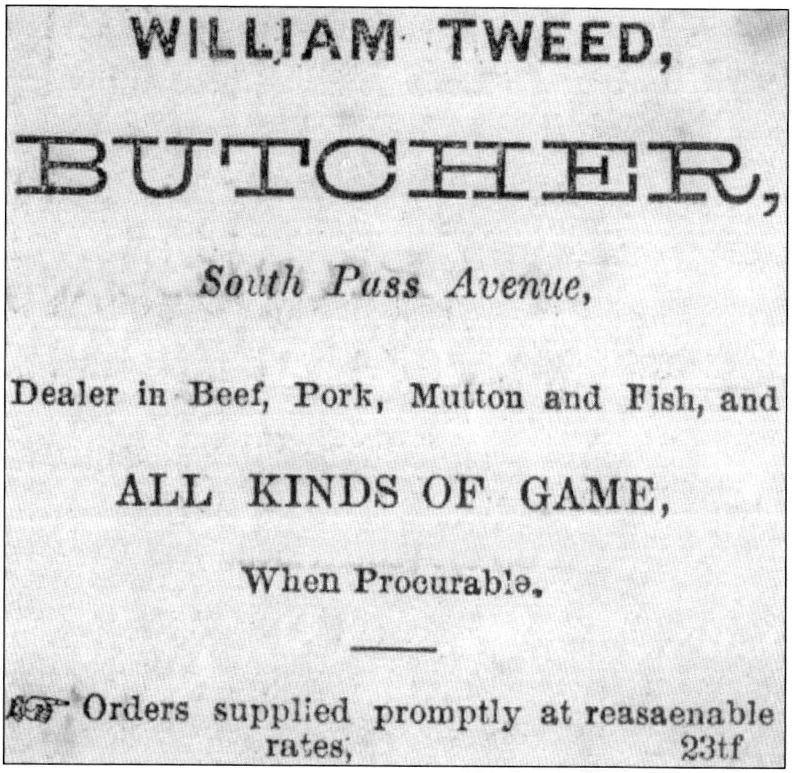

WILLIAM TWEED,

BUTCHER,

South Pass Avenue,

Dealer in Beef, Pork, Mutton and Fish, and

ALL KINDS OF GAME,

When Procurable.

Orders supplied promptly at reasaenable rates; 23tf

South Pass News, April 5, 1871. Tweed's advertisement in the *South Pass News* reminds readers that, like most meat markets of the time, wild game was often made available through the efforts of market hunters.

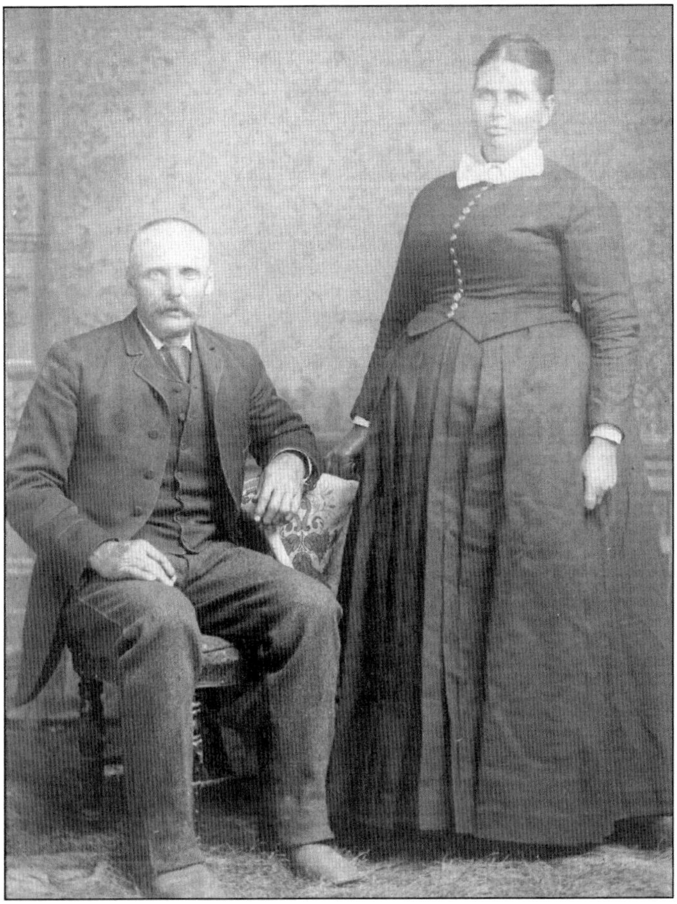

JOHN AND LUCY REID. Reid was born and raised in Indiana, serving with the 87th Indiana Volunteers in the Civil War. Attracted by the flurry of activity created by the gold rush of 1968, Reid set up a blacksmith shop in the area. Later, Reid engaged in freighting wood and hay for the military forts in the area. Reid homesteaded a tract of land between Red Canyon and Lander, located on Willow Creek. (Courtesy of Lander Pioneer Museum.)

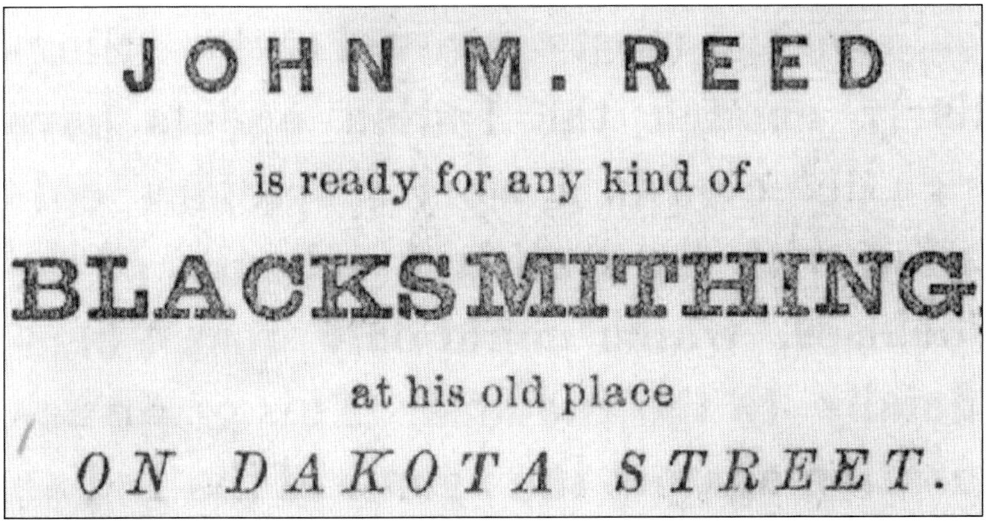

JOHN M. REED

is ready for any kind of

BLACKSMITHING,

at his old place

ON DAKOTA STREET.

SOUTH PASS NEWS, SEPTEMBER 7, 1871. In high demand, blacksmiths alone could fabricate and repair the wide array of metal objects needed in remote mining districts far from heavy industry and factories. Particularly, miners relied upon blacksmiths to sharpen and temper the drills they used to bore blast holes into the area's gold-bearing rock.

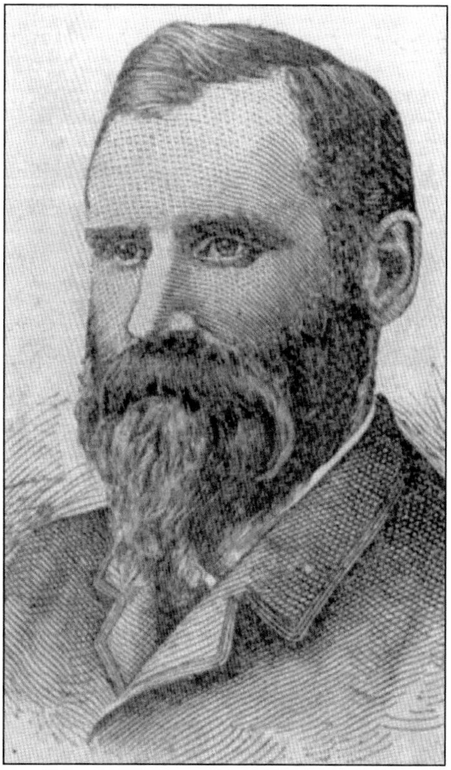

JAMES A. MCAVOY. Born in 1842 in Cambridge, Ohio, McAvoy freighted between Ohio and Baltimore before railroads were constructed. He later came to Wyoming as a clerk for the Union Pacific Railroad. After finishing the section on which he was engaged, McAvoy decided to investigate the South Pass gold country, arriving in 1869. McAvoy mined in the area for two years. Around 1873, he partnered with fellow gold-rusher John Reid in a potato farm outside Lander. Two out of three years' crops were destroyed by grasshoppers. In 1900, McAvoy and his partners secured a patent on the Diana Lode gold claim outside Atlantic City.

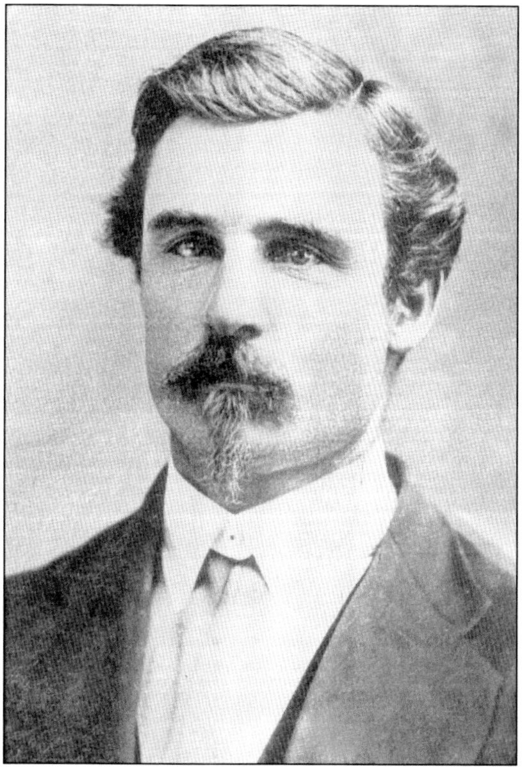

FINCELIUS G. "FINN" BURNETT. Born in April 1844, in Lewis County, Missouri, Burnett served in the Confederacy in the Civil War with the Monticello Grays. After the war, he went west in the Powder River Expedition led by General Conner. In 1869, he settled in South Pass City. He married Eliza A. McCarty in Atlantic City on March 2, 1870. In 1871, Burnett ended his time at the Sweetwater Mines.

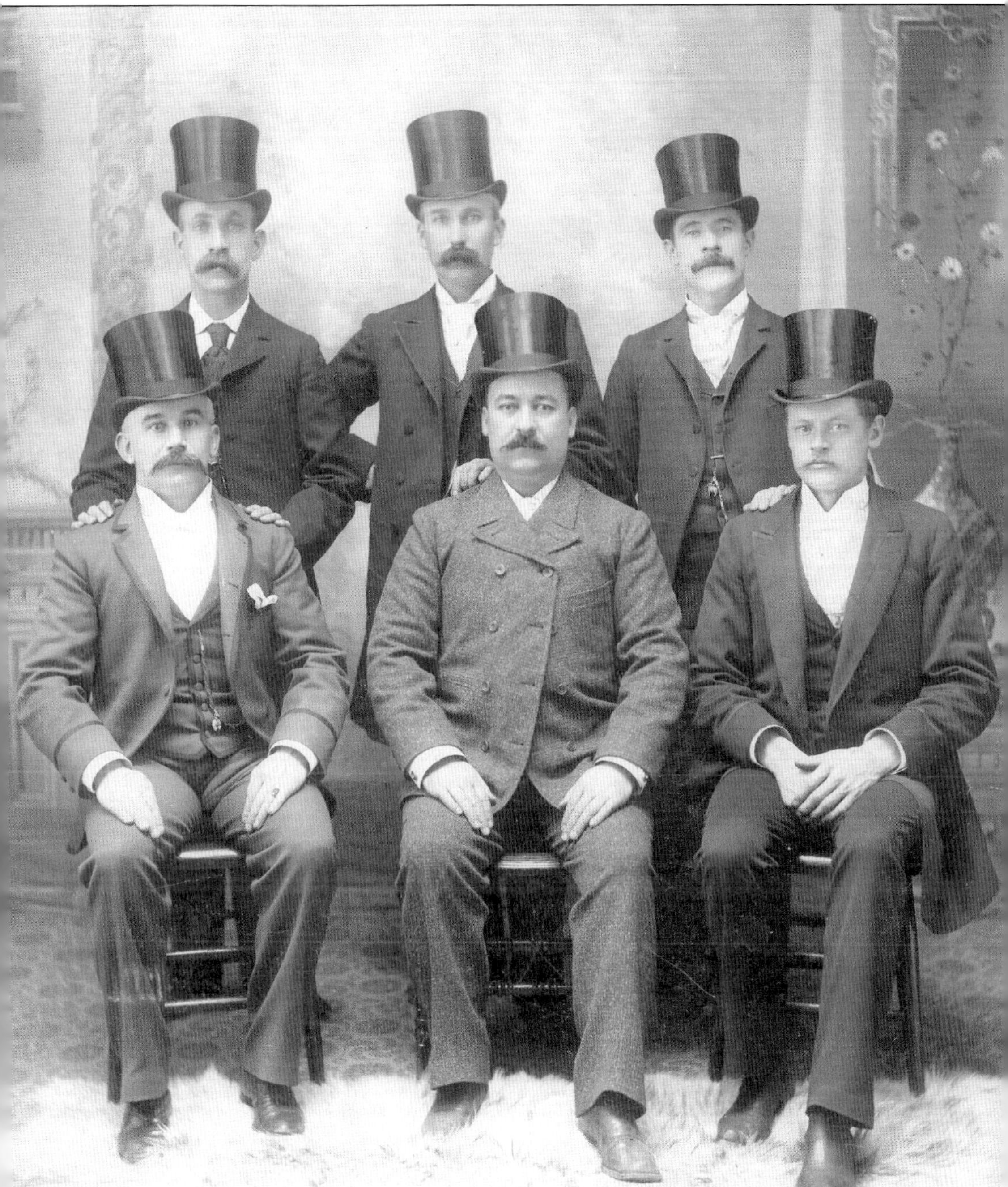

ROCK SPRINGS CITY COUNCIL, DECEMBER 1893. Charles Swanson is seated in the center. Swanson was born in Sweden in 1860. He immigrated to Wisconsin in 1878,where he was employed as a logger. He began his mining career in 1880 when he moved to Telluride, Colorado. By 1885, Swanson had come to the South Pass area where he opened The White Swan saloon. He left South Pass after 1887 and went to Blairtown, Wyoming, where he again operated a saloon. Swanson was elected to the Wyoming Legislature in 1896.

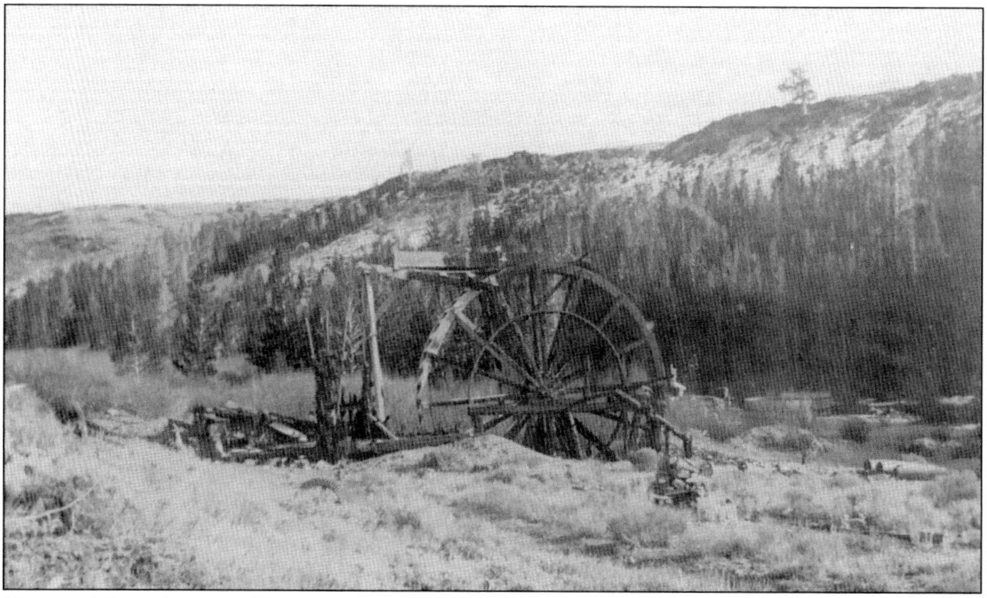

Carissa Mill: Sunday, November 13, 1898. A short distance below South Pass City on Willow Creek, only the waterwheel remained of the Carissa Mill after a July 1896 fire. During the early 1870s, the mill had crushed the ores of several nearby mines, including the Carissa and the Carrie Shields. On September 17, 1896, the *Rock Springs Miner* noted that Frank Sheldon reprocessed the mill's gold rush tailings piles using cyanide solution, which selectively leached the remaining gold from the worthless sands. Sheldon recovered about 75 ounces of gold for his risk in using the lethal chemical.

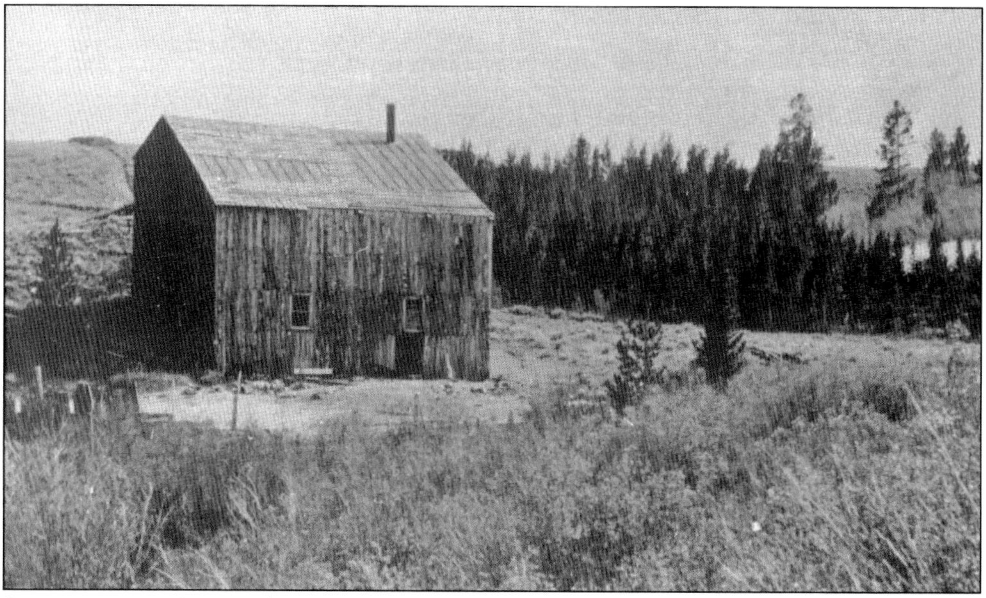

Sturman Mill. During the boom, Moses E. Sturman erected a sawmill on this site. In March 1896, a 10-stamp steam-powered mill was installed by J.J. Marrin and Peter Sherlock. Later still, the mill was purchased by the B&H Mining Company and moved two miles east to Palmetto Gulch. The original stamps from this mill are the last set in the Sweetwater Mines and were moved to South Pass City State Historic Site in 1976 to preserve them.

ALBERT LYMAN HOUGHTON. Born on September 24, 1839, in Massachusetts, he rushed to South Pass City in 1868. Houghton set up a mercantile with Thomas Cotter. Named the Sheriff of Carter County in 1868, Houghton also served as a tax collector. Real estate and mine dealings in 1869 soured Houghton's view of the Sweetwater Mines, for, by the early spring of 1870, records indicate that he was no longer sheriff. Houghton relocated to Manhattan, Kansas, to join his brother in business. In November 1877, Houghton was elected sheriff of Riley County, Kansas; a post that he held honorably for 12 years. (Courtesy of Edwina Anderson.)

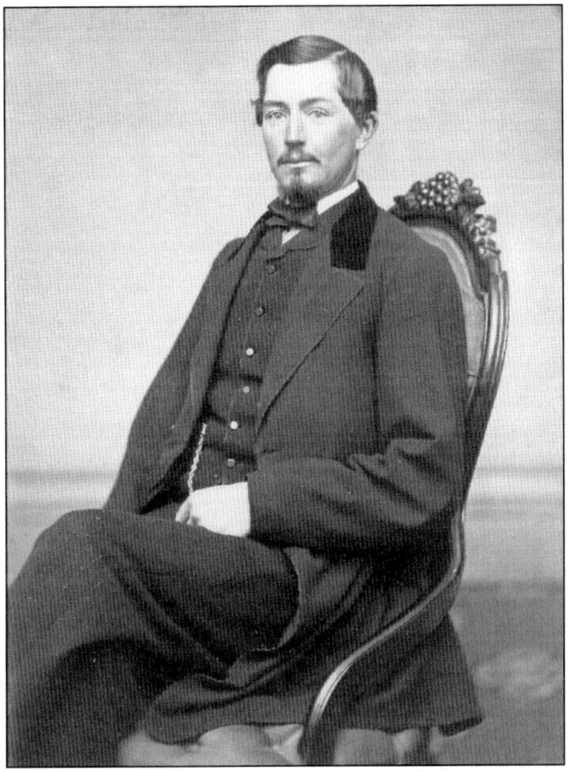

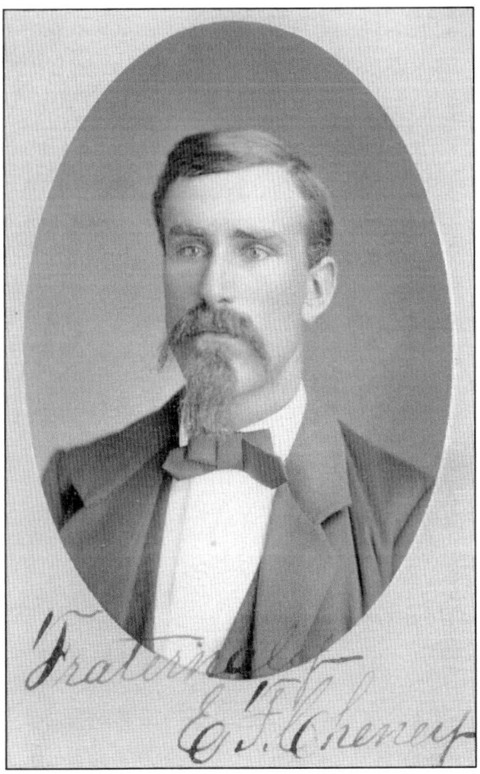

ERVIN F. CHENEY. Born in New York State in 1844, Cheney journeyed to South Pass City in 1869, where he established a wagon and blacksmith shop. Cheney also made coffins for the community. As the promise of the mines faded, Cheney relocated to Lander. A Republican, Cheney served the people of Sweetwater County in the Fifth Legislative Assembly. Following Wyoming statehood in 1900, Cheney was named one of the US Commissioners for Fremont County. (Courtesy of Lander Pioneer Museum.)

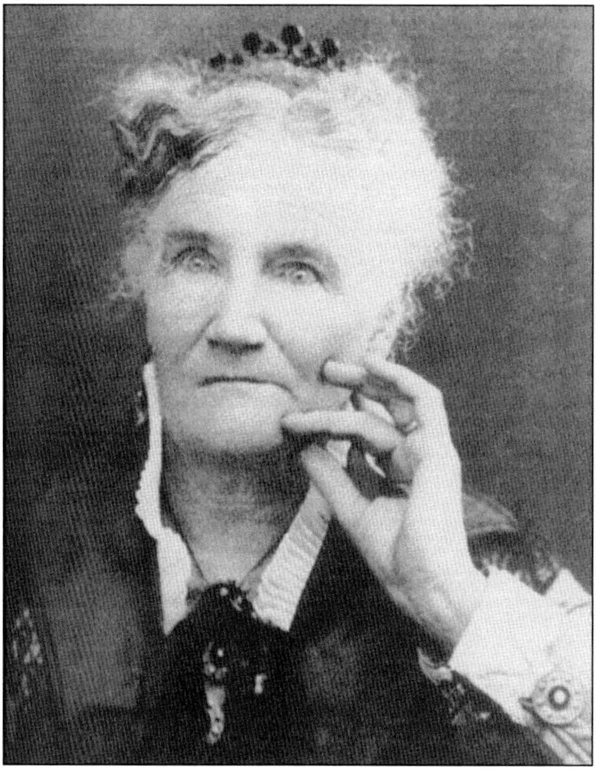

Esther Morris. Born August 8, 1814, in Tioga County, New York, Morris moved to South Pass City with her husband and three sons in 1869. Secretary of State Edward Lee appointed her as justice of the peace in 1870. Morris became the first woman to hold public office in the United States. She served for nine months hearing 26 cases; 12 were criminal and 14 were civil. In 1890, Wyoming entered the Union as the Equality State for being the first to enfranchise women.

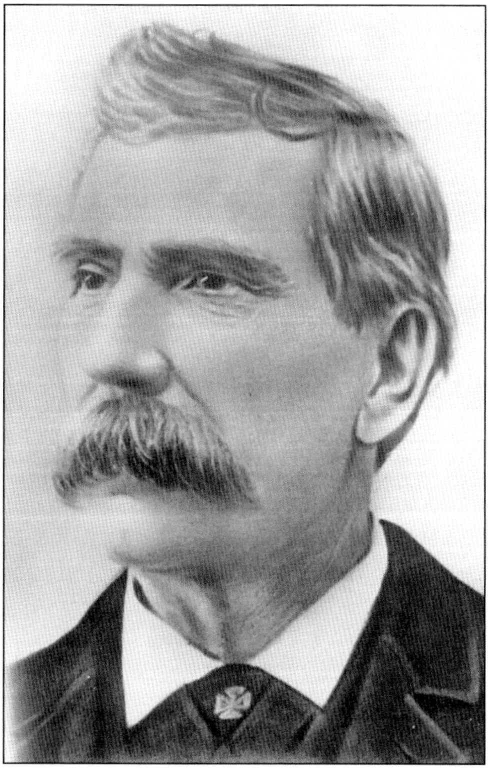

William Bright. A major in the Union Army, the Virginian moved to Salt Lake City after the conflict to serve as a postal inspector. News of gold strikes drew Bright to Miners Delight in 1867, where he served as justice of the peace. There, he operated the Bon Ton Saloon. Bright, a Democrat, won a seat in the First Wyoming Territorial Legislature in 1869. He introduced, and helped pass, a bill enfranchising women.

Edward Archibald "Archy" Slack. The son of Esther Morris by her first marriage to Artemus Slack, "Archy" moved with his mother to Peru, Illinois, after the death of his father. He took work in a print shop and built a lifelong connection with newspapers. Slack served from 1861 to 1864 in the 19th Illinois Infantry. Afterward, he attended Chicago University for two years prior to embarking for South Pass with his stepfather John Morris. Slack's work was diverse; town constable, sawmill operator, newspaper publisher, and clerk of his mother's court. In 1871, Slack moved first to Laramie and then Cheyenne in order to publish newspapers.

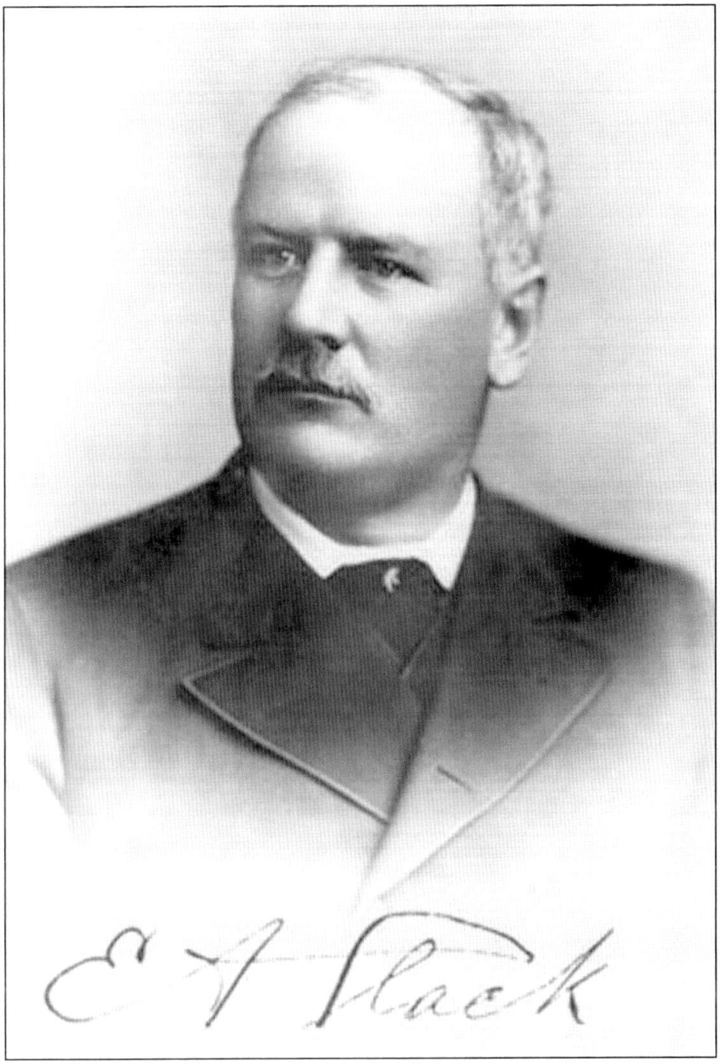

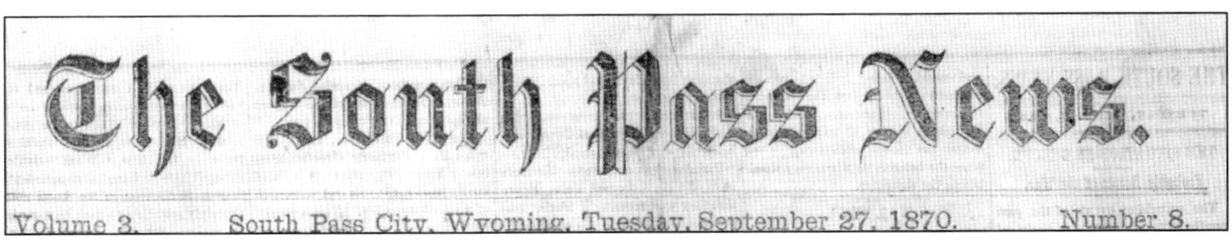

The South Pass News.

Volume 3. South Pass City, Wyoming, Tuesday, September 27, 1870. Number 8.

Frontier Newspaper, 1869–1871. Founded in 1869, the paper was issued twice weekly. It was originally published by Nathan Baker, who also established the *Cheyenne Daily Leader*, Wyoming's first newspaper, and the *Daily Sentinel* in Laramie.

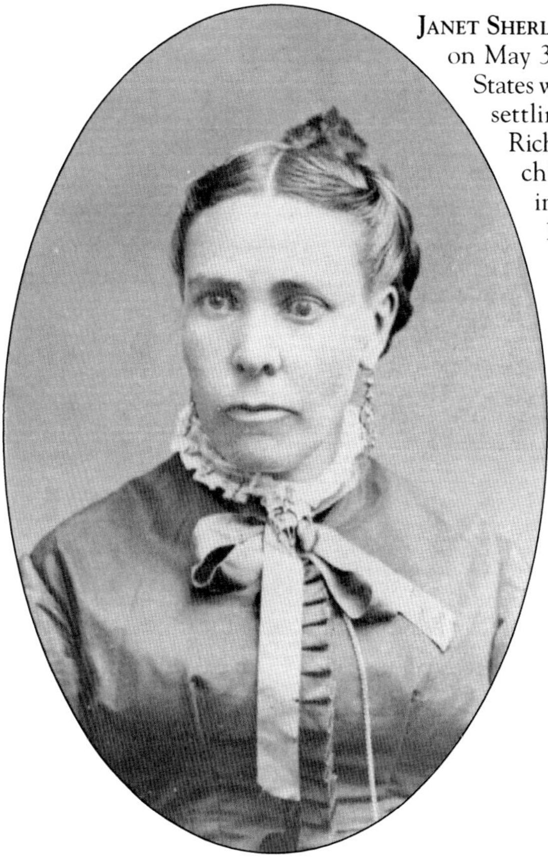

JANET SHERLOCK-SMITH. Born in Edinburgh, Scotland, on May 3, 1844, Janet immigrated to the United States with her brother John and his family in 1861, settling in Salt Lake City, Utah. She married Richard Sherlock on February 3, 1862. Her three children, Maggie, Peter, and Jennie were born in Utah. They moved to South Pass City in 1868, where two more children, John and William, were born. Richard died in 1873. She became the postmistress of South Pass City in 1873, the same year that she purchased the South Pass Hotel. Janet married James Smith in 1875 and they had two children, Anna and James Ernest. In 1895, the couple built the Smith–Sherlock Company Store.

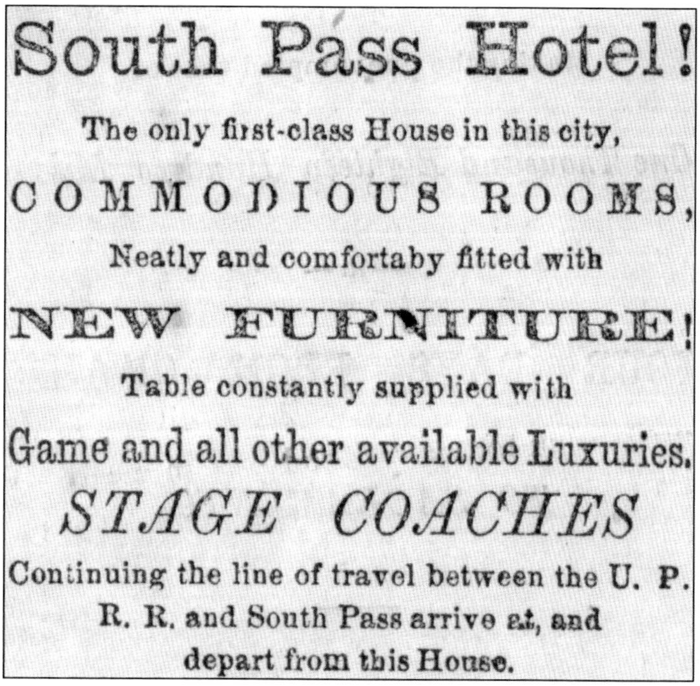

South Pass Hotel!

The only first-class House in this city,

COMMODIOUS ROOMS,

Neatly and comfortaby fitted with

NEW FURNITURE!

Table constantly supplied with

Game and all other available Luxuries.

STAGE COACHES

Continuing the line of travel between the U. P. R. R. and South Pass arrive at, and depart from this House.

SOUTH PASS NEWS, FEBRUARY 8, 1871. Economic opportunities in a gold rush boomtown were limited for the newly widowed mother of five. Friends encouraged her to take over the South Pass Hotel from Catherine Ervin. Hotels were seen as extensions of what was then viewed as a woman's proper place in the home. Relatively safe and sanitary hotels were considered essential to a thriving business community.

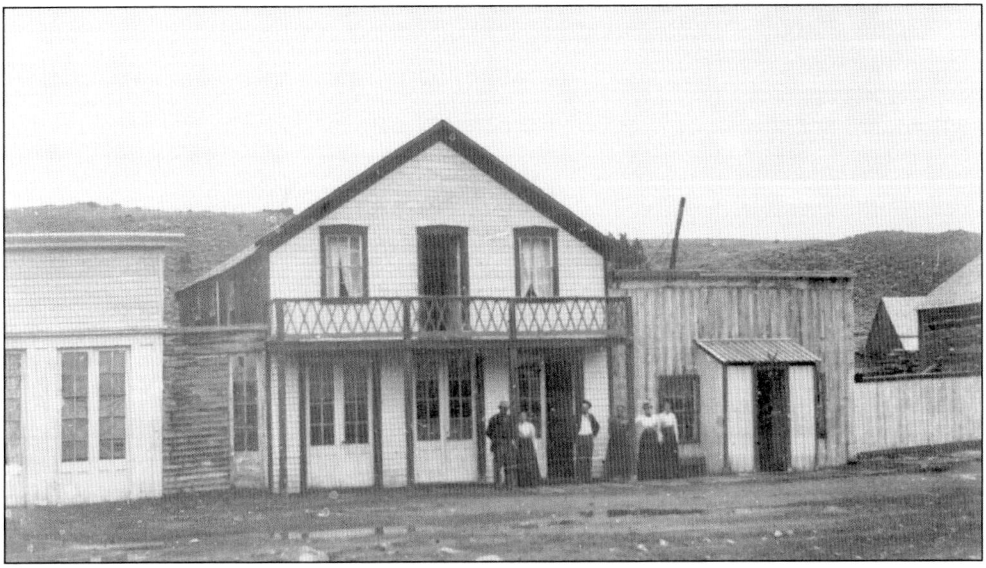

SOUTH PASS CITY, 1899. The buildings pictured are, from left to right, Ervin Store, South Pass Hotel, and Grecian Bend Saloon. Little is known of the Ervin Store building, other than it was a retail grocery during the gold rush and was later used, in part, as a meat locker due to a specially insulated corner of the building. Janet Sherlock bought the hotel from Catherine Ervin in 1873. According to newspaper accounts, the Grecian Bend was "crowded day and night with lovers of good music, and superior brands of liquor and cigars." It was replaced by Janet Sherlock's new restaurant in 1899.

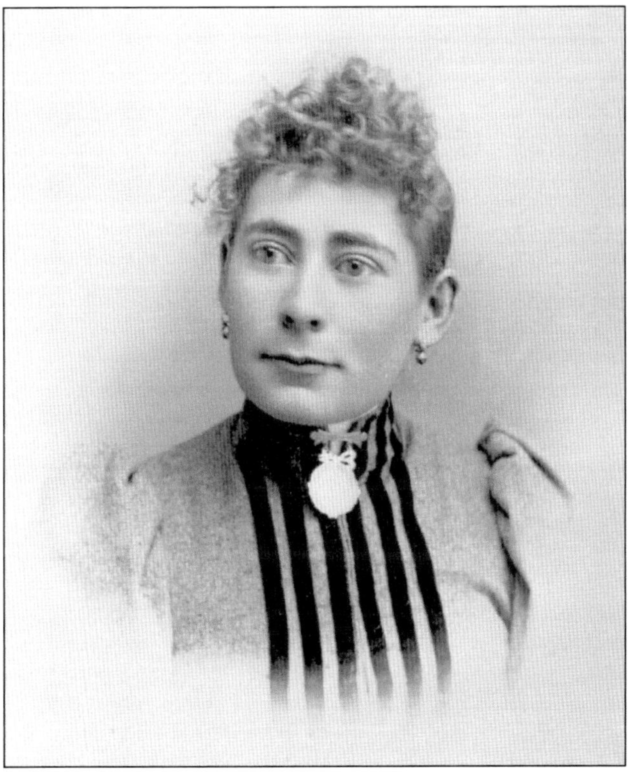

JENNIE SHERLOCK. Born on September 7, 1867, in Salt Lake City, Utah, Jennie came to South Pass City with her family in 1868. She finished primary school in South Pass City, later attending St. Mary's Academy in Salt Lake City. She helped her family to operate the South Pass Hotel and restaurant, as well as the Smith-Sherlock Company Store. Jennie never married. She died in 1938.

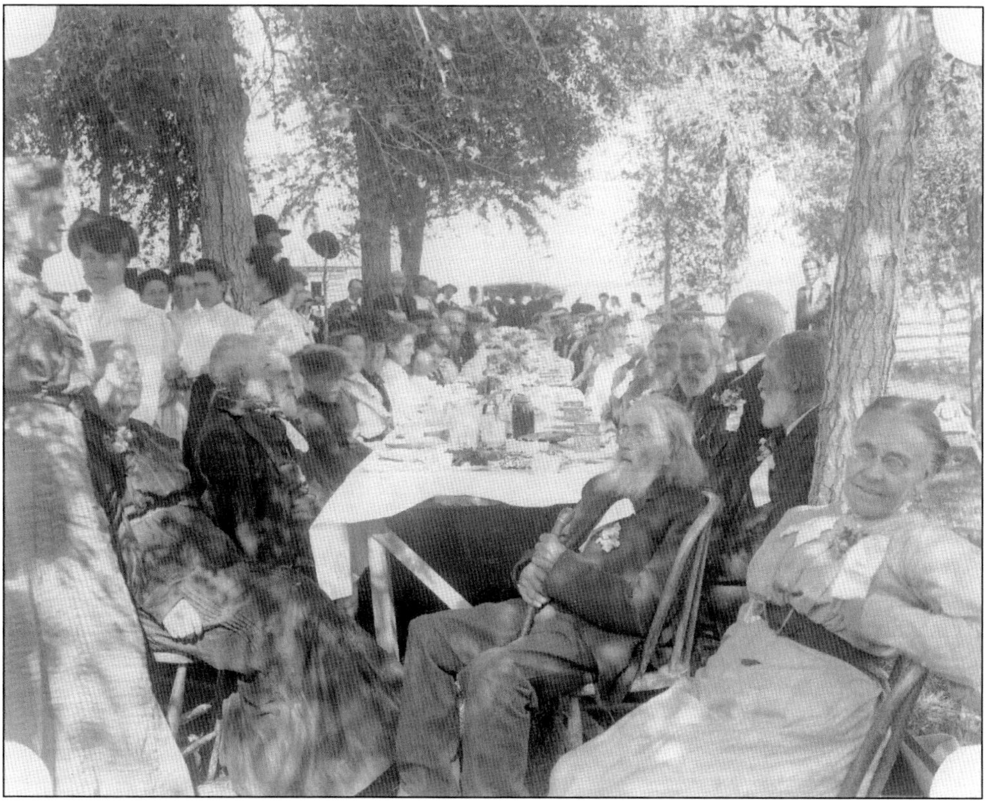

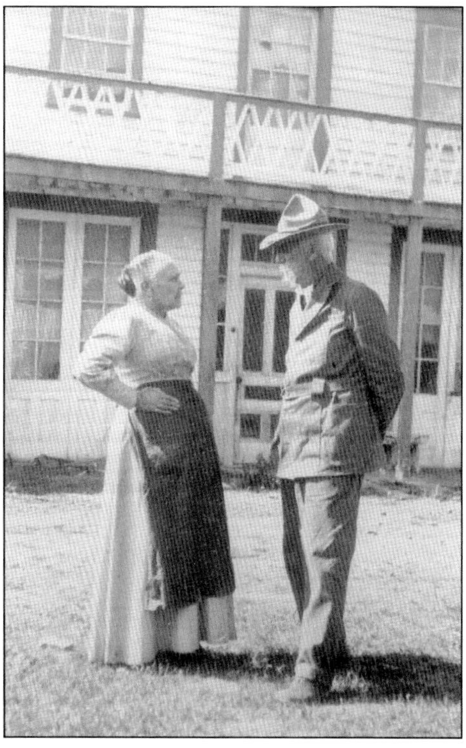

PIONEER PICNIC. Janet Sherlock-Smith is seen in the front right of the photograph. From an early time, the area's founders celebrated their accomplishments in opening up a new territory and putting down roots. Many of them had endured war, hardship on westbound trails, loss of family, and natural disasters in order that their children might reap the rewards. Janet herself lost two husbands, one teenaged child who froze to death, another child that was blinded in a mining blast, and the death of her brother in a saloon shooting.

JANET SHERLOCK-SMITH AND HERMAN NICKERSON, C. 1920. Both had been among the first to the boomtown, and more than half a century later were among the last surviving. Janet had stayed on, enduring, and even prospering, in the place so many others had failed. "Cap" Nickerson was a Civil War veteran turned prospector at Miners Delight. An entry in South Pass City's Exchange Bank Gold Dust Book records a deposit made by Nickerson in 1870.

Two

Federal Gold Mining Company

The Carissa Mine's best documented years of development took place in the years immediately on either side of 1900. Federal Gold Mining Company was the corporate creation of Chicago timber tycoon John C. Spry. Not a mining man himself, Spry entrusted the location and development of a Western mining property with potential to his agent, Barney Tibbals. With some mining experience in Lead and Deadwood, South Dakota, Leadville and Aspen, Colorado, and the Fall River district in Idaho, Tibbals also acquired a modicum of academic training in assay work at the University of Michigan. Tibbals reviewed properties among the Sweetwater Mines, settling on the Carissa by 1897.

Federal Gold Mining Company was the first to erect a mill at the mine site. Its small mill incorporated some of the most recent advances in gold recovery. Underground, Tibbals sank deeper shafts and extended tunnels, or drifts, along thousands of feet of mineralized rock. Wood-fired boilers at the surface powered modern air drills and steam driven pumps, allowing development of the mine on a scale undreamed of by the gold rushers only three decades earlier. Science and technology held great promise at the Carissa.

However, Spry's goal at the Carissa was essentially to improve the property to a point where he could sell out to a buyer who would pay a premium for Federal Gold Mining Company's efforts. Conversely, Tibbals hoped to actually operate the property as an ongoing proposition with himself at the helm. Spry and Tibbals sparred over the future of the Carissa with a predictable outcome. Rather than sink his chances of a quick sale by allowing Tibbals to mine out the rich ore he had exposed, Spry elected to close the mine and leave the valuable ore in place as an enticement to possible buyers. Only the mine pumps were left running.

Federal Gold Mining Company shuttered the property until after Spry's death in 1926. His heirs immediately attempted to unload the property, but Tibbals intervened through the courts. Federal Gold Mining Company's tenure at the Carissa was its most industrious period of combined surface and underground work, but ultimately ended in decades of lawsuits.

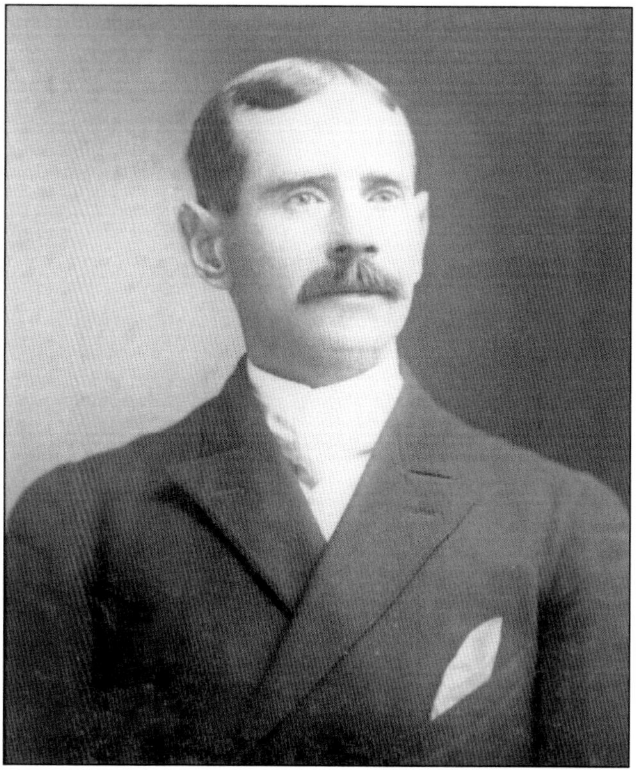

Barney N. Tibbals, 1895. Born on December 18, 1857, in Bay City, Michigan, his first job was in the timber industry as a tally clerk. In 1876, Tibbals joined the Black Hills gold rush, taking the railroad as far as Cheyenne, Wyoming, and then navigating the final 275 miles to the heart of Sioux Indian country on foot. While Tibbals did not strike it rich in the Hills, his enthusiasm for Western mining only grew. Tibbals headed to Leadville, Colorado, with one foot in mining and the other in saloon keeping. In 1896, John C. Spry hired him to locate an undervalued mine that could be made to pay dividends. Tibbals decided on the Carissa Mine and became the driving force in its development.

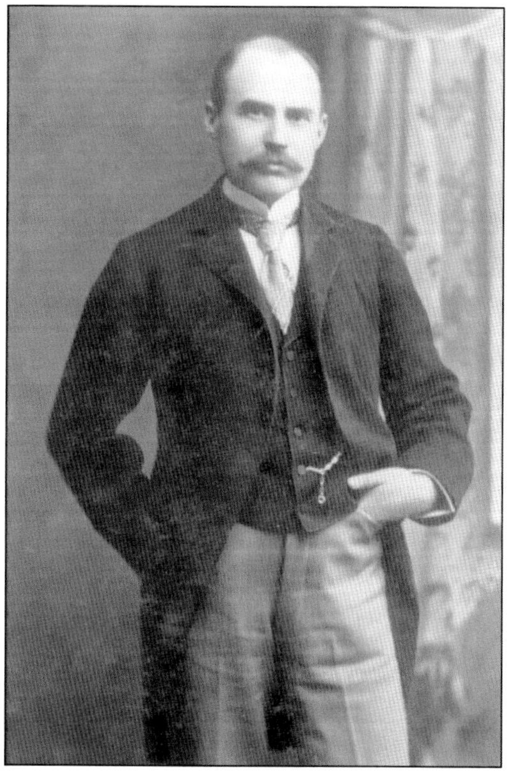

John C. Spry, 1900. Born in Chicago, Illinois, on February 25, 1857, he went on to attend business school. Spry incorporated the John C. Spry Lumber Company in 1891, installing himself as president. The company held extensive wooded tracts and a fleet of lumber hookers shipped the building material to Chicago. His interest in Western mining exceeded his knowledge. After he acquired the Carissa in 1897, Spry invested heavily, became disenchanted with the constant expenditures, and finally closed operations. He owned the mine until his death in 1926.

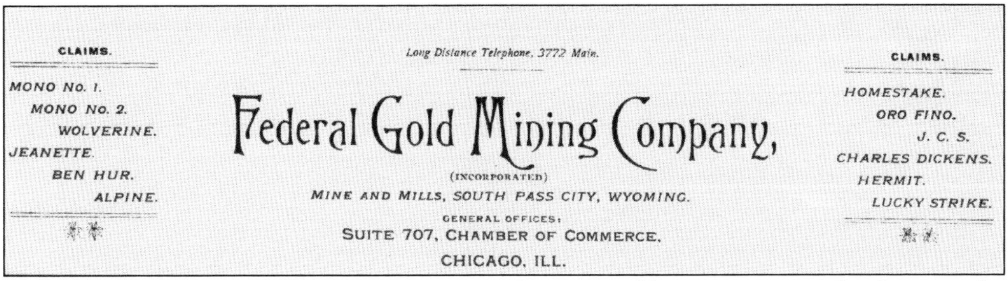

CLAIMS.
MONO No. 1.
MONO No. 2.
WOLVERINE.
JEANETTE.
BEN HUR.
ALPINE.

Long Distance Telephone, 3772 Main.

Federal Gold Mining Company,
(INCORPORATED)
MINE AND MILLS, SOUTH PASS CITY, WYOMING.
GENERAL OFFICES:
SUITE 707, CHAMBER OF COMMERCE,
CHICAGO, ILL.

CLAIMS.
HOMESTAKE.
ORO FINO.
J. C. S.
CHARLES DICKENS.
HERMIT.
LUCKY STRIKE.

FEDERAL GOLD MINING COMPANY LETTERHEAD. Spry wanted his operations at the Carissa to be viewed as first rate. His corporate letterhead lists the mining claims that he consolidated through shrewd dealings with the owners who held them previously. Spry successfully avoided instigating a bidding war by using multiple agents to acquire the properties under their names, and then assuming their interests under his new mining corporation.

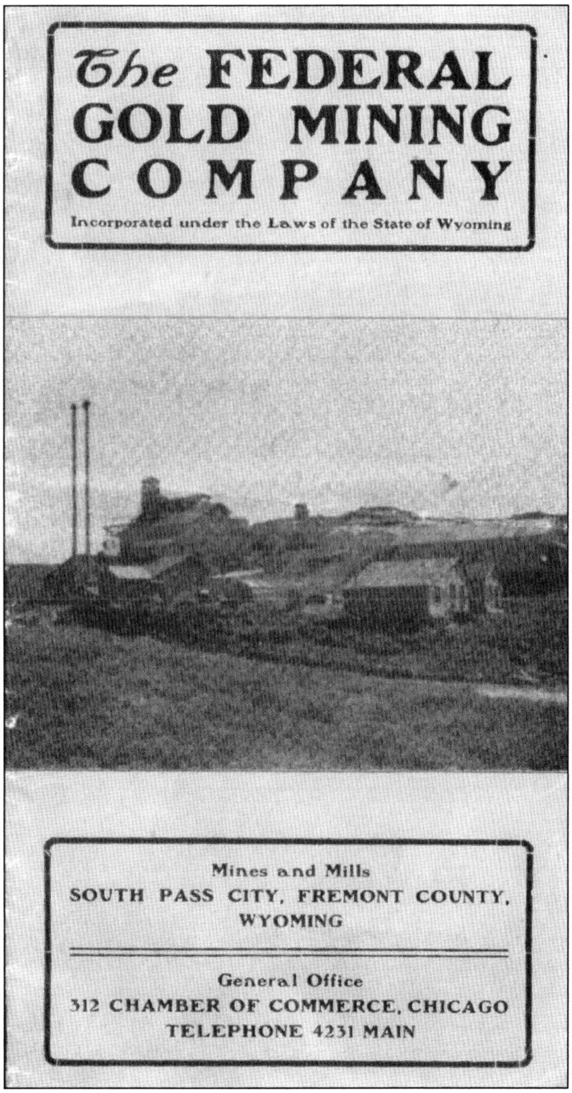

PROSPECTUS, 1901. Investors in the Federal Gold Mining Company could learn of the property with a bit of reading. The cover of the brochure depicts the new mill that Tibbals erected, beginning in 1898. The twin smokestacks funneled exhaust from the locomotive boilers that provided steam to a Corliss engine in the heart of the facility. Smaller structures surrounding the mill include storage sheds, an office building, bunkhouse, and manager's residence.

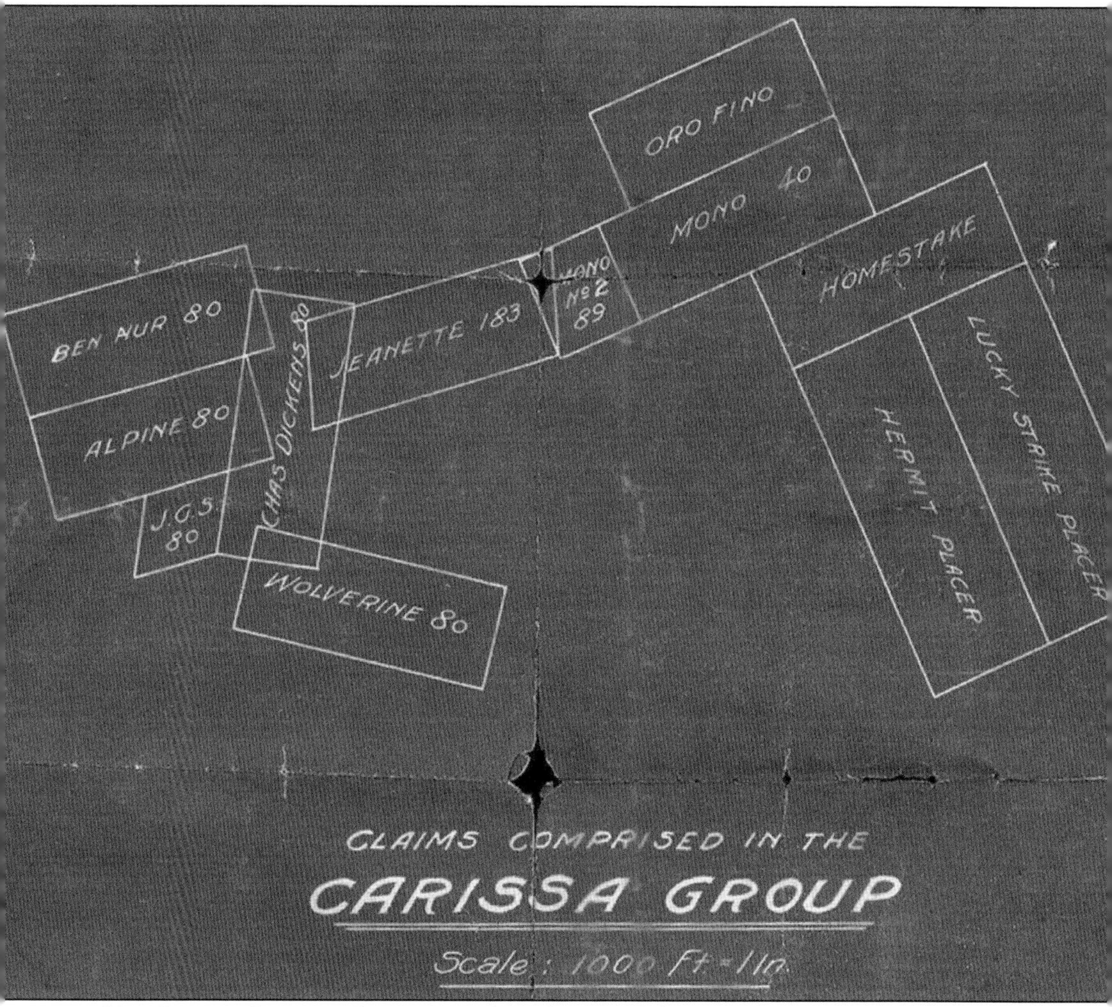

THE CARISSA CLAIMS. The Mono Lode is the site of the Carissa Mine. The Wolverine Lode is essentially the town site of South Pass City. In 1901, Federal allowed the residents of town to buy the ground under their businesses and homes for a nominal amount. The mineral rights to these properties remained with the private owners of the Carissa until the mine itself was purchased by the State of Wyoming in 2003.

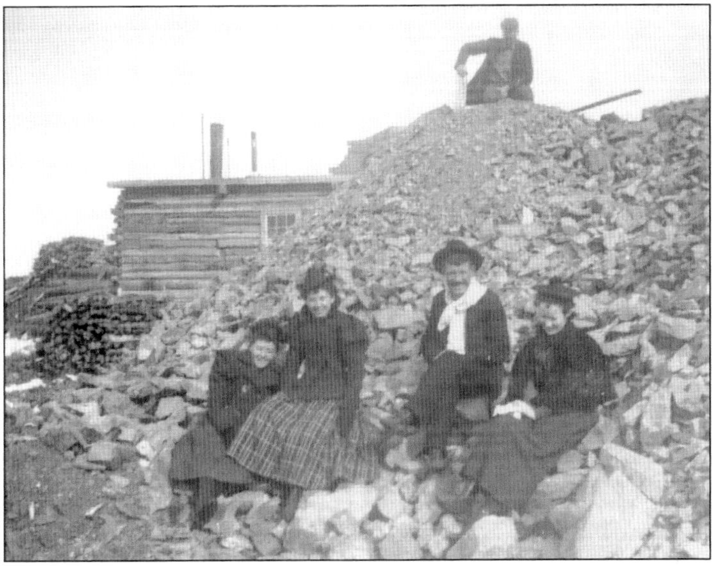

Carissa Mine, 1897. Pictured are, from left to right, two unknown girls, Dan Carmody, and Josie Billcox. The man on the dump is unknown. Evidence of recent work at the Carissa under various lessees and Bolivar Roberts abounds in the ore dumps. A log shaft house and blacksmith shop in the background were modified, or enlarged, under the management of Tibbals.

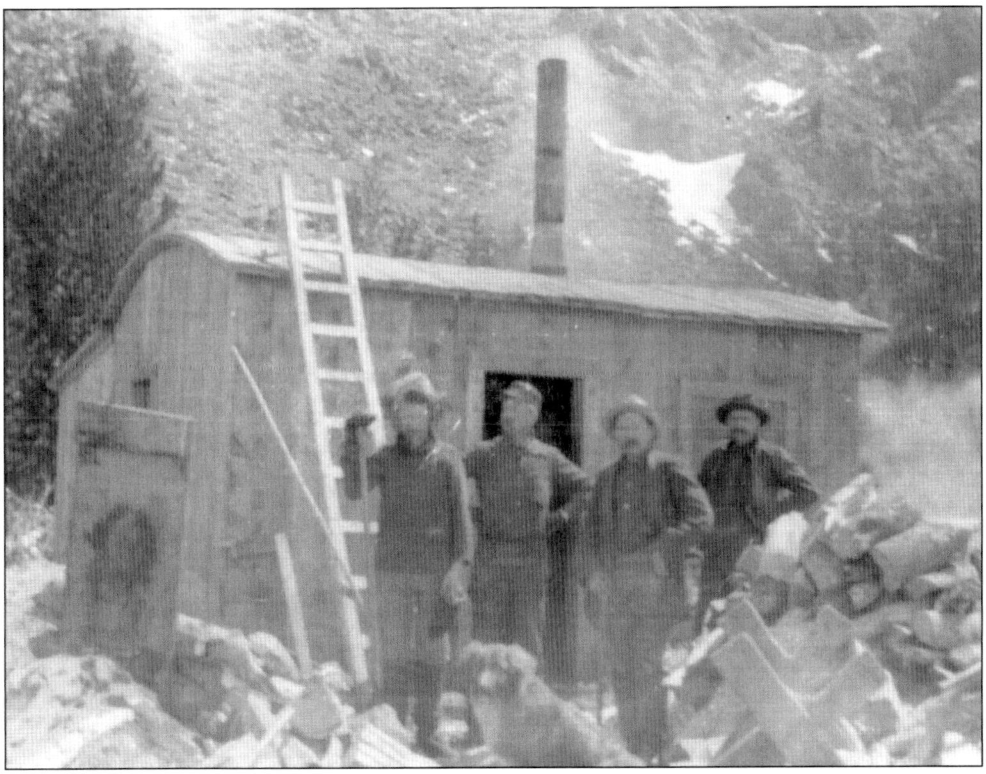

Carissa Mill Pond Pump House, 1900. Pictured are, from left to right, Dan Carmody, Frank Rottgen, Maurice "Casey" Llewellyn, and George Schear. Grinding ore in order to free the gold particles inside required vast quantities of water, but since the Carissa Mine was relatively dry, the company had to locate another source. Neighboring Hermit Gulch was dammed and its waters supplied to the mill from a pipeline filled by pumps housed in this shed.

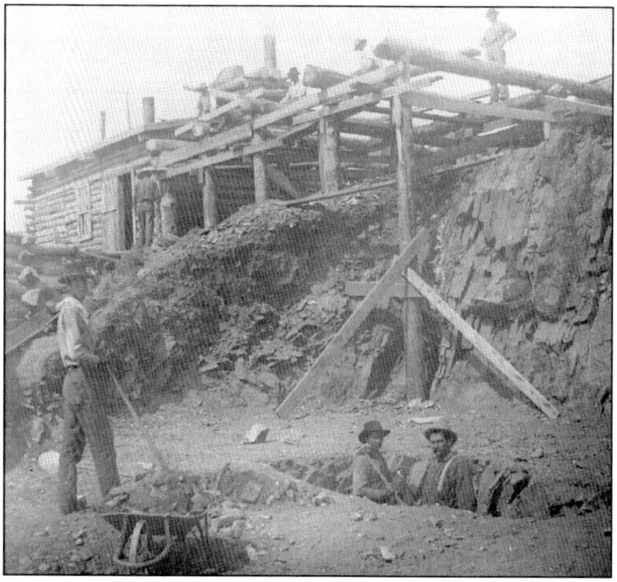

Mill Foundation Work, 1898. Three unidentified men below excavate foundations, possibly in preparation for the 10-stamp quartz mill that Tibbals had specified. Five unidentified men above frame up ore bins. One of the old log mine buildings that belonged to Bolivar Roberts stands in the background.

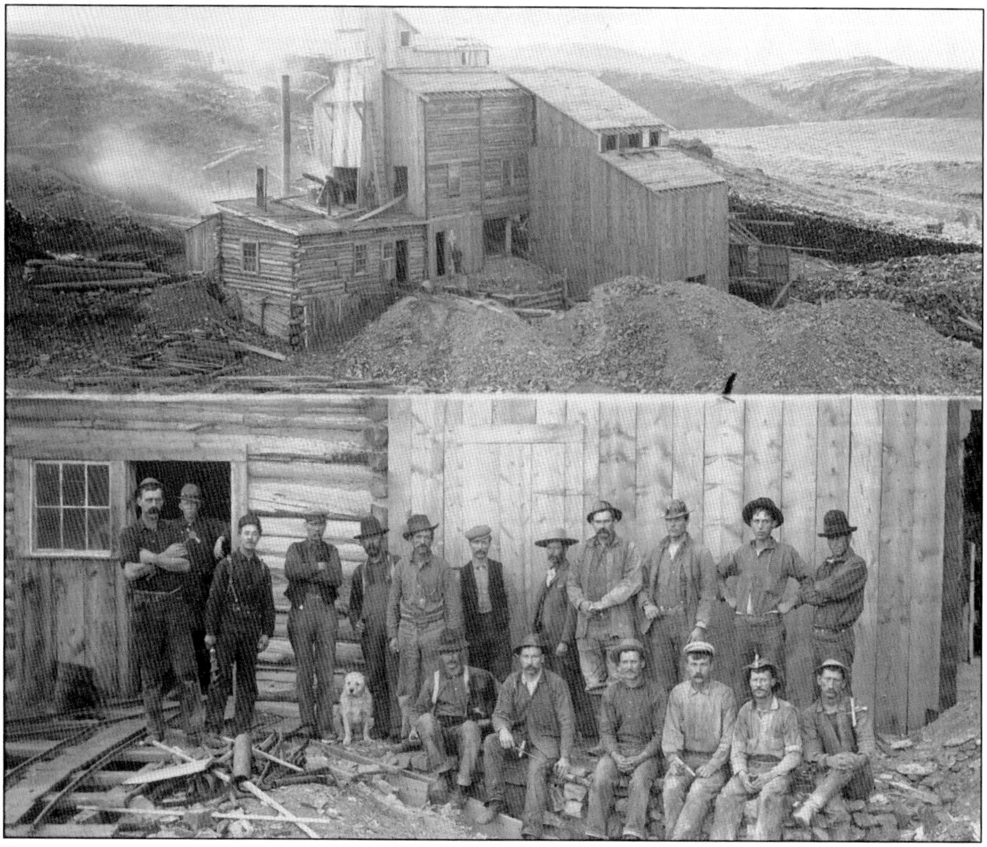

Promotional Photograph, 1898. This split view of the new mill building and the work crew were intended to show possible investors what they were buying. Light colored quartz gold ore is seen stockpiled for future milling in front of the mill building. Tibbals is seen in the center of the lower image, right of the man with the black vest.

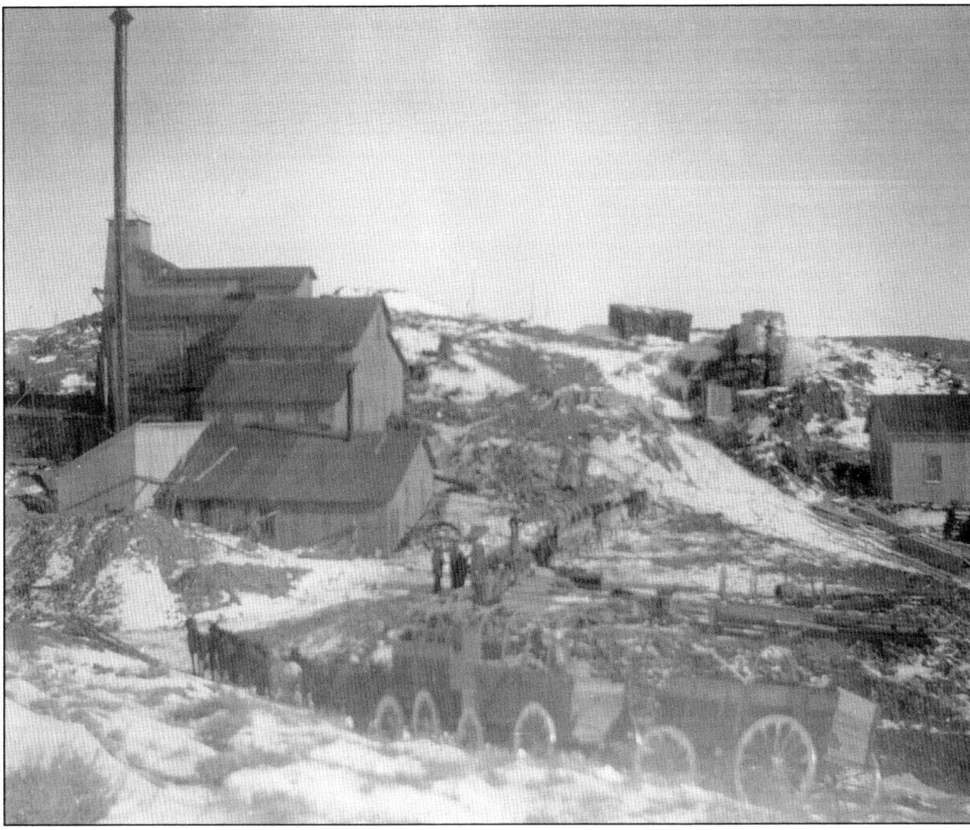

FREIGHT DELIVERY, 1900. Whether explosives, chemicals, building supplies, or winter provisions, all freight to the Carissa Mine had to arrive before roads became impassable for the season. The Union Pacific Railroad's station at Point of Rocks was nearly 80 miles away. Stacks of cordwood for the Carissa's boilers and stoves lay stacked in the center of the image near the skyline.

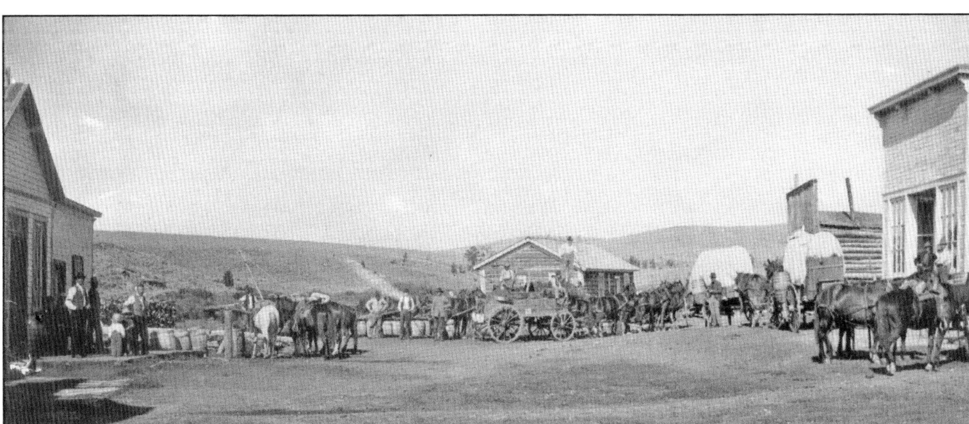

FREIGHTING THROUGH SOUTH PASS CITY, 1899. A major convoy of supplies destined for the Carissa Mine stops to water its horses at Willow Creek in preparation for the final hill ahead. Refreshment options abounded for the teamsters in the heart of town as well. Pictured are, from left to right, the Exchange Saloon, Carr Butcher Shop center, White Swan Saloon, and Smith-Sherlock Co. Store.

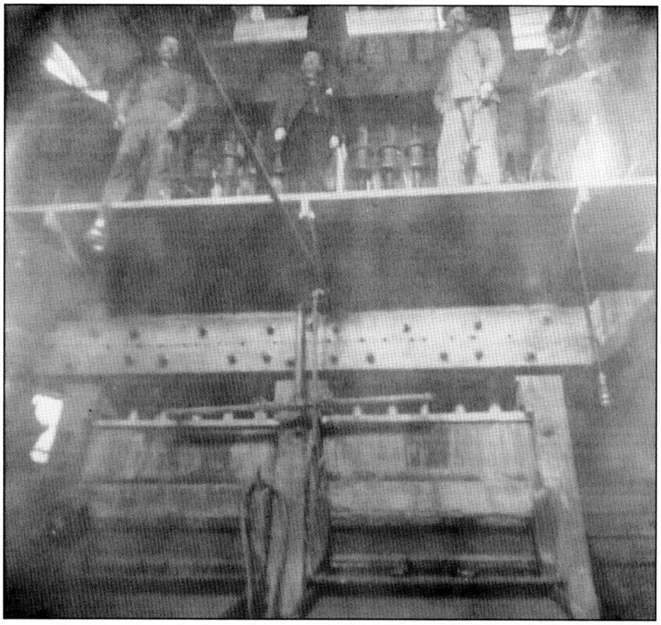

TEN STAMP MILL, 1900. Barney Tibbals (center) is seen wearing a dark suit; the rest of the men are unidentified. Stamp mills essentially used heavy hammers to pulverize the gold-bearing quartz ore into very fine particles small enough for the mill's operators to recover the gold and discard the wastes. Mercury, or quicksilver, was used extensively in this process because it readily held the fine gold particles, yet allowed the sand to slide past.

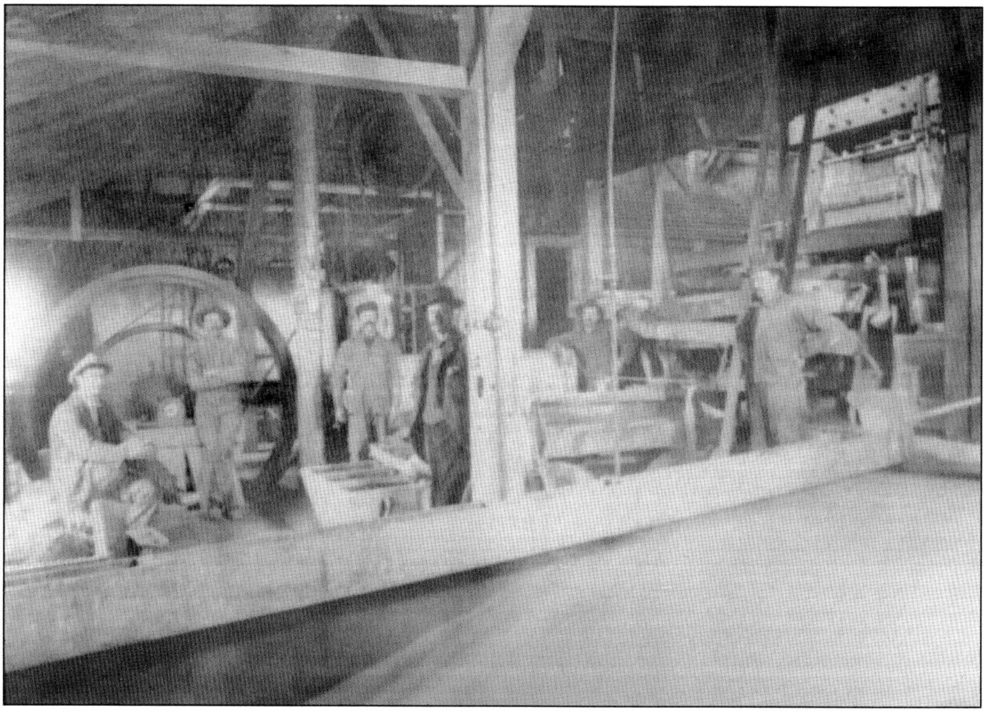

1898 FEDERAL GOLD MINING COMPANY MILL INTERIOR. Barney Tibbals (dark suit at center) is overseeing the mill in operation. Erie Boiler Company locomotive boiler (left, background) powers a Corliss engine, its large flywheel a blur of motion. From the engine, energy was transmitted to the stamps at the far right background to pulverize the ore. The finely ground material was flushed from the stamps with a steady flow of water into a Frue Vanner, which produced a rich concentrate of gold and associated heavy minerals. A Wilfley table, which also produced concentrates to be reduced at smelters in Denver or the Salt Lake Valley, fills the foreground.

Work Break at the Carissa, 1901. From left to right are Jennie Sherlock, Harry Kronberg, John McOmie, Frank Rottgen, Barney Tibbals, and Tip the dog. Women rarely paid official visits to mine sites, and were positively prohibited underground; an example of a centuries old European mining taboo brought to America. The chemical reagent bottle in the hand of Barney Tibbals suggests he may have been caught in the middle of assay work.

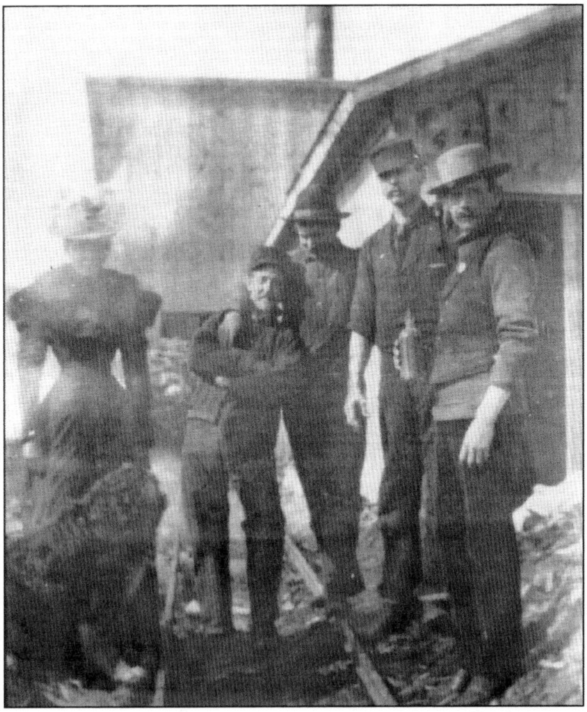

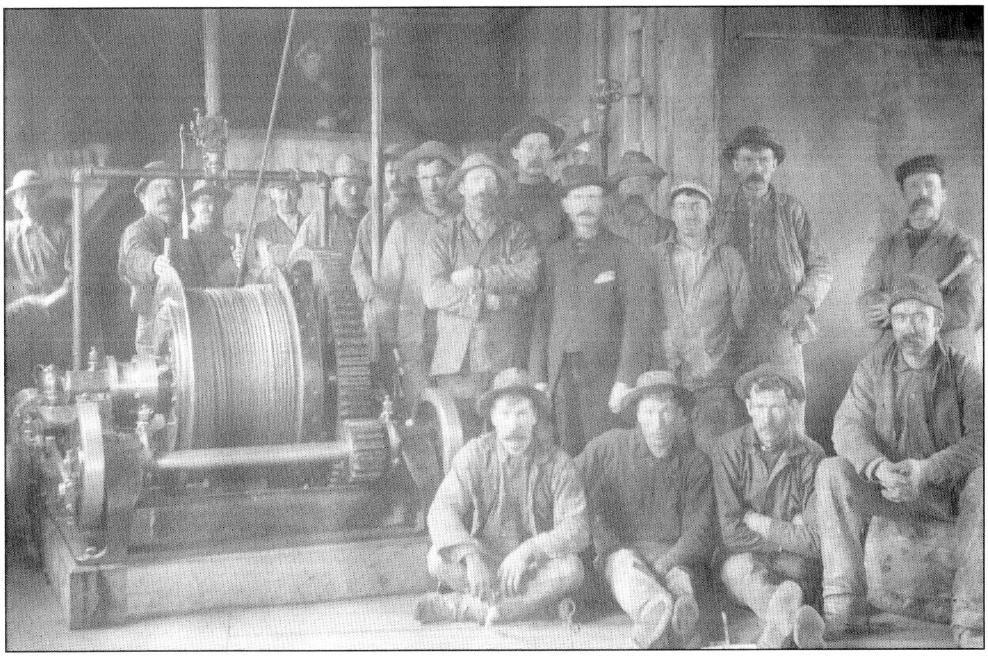

Steam Hoist, 1899. Barney Tibbals gathered his crew for a promotional photograph that he hoped would not only capture the modernity of the Carissa's facilities, but also the dollars of potential investors in the Federal Gold Mining Company. At the brake levers of the new hoist stands J.J. Marrin. During his tenure at the mine, Tibbals guided the development of the Carissa beyond the shallow, ad hoc, gold rush–era "gopher holes" to a systematically planned excavation more than 400 feet deep. At such depths, steam hoists were required to move men and ore.

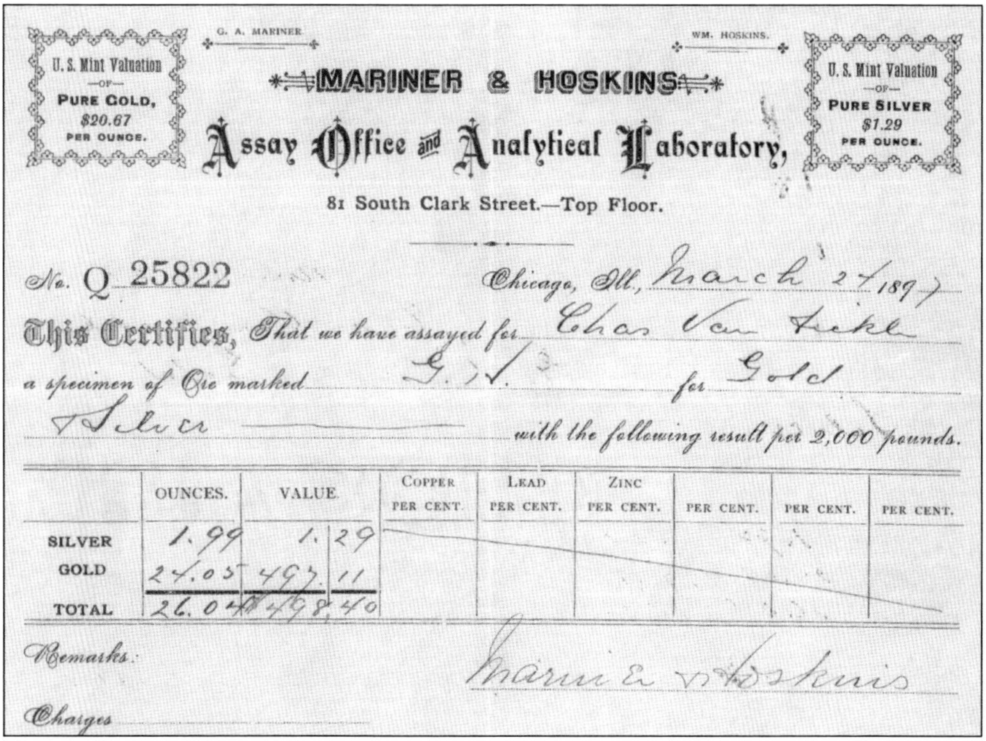

G. A. MARINER WM. HOSKINS.

U. S. Mint Valuation —of— Pure Gold, $20.67 per ounce.

MARINER & HOSKINS

Assay Office and Analytical Laboratory,

U. S. Mint Valuation —of— Pure Silver $1.29 per ounce.

81 South Clark Street.—Top Floor.

No. Q 25822 Chicago, Ill., March 27/1897

This Certifies, That we have assayed for Chas Van Sickle

a specimen of Ore marked G. T. for Gold

& Silver with the following result per 2,000 pounds.

	OUNCES.	VALUE.	COPPER PER CENT.	LEAD PER CENT.	ZINC PER CENT.	PER CENT.	PER CENT.	PER CENT.
SILVER	1.99	1.29						
GOLD	24.05	497.11						
TOTAL	26.04	498.40						

Remarks: Mariner & Hoskins

Charges

ASSAY REPORT, 1897. Federal Gold Mining Company shareholder Charles Van Sickle must have been ecstatic when one of Denver, Colorado's major assayers returned Carissa results that revealed over one ounce of gold per ton. Results like these from a reputable assay firm were certainly rich enough to attract investors.

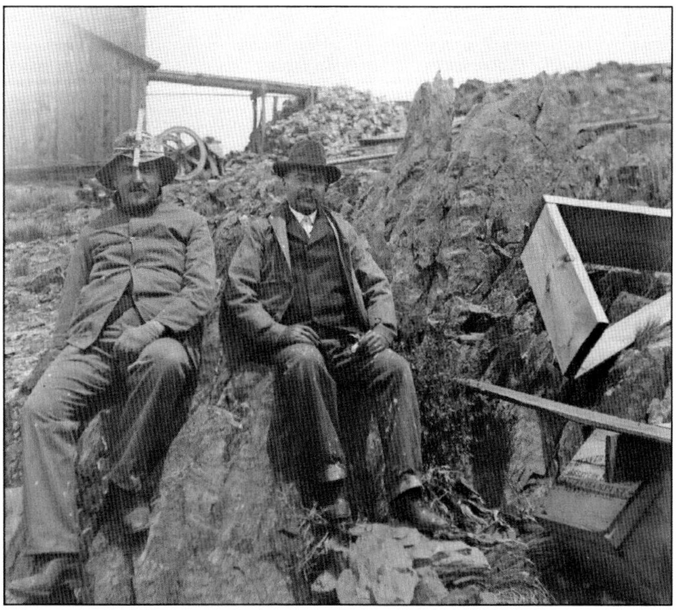

MINE INSPECTION TOUR, 1899. Spattered with candle wax, an unknown man (left) and John C. Spry had just completed an underground tour. Safe, cheap, and well understood, candles remained a mainstay at the Carissa well into the 20th century. Metal holders called miners' candles allowed men to affix the candle to mine timbers, or to their hats for hands-free use. The flywheel in the background is part of a jaw crusher used to break large ore into pieces suitable for feeding a stamp mill.

Fred Lovejoy. Fred was born on November 13, 1868, in Old Rippey, Iowa. Fred came to Wyoming in 1888, joining his brother Walter. Fred and Walter owned or worked a number of mines in the area, including the Caribou, Irish Poet, Lone Wolf, and Charles Dickens. Fred enjoyed social activities like the local Whist Club, community dances, and parties. By 1898, Fred and Walter relocated to Kemmerer, Wyoming. Fred offered scenic outfitting trips to Yellowstone National Park, then only 25 years old. He homesteaded on the Gros Ventre River north of Jackson, Wyoming. Once there, he became known for bringing telephone service to the area.

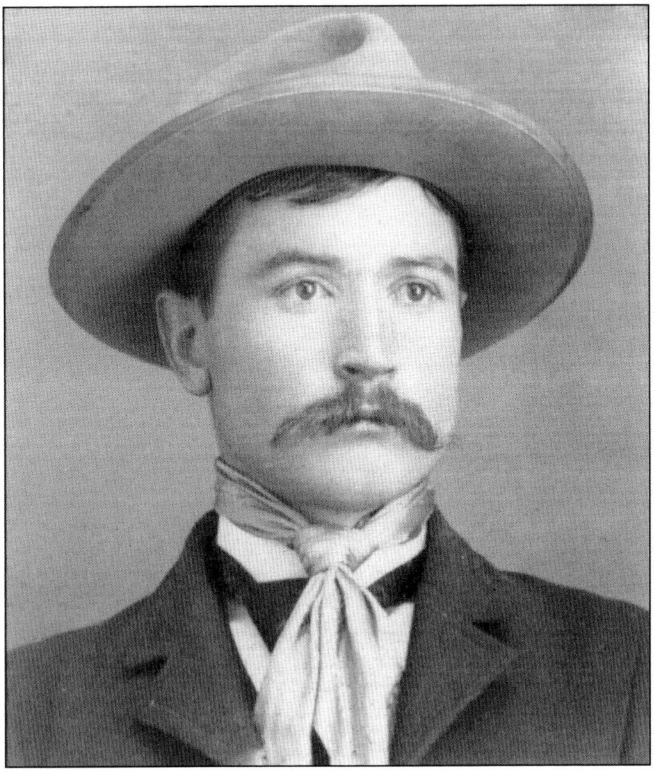

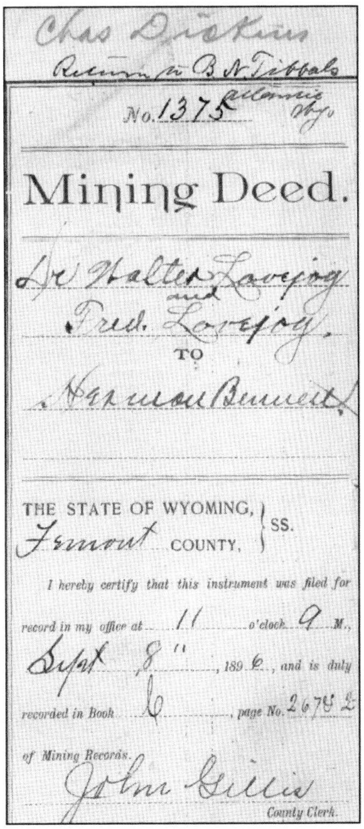

Chas Dickens
Return to B. N. Tibbals
No. 1375 Atlantic Wyo

Mining Deed.

Dr Walter Lovejoy and Fred. Lovejoy.
TO
Herman Bennett

THE STATE OF WYOMING, Fremont COUNTY, SS.

I hereby certify that this instrument was filed for record in my office at 11 o'clock a M., Sept 8", 1896, and is duly recorded in Book 6, page No. 267 & 2 of Mining Records.

John Gillis
County Clerk.

Mining Deed for the Charles Dickens Lode. Walter and Fred Lovejoy owned the Charles Dickens Lode, about a quarter mile north and west of South Pass City. They sold out to Herman Bennett on September 8, 1896. Tibbals and Bennett, on orders from John Spry, were quietly buying up claims that adjoined the Carissa. The Lovejoy brothers received $2,000 for their claim.

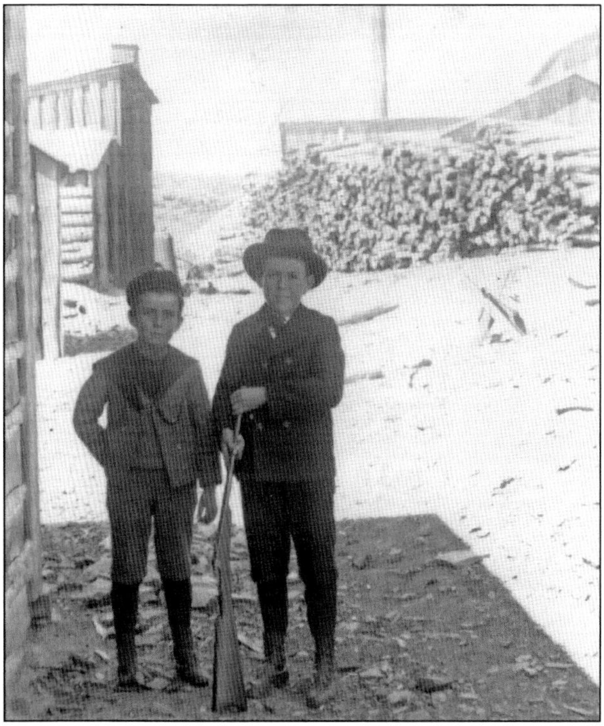

Hugh and Evan Williams at the Carissa Mine, 1900. The boys, aged 8 and 12, are shown with a prized possession, a rifle. Their father, Evan J. "Baldy" Williams, ran a sawmill for the Carissa. The Carissa's wood burning boilers had an unending appetite for cordwood, with more than one abandoned gold rush–era structure from South Pass City going up the Carissa's smokestacks.

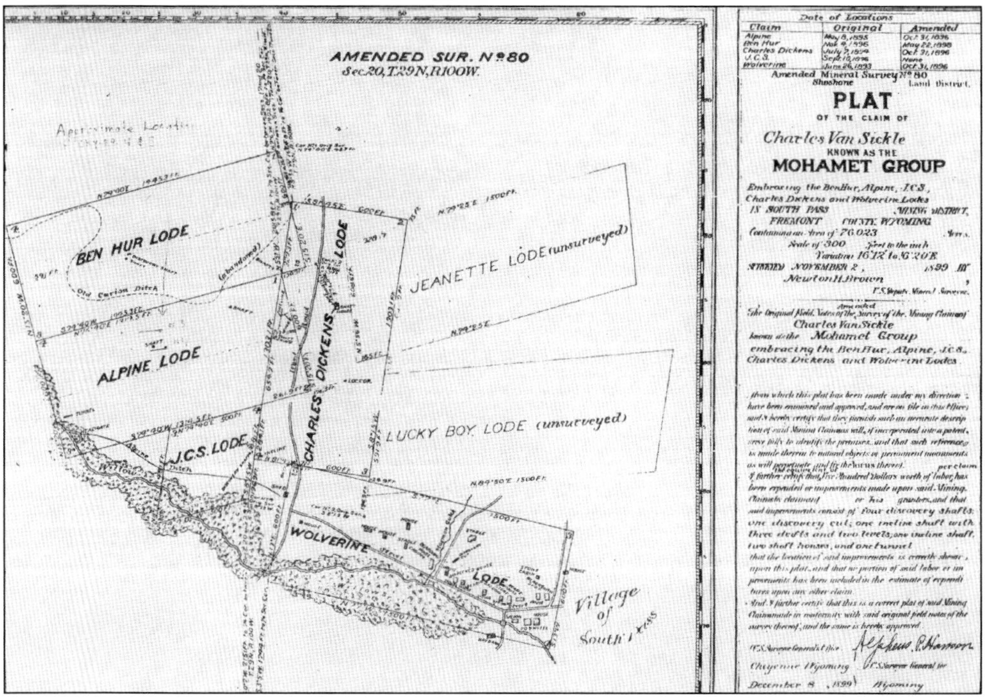

Mohamet Group. Charles Van Sickle, an associate of John Spry was also buying claims and quietly consolidating them on behalf of the Federal Gold Mining Company. The Mohamet Group was located at the westernmost edge of the Carissa. The Village of South Pass can be seen at the lower right of the map. At the time, the Jeanette Lode belonged to Janet Sherlock.

HAROLD ABBOT "HAT" TITCOMB, MINING ENGINEER. Harold was born in Brooklyn, New York, on April 26, 1874. HAT graduated from the Columbia University, School of Mines in 1898. One of his first jobs was as an assistant manager of the Carissa. Later, Titcomb was a consulting and examining engineer at mines all over the world, including Australia, Russia, and Macedonia. He was also an accomplished archer and hunter, returning to the Wind River Mountains with his sons to hunt elk and bighorn sheep.

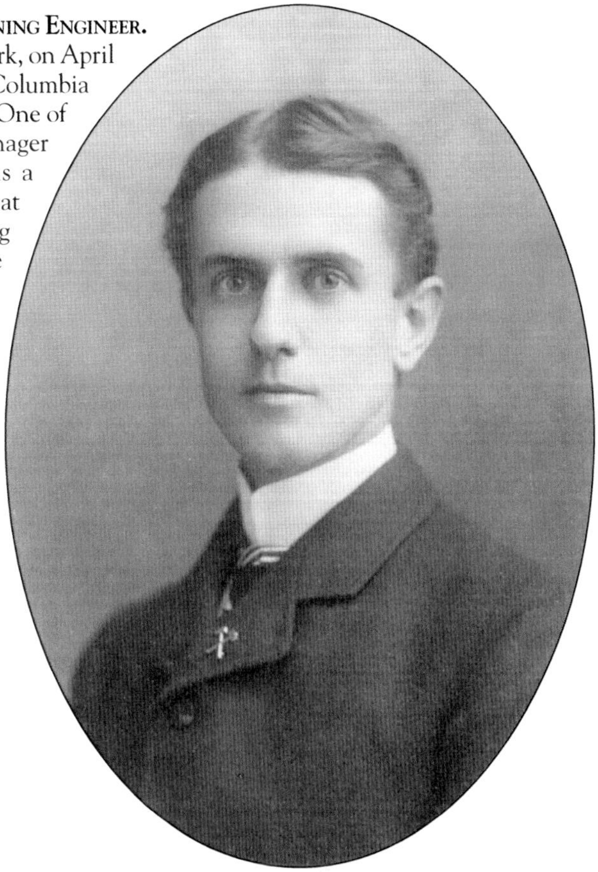

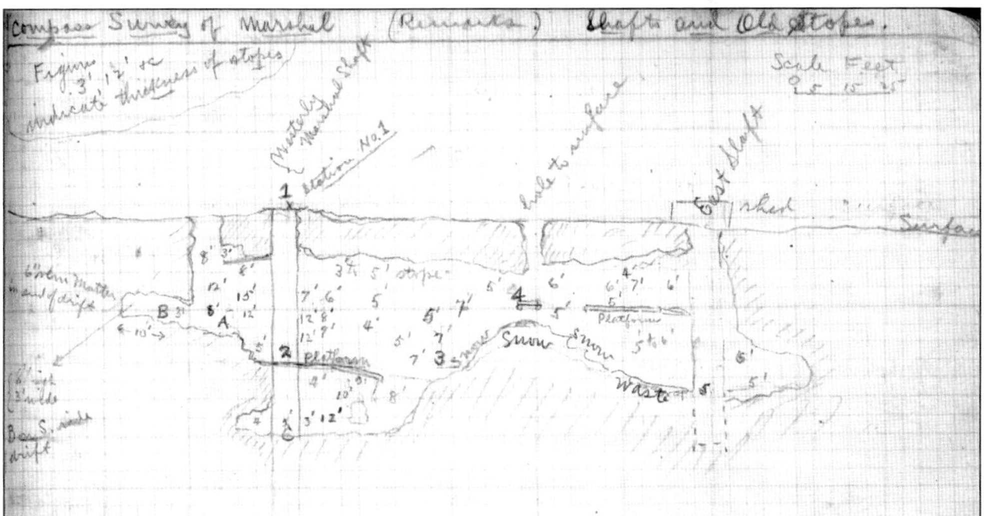

SURVEY OF THE CARISSA, 1900. Titcomb sketched out the shafts, stopes, and drifts using a compass and measuring tape. HAT then sampled the ore at various locations for assay in order to better inform future mining development. The features shown in this sketch are the gold rush–era Marshall Workings.

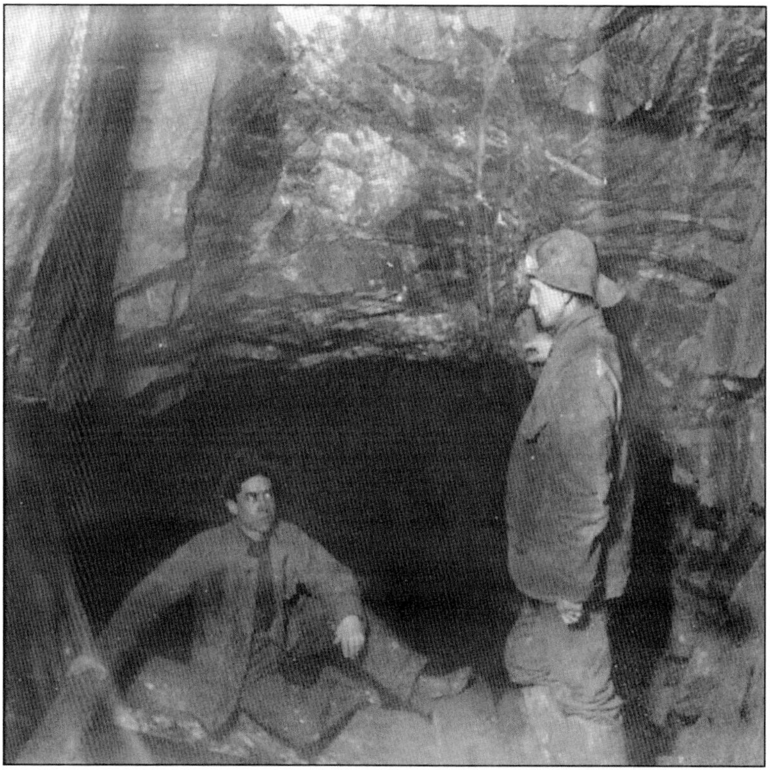

CHARLES AND HAROLD TITCOMB UNDERGROUND AT THE CARISSA, 1900. HAT's younger brother, Charles, spent some time working at the Carissa as an assistant in the mapping and assaying. The quest for gold barely curtailed their drive for adventure, and in 1901 they climbed the 13,745-foot-high Fremont Peak in only the second ascent since Capt. John C. Frémont first stood on the summit in 1842.

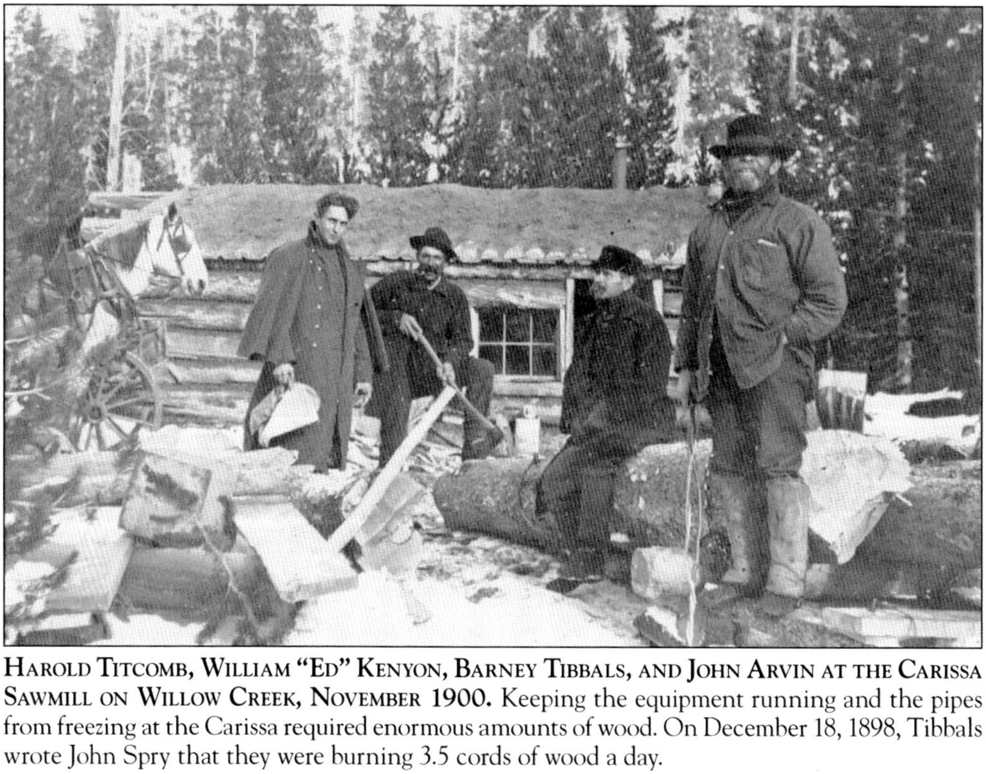

HAROLD TITCOMB, WILLIAM "ED" KENYON, BARNEY TIBBALS, AND JOHN ARVIN AT THE CARISSA SAWMILL ON WILLOW CREEK, NOVEMBER 1900. Keeping the equipment running and the pipes from freezing at the Carissa required enormous amounts of wood. On December 18, 1898, Tibbals wrote John Spry that they were burning 3.5 cords of wood a day.

SAMPLING THE MINE, 1901. Carl Gunderson (left), Harold A. Titcomb (center) and an unknown man are pictured here. Gunderson holds a hammer and moil used to gouge out samples for assay. Ore samples taken from the underground workings sit at HAT's feet, each one labeled and sealed against tampering. The miner at right hefts a heavy iron muller used for finely crushing the samples, as well as a wire mesh screen for sorting oversize. Sampling a mine accurately was as much art as science, with all parties looking to preserve their own interests at the expense of others.

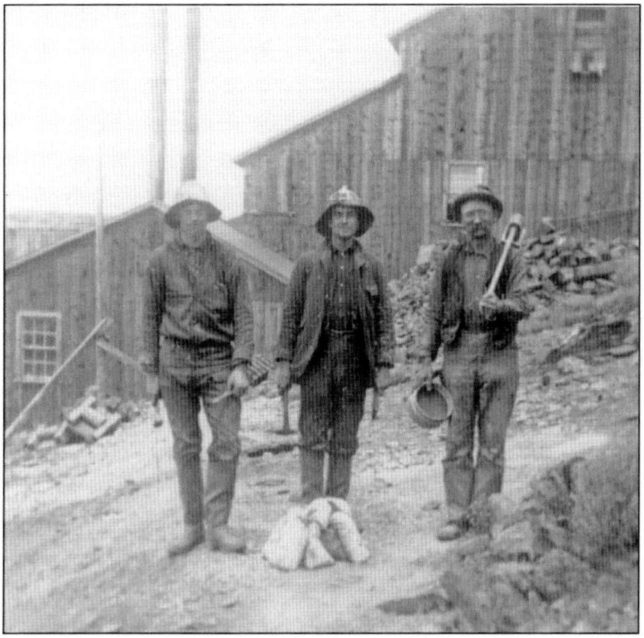

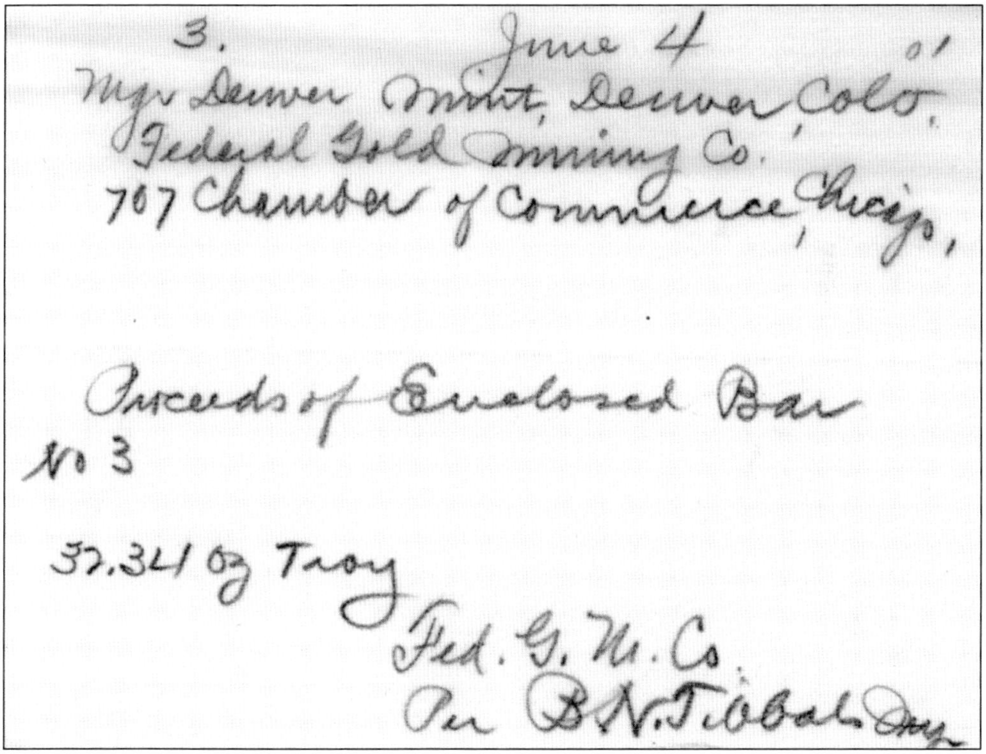

3. June 4 '01
Mgr Denver Mint, Denver, Colo.
Federal Gold Mining Co.
707 Chamber of Commerce, Chicago,

Proceeds of Enclosed Bar
No 3

32.341 Oz Troy
Fed. G. M. Co
Per B.N. Tibbals Sup

THE GOLD. During Federal's operations at the Carissa, the mill captured free milling gold through amalgamation with mercury. The amalgam was heated in a heavy iron vessel known as retort, releasing the mercury as a vapor and leaving behind a material called doré. Doré was an alloy containing both gold and silver. If historical gold-silver ratios at the Carissa hold for the 32.34-ounce bar noted here, the value today would be about $41,000.

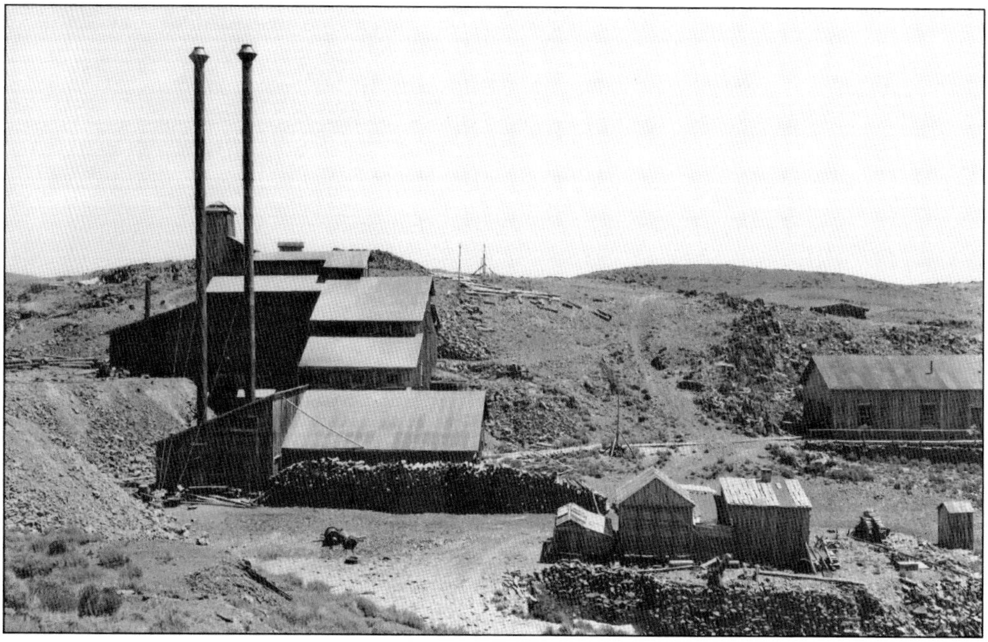

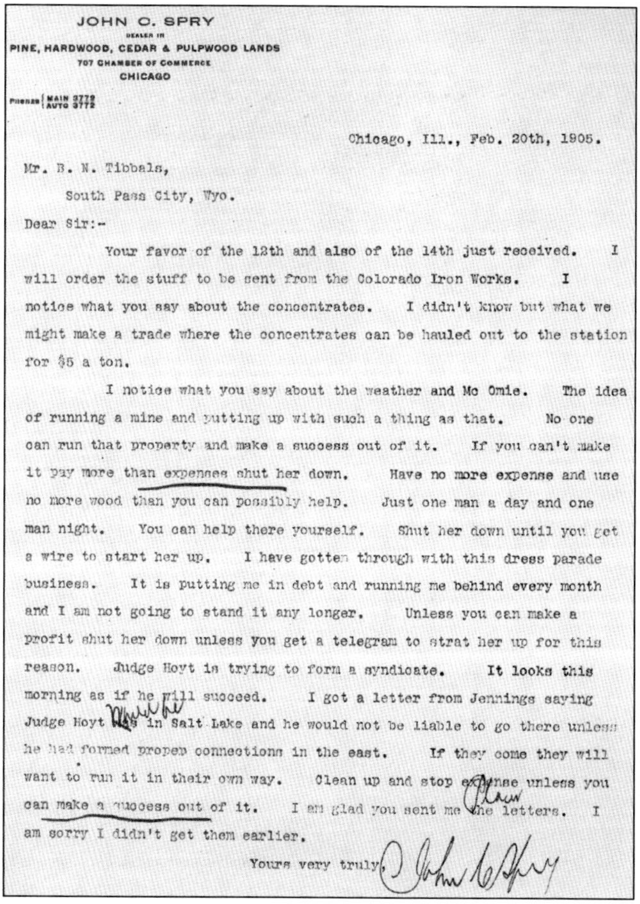

JOHN C. SPRY
DEALER IN
PINE, HARDWOOD, CEDAR & PULPWOOD LANDS
707 CHAMBER OF COMMERCE
CHICAGO

Phones { MAIN 3772 / AUTO 3772

Chicago, Ill., Feb. 20th, 1905.

Mr. B. N. Tibbals,
South Pass City, Wyo.

Dear Sir:-

Your favor of the 12th and also of the 14th just received. I will order the stuff to be sent from the Colorado Iron Works. I notice what you say about the concentrates. I didn't know but what we might make a trade where the concentrates can be hauled out to the station for $5 a ton.

I notice what you say about the weather and Mc Omie. The idea of running a mine and putting up with such a thing as that. No one can run that property and make a success out of it. If you can't make it pay more than expenses shut her down. Have no more expense and use no more wood than you can possibly help. Just one man a day and one man night. You can help there yourself. Shut her down until you get a wire to start her up. I have gotten through with this dress parade business. It is putting me in debt and running me behind every month and I am not going to stand it any longer. Unless you can make a profit shut her down unless you get a telegram to strat her up for this reason. Judge Hoyt is trying to form a syndicate. It looks this morning as if he will succeed. I got a letter from Jennings saying Judge Hoyt was in Salt Lake and he would not be liable to go there unless he had formed proper connections in the east. If they come they will want to run it in their own way. Clean up and stop expense unless you can make a success out of it. I am glad you sent me the letters. I am sorry I didn't get them earlier.

Yours very truly,
John C. Spry

Shut Her Down. There are no smoke puffs from the twin stacks of the Federal Mill in this photograph. The work crews had all been dismissed and the prospects for the future looked bleak. Spry once again focused on his timber business and Tibbals realized his lifelong dream of establishing himself as a Western ranchman at nearby Boulder, Wyoming.

End of an Era. By 1905, the unrestrained dreams of Tibbals had exhausted Spry's patience, and the bounds of his pocketbook. Perhaps Spry sensed that his trust in advice from Tibbals was misplaced. Over the years, Spry's letters to Tibbals became increasingly disenchanted with the prospects of the Carissa. At one point, Spry laments having been distracted by the Carissa, when he should have instead been taking part in the Klondike gold rush.

Three

Carissa Mine

Tom Ryan, a member of the 1st Nevada Volunteer Cavalry stationed at Fort Bridger is credited with the discovery of what was to become known as the Carissa Mine in 1865 during an assignment in the South Pass area. Unfortunately for Ryan, he was unable to follow up on his discovery on account of his military duties, and another party outfitted from Fort Bridger took legal right to the property by reporting the discovery in public record in 1867. Fourteen men were named on the location of the Cariso Lode, including Homer Roberts. His brother Bolivar Roberts was apparently Homer's financial backer.

On June 8, 1870, Bolivar is credited with a 65 ounce gold deposit at South Pass City's Exchange Bank worth nearly $91,000 today. Bolivar Roberts bought up the other shares at the Carissa and incorporated the Carissa Gold Mine Company, with himself as president and principal shareholder. Having achieved some early notoriety for the mine, Roberts patented his 20-acre claim from the public domain in 1886, but the workings remained fairly limited. As a further testament to Robert's waning interest in the property, he leased the Carissa to a number of local men over the years, content to take a share of their cleanup.

Federal Gold Mining Company took over the Carissa in 1897 and initiated a massive development scheme. With no buyer in sight for the mine, despite the improvements, the Carissa sat idle for 20 years until the arrival of Midwest Mines Corporation of Chehalis, Washington. The firm embarked on extensive improvements to the surface plant, but creditors refused to be delayed in their payments at the outset of the Great Depression. The Carissa was closed during the Depression as attorneys wrangled in courts from Lander to Cheyenne.

Mica Mountain Mines revived the Carissa in 1946, totally reequipping the mine and mill with modern tools and gold recovery technologies. Pent up consumer demand caused runaway price inflation, raising the costs of gold production beyond what could be recouped in the government-controlled gold market. The last recorded production at the Carissa took place in 1955 under Pioneer Carissa Gold Mines, Incorporated.

A number of examinations of the property took place in the 1970s through the 1990s, with no production occurring. The State of Wyoming was offered the property for sale in 2003.

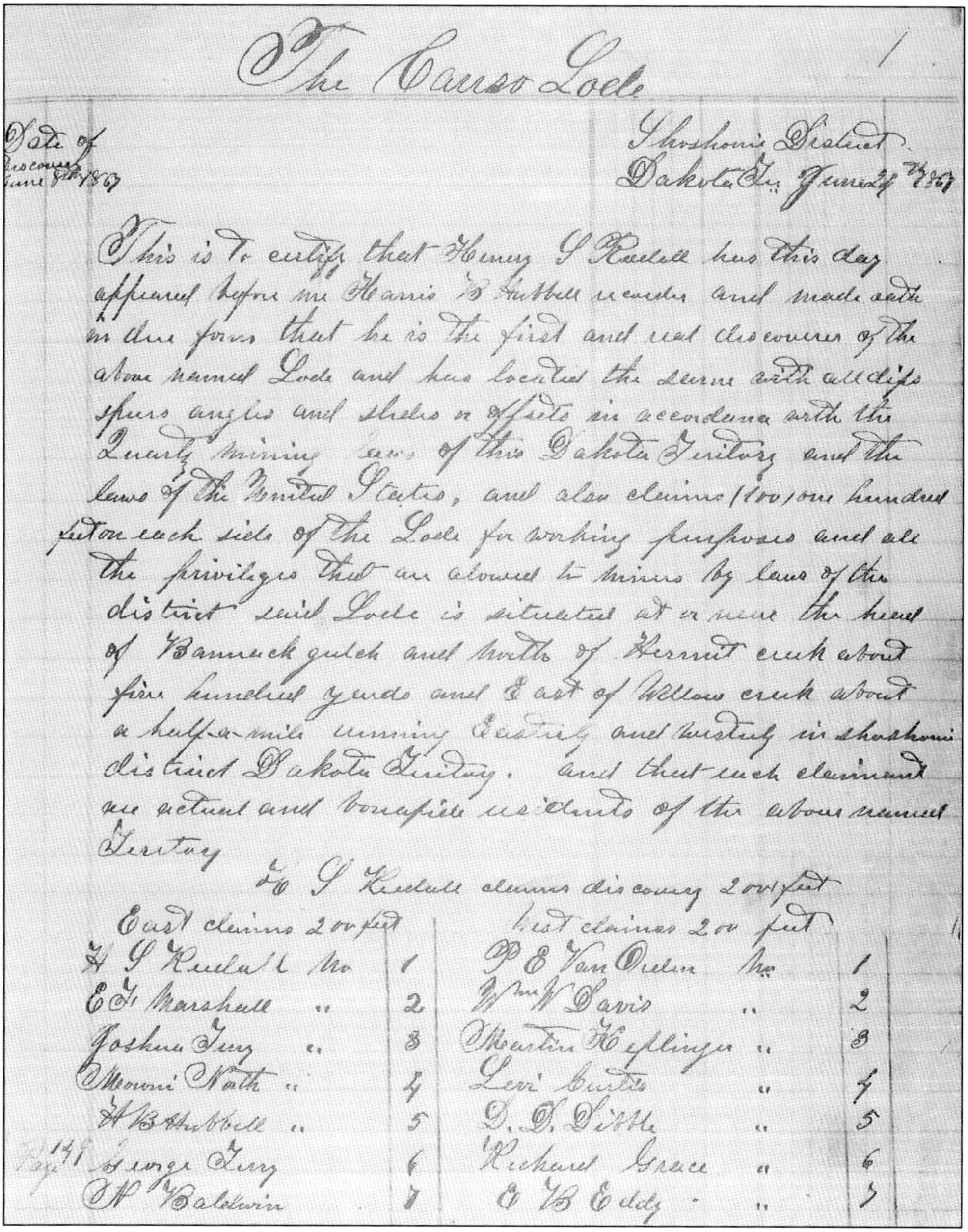

The Cariso Lode 1

Date of discovery June 8th 1867

Shoshonie District
Dakota Ty. June 24th 1867

This is to certify that Henry S Reedall has this day appeared before me Harris B Hubbell recorder and made oath in due form that he is the first and real discoverer of the above named Lode and has located the same with all dips spurs angles and sheers or offsets in accordance with the Quartz mining laws of this Dakota Territory and the laws of the United States, and also claims (100) one hundred feet on each side of the Lode for working purposes and all the privileges that are allowed to miners by laws of the district said Lode is situated at or near the head of Bannock gulch and North of Hermit creek about five hundred yards and East of Willow creek about a half a mile running Easterly and westerly in Shoshonie district Dakota Territory. And that each claimant are actual and bonafide residents of the above named Territory

H S Reedall claims discovery 200 feet

East claims 200 feet			West claims 200 feet		
H S Reedall	No	1	P E Van Ordin	No	1
E T Marshall	"	2	Wm W Davis	"	2
Joshua Terry	"	3	Martin Kefflinger	"	3
Moroni North	"	4	Levi Curtis	"	4
H B Hubbell	"	5	D. D. Dibble	"	5
Page 149 George Terry	"	6	Richard Grace	"	6
W Baldwin	"	7	E B Eddy	"	7

The Cariso Lode. This was the first claim filed in the Shoshonie Mining District. Henry Reedall, and associates, located the claim on June 8, 1867, and recorded it publicly on June 24. The origin of the name "Cariso" is not known. Bolivar Roberts purchased a portion of the Cariso and sank a shaft in 1870. About $75,000 in gold was produced in 1867.

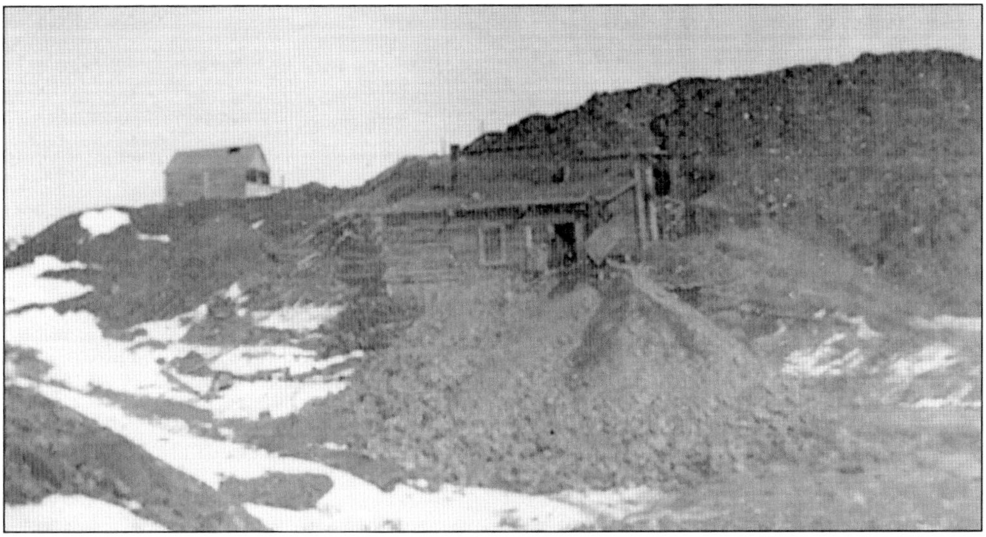

Bolivar Roberts Era. Bolivar was born on July 4, 1831, in Scott County, Illinois. In his lifetime, he was Utah Territorial Treasurer, superintendent of the Pony Express, a merchant, and mine owner. In 1883, he patented the Mono Lode, also known as the Carissa Mine. Roberts sold the holdings of his Carissa Gold Mining Company to Federal Gold Mining Company in 1899.

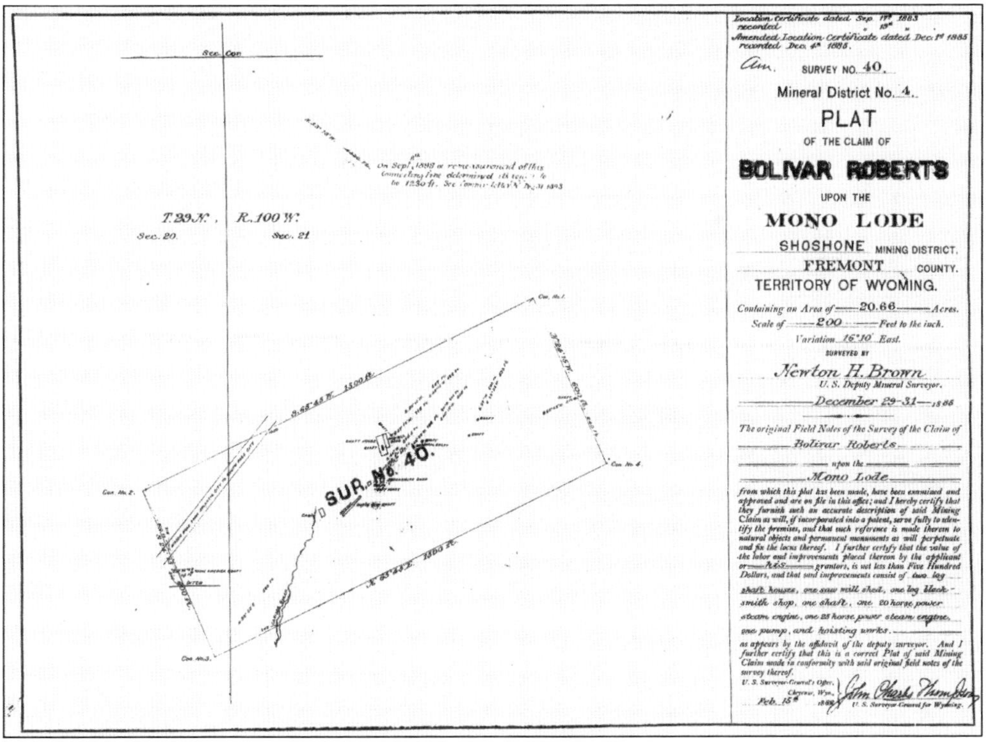

Plat of the Mono Lode. Like homesteading on agricultural lands, mineral claims could be taken up by private citizens and, after sufficient improvements had been performed, the claimant could petition to have them made private property. An official survey of the property was conducted prior to patent and improvements like structures, mineshafts or tunnels, and workshops were listed on the survey.

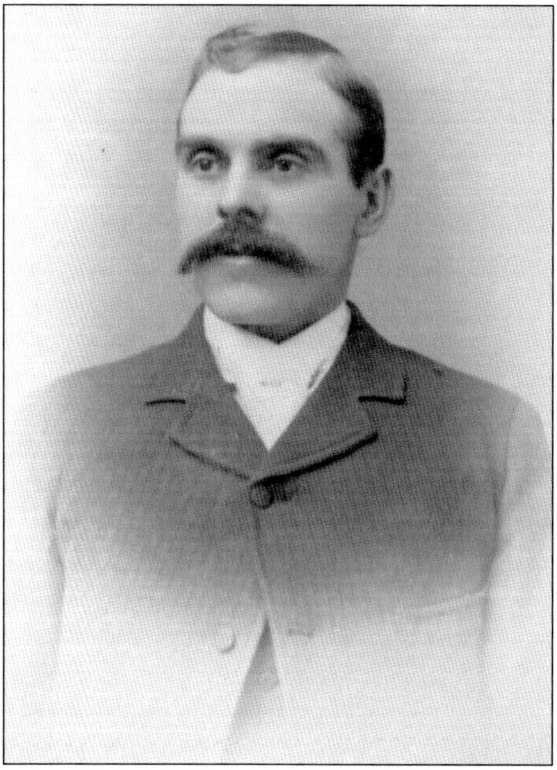

Sam Leckie. A homesteader in the area, Leckie leased the Carissa from Bolivar Roberts in 1895. The season for Leckie ended on October 31, 1895, when he deposited his share, a gold retort weighing about 30 ounces with the Rock Springs National Bank. Today, the value of Leckie's deposit would be $40,000. He returned to sheep raising west of South Pass City on the Big Sandy. Leckie was shot and killed at his saloon in the town of Leckie in 1905. He had run off a sheepherder from his saloon and fired a warning shot from a pistol as the man returned. The sheepherder fired a single shot from his Winchester, striking Leckie in the head.

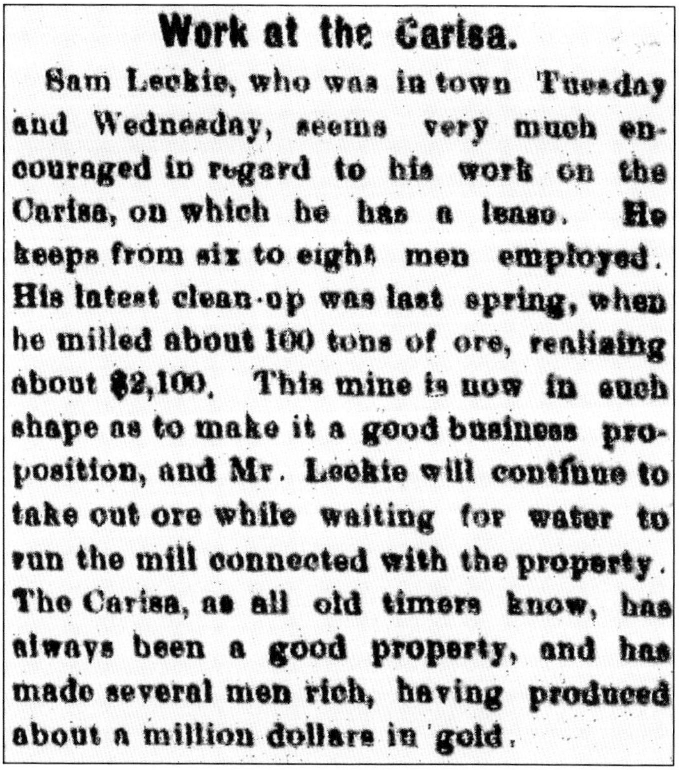

Work at the Carisa.

Sam Leckie, who was in town Tuesday and Wednesday, seems very much encouraged in regard to his work on the Carisa, on which he has a lease. He keeps from six to eight men employed. His latest clean-up was last spring, when he milled about 100 tons of ore, realizing about $2,100. This mine is now in such shape as to make it a good business proposition, and Mr. Leckie will continue to take out ore while waiting for water to run the mill connected with the property. The Carisa, as all old timers know, has always been a good property, and has made several men rich, having produced about a million dollars in gold.

***The Fremont Clipper,* August 16, 1895.** The Carissa, often called the "Carisa" by locals, always enjoyed a good reputation with those who knew that the mine could produce rich pockets of bonanza ore. The terms of mining leases varied, but lessees often gained a bad reputation with absentee owners for haphazardly drilling and blasting while seeking out rich high-grade ore shoots. In 1887, Leckie's brother Andrew plunged to his death at the Carissa when the ore bucket he was riding in came free from a primitive hand-cranked hoist.

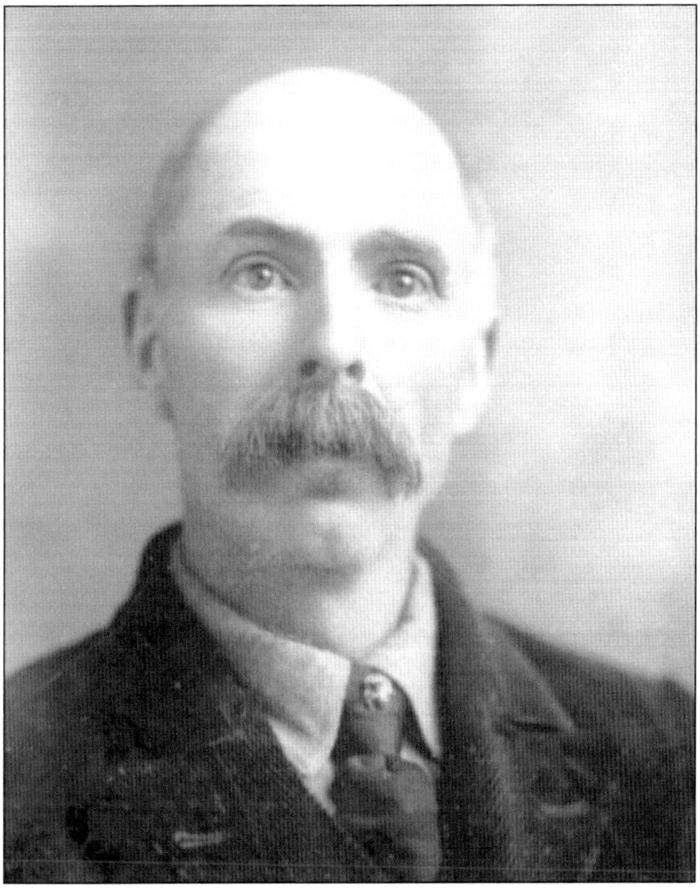

Evan J. "Baldy" Williams. Born in Wales in 1852, Williams stowed away on a ship heading for America when he was nine years old. He apprenticed with a carpenter. Williams came to South Pass City in 1885 and homesteaded on the Sweetwater River. He operated a sawmill in the area for a number of years, supplying lumber to the Carissa.

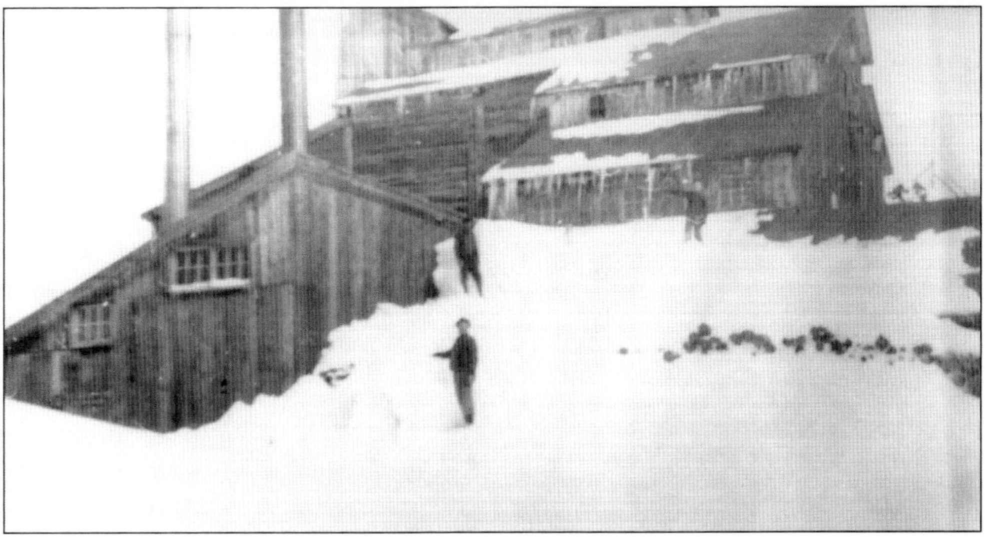

Snowed in at the Federal Gold Mining Company Mill. Winter weather has always been a challenge with which miners have had to contend. Snow made transportation of supplies, mail, and spare parts more difficult. Boilers had to be kept running day and night, whether mining operations were active or suspended, in order to keep water pipes from freezing.

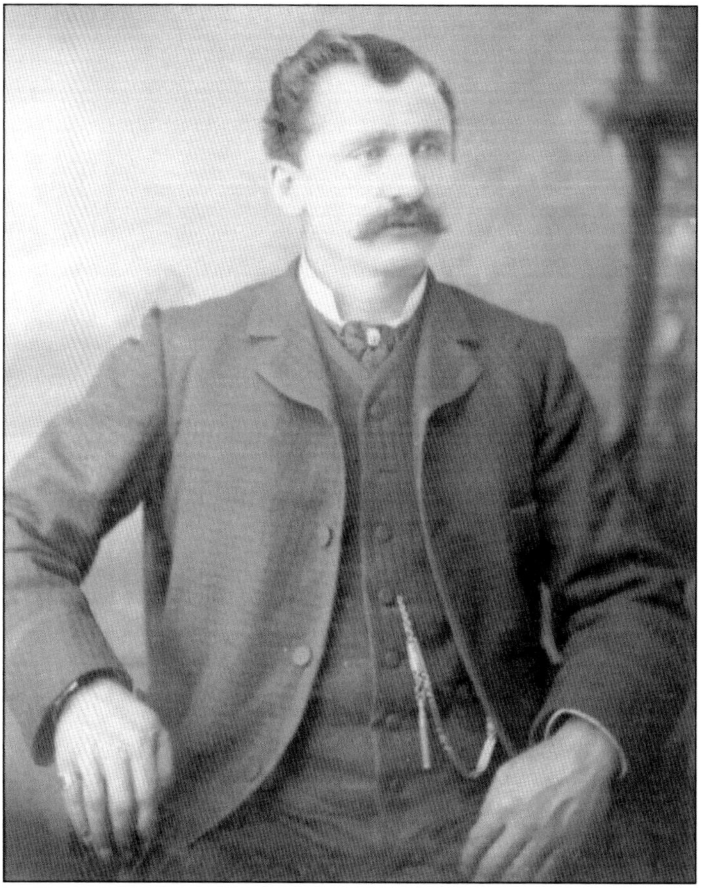

John J. Marrin. The native Pennsylvanian was born in 1860. Marrin moved to Utah in 1883, going to work for Bolivar Roberts at his Sampson Mine at Park City. When Roberts consolidated the Carissa in 1885, he transferred Marrin, an engineer, to South Pass City. When Roberts sold out, Marrin went to work for Federal Gold Mining Company as the hoist operator. Later, Marrin operated the Carissa Saloon and partnered in ranching, but gave those up to return to his work as hoist engineer until his retirement.

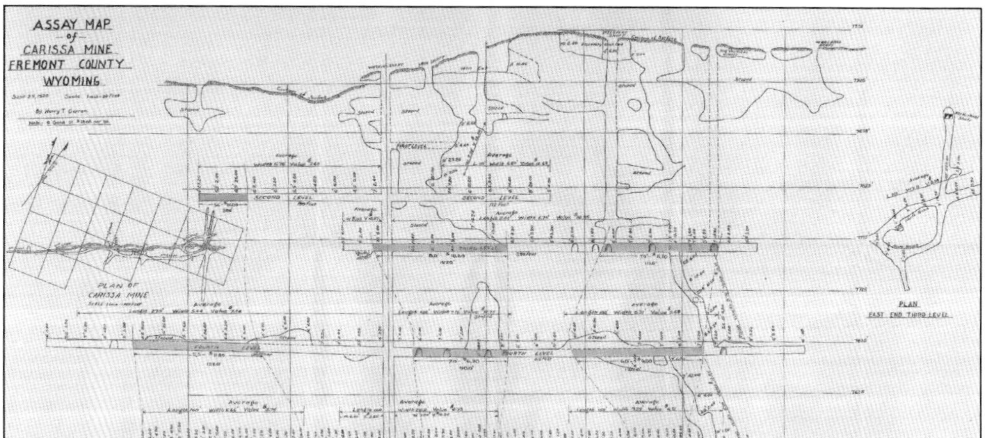

Underground Workings. When looking for a buyer, Federal Gold Mining Company hired South Dakota School of Mines graduate Harry T. Curran as manager for the Carissa. Curran was a well-known mining engineer, having worked in Jalisco, Mexico, the Oregon Bureau of Mining and Geology, and Idaho Springs, Colorado. As a consultant, Curran surveyed and sampled the Carissa's underground workings for this 1920 map. Later, Curran was manager of the Carissa from 1922 until 1927.

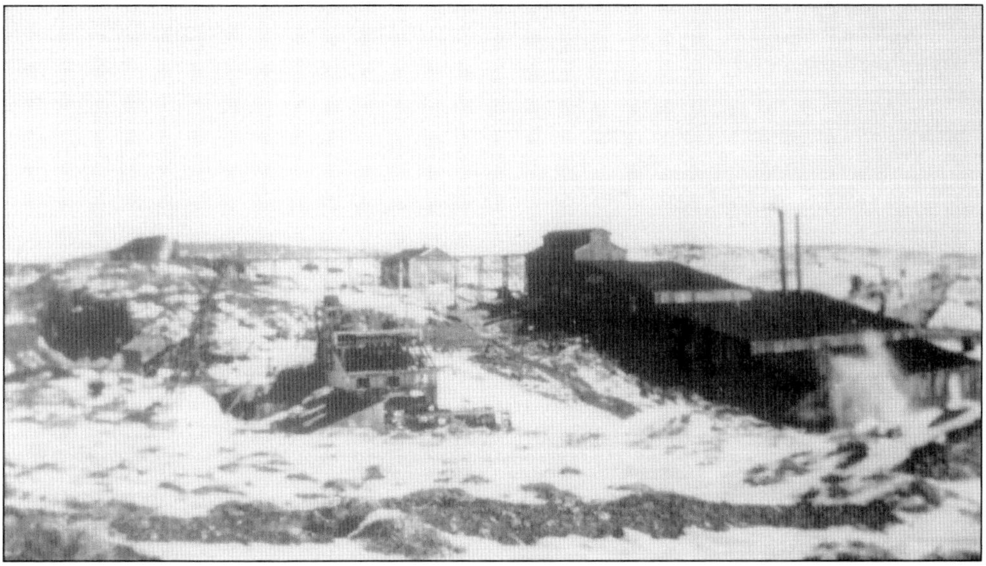

Carissa Mill, 1929. After years of sitting idle, Midwest Mines Corporation purchased Atlantic City's Dexter Mill, tore it down, and reassembled it to become the new Carissa Mill. Midwest scavenged materials from Federal Gold Mining Company's mill still visible at left center. The Chehalis, Washington, corporation erected a number of new structures at the Carissa during their short period of operations, ending in 1931.

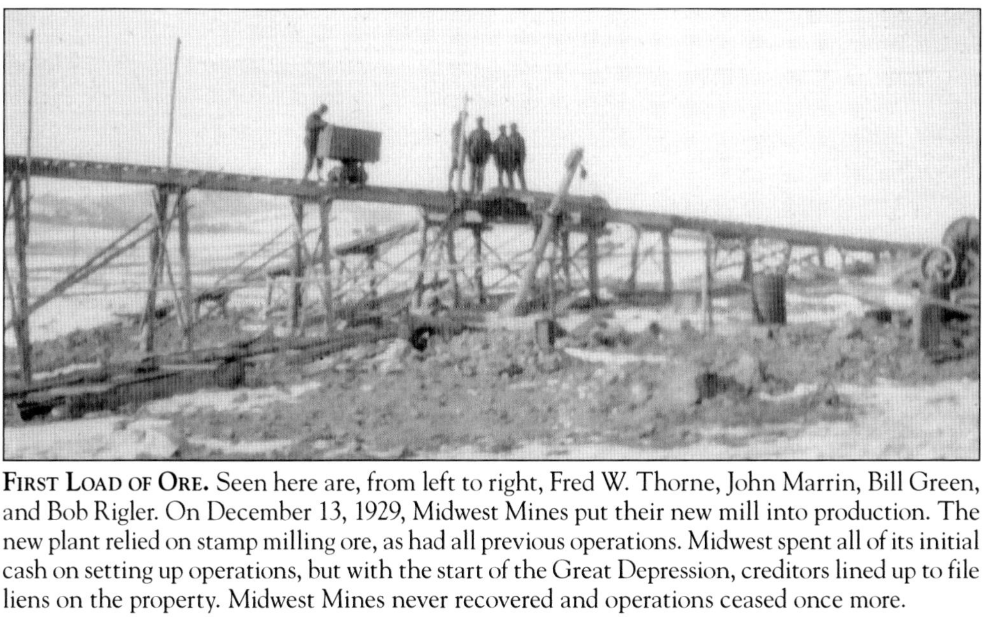

First Load of Ore. Seen here are, from left to right, Fred W. Thorne, John Marrin, Bill Green, and Bob Rigler. On December 13, 1929, Midwest Mines put their new mill into production. The new plant relied on stamp milling ore, as had all previous operations. Midwest spent all of its initial cash on setting up operations, but with the start of the Great Depression, creditors lined up to file liens on the property. Midwest Mines never recovered and operations ceased once more.

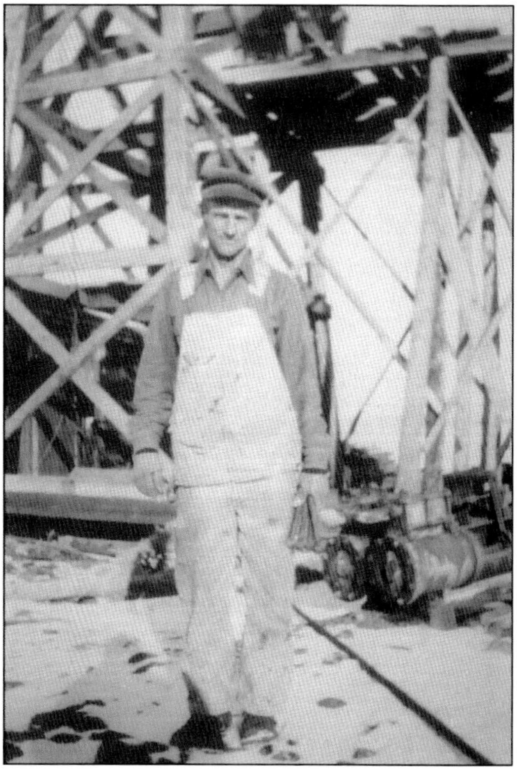

HARRY MILLS, DECEMBER 13, 1929. Mills was an Iowa-born carpenter for Midwest Mines who helped reassemble the Dexter Mill at the Carissa. The 1930 census states Mills was a 49-year-old bachelor living at the Carissa's bunkhouse. In this photograph taken at the enlarged Operating Shaft, the new derrick-style headframe rises behind Mills and the cylinders for a duplex steam pump used for dewatering the main shaft are seen at the lower right.

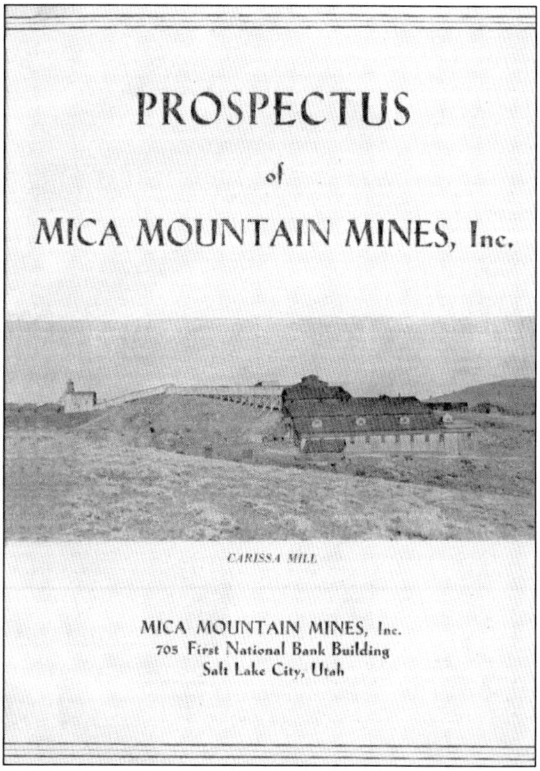

PROSPECTUS

of

MICA MOUNTAIN MINES, Inc.

CARISSA MILL

MICA MOUNTAIN MINES, Inc.
705 First National Bank Building
Salt Lake City, Utah

MICA MOUNTAIN MINES, INC. The Carissa was snarled in litigation all through the Great Depression. The War Production Board then closed all gold mines nationwide during World War II. Ray E. Tower, a mining engineer from Butte, Montana, took over management of the Carissa for Mica Mountain Mines in 1946. Tower reequipped the mill with the latest technology. The new ball mill was followed by a mineral jig, flotation, and cyanide systems.

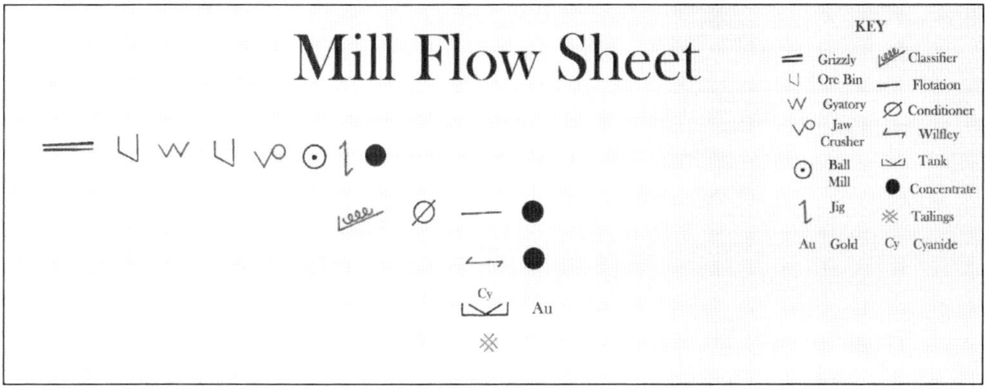

1946 Mill. This is a technical drawing, in shorthand, of the mill set up. Records from the postwar boom at the Carissa state that both concentrates and bullion were sold. Concentrates were a crude product resulting from heavy metallic particles being captured due to their density. Concentrates were transported to a smelter in Garfield, Utah, to recover the gold. Gold bars went to the US Mint in Denver, Colorado.

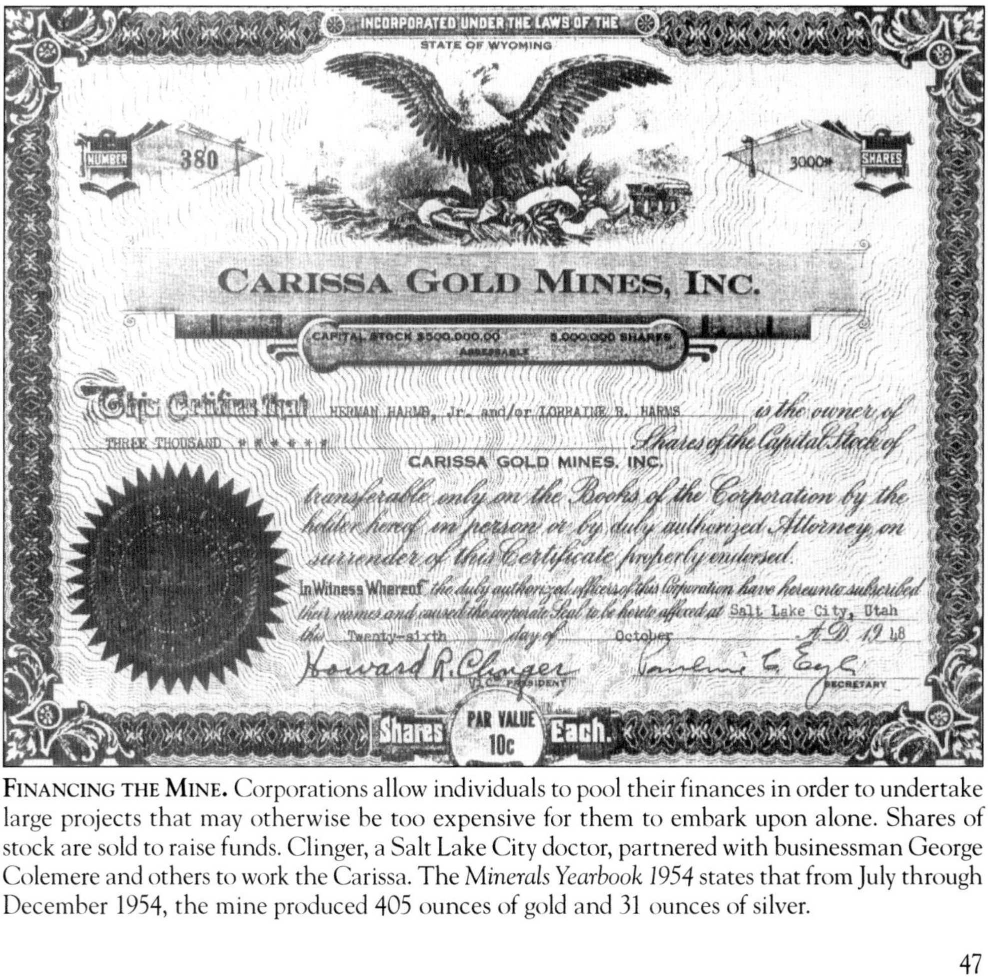

INCORPORATED UNDER THE LAWS OF THE STATE OF WYOMING

NUMBER 380

3000# SHARES

CARISSA GOLD MINES, INC.

CAPITAL STOCK $500,000.00 5,000,000 SHARES ASSESSABLE

This Certifies that HERMAN HARMS, Jr. and/or LORRAINE R. HARMS is the owner of THREE THOUSAND ****** Shares of the Capital Stock of CARISSA GOLD MINES, INC. transferable only on the Books of the Corporation by the holder hereof in person or by duly authorized Attorney on surrender of this Certificate properly endorsed.

In Witness Whereof the duly authorized officers of this Corporation have hereunto subscribed their names and caused the corporate Seal to be hereto affixed at Salt Lake City, Utah this Twenty-sixth day of October A.D. 1948

Howard R. Clinger, PRESIDENT — SECRETARY

Shares PAR VALUE 10c Each.

Financing the Mine. Corporations allow individuals to pool their finances in order to undertake large projects that may otherwise be too expensive for them to embark upon alone. Shares of stock are sold to raise funds. Clinger, a Salt Lake City doctor, partnered with businessman George Colemere and others to work the Carissa. The *Minerals Yearbook 1954* states that from July through December 1954, the mine produced 405 ounces of gold and 31 ounces of silver.

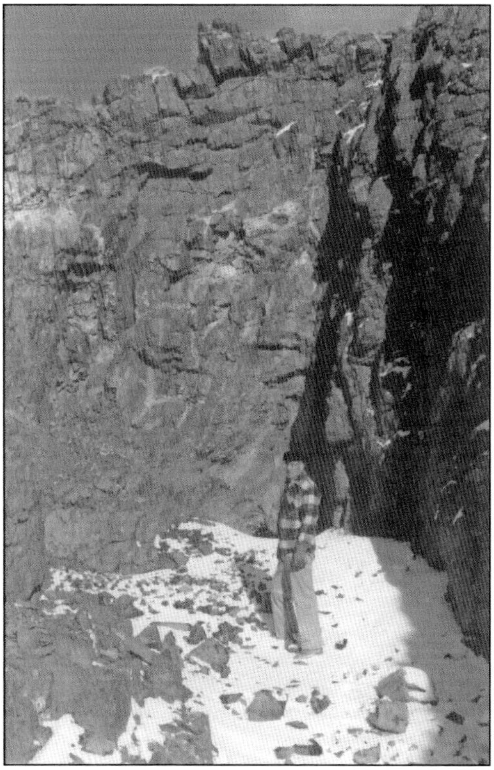

Open Pit. Griff Williams, owner of Carissa Gold Inc., inspects a mine feature at the Carissa. Williams, a Salt Lake City businessman involved in the commercial metals industry, worked in the same office building as George Colemere. The two visited about Colemere's property in Wyoming and came to terms of sale. Williams could not develop the Carissa on his own, so he entered into a partnership with a Canadian firm that eventually wrested control of the mine from him.

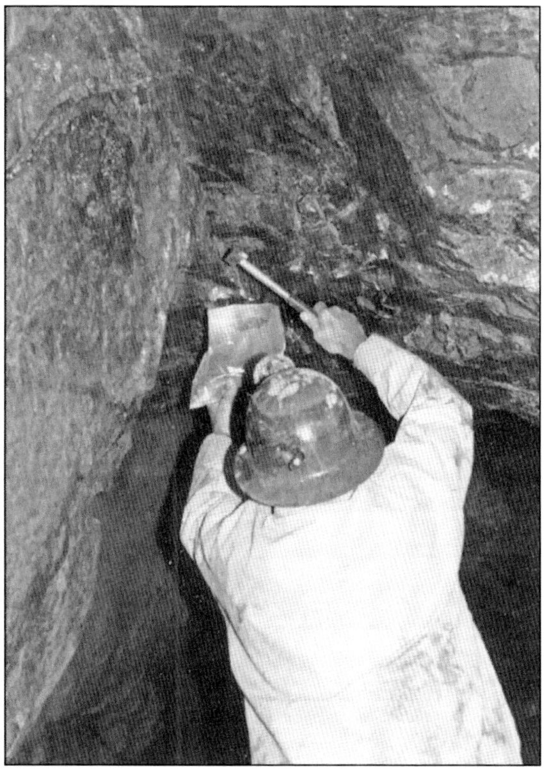

Sampling the Carissa. Carissa Gold, Inc., hired mining geologist Steve Gyorvary to sample the mine in the late 1980s. In this image, Gyorvary chip samples ore 150 feet below ground on the third level of the mine and about 199 feet from the production shaft. Gyorvary was one of the last people to go underground before the pumps were turned off, allowing the workings to flood. Despite optimism expressed by Gyorvary and others, the Carissa was not put back into production.

Core Drilling. Consolidated McKinney Resources, Inc., of Vancouver, British Columbia, succeeded Griff Williams at the Carissa. The Canadians initiated a core-drilling program geared to pulling thousands of feet of rock cores from the Carissa beyond the mine workings. A Nevada firm carried out the work with promising samples being examined on-site. The most valuable samples were forwarded to an assay laboratory in Colorado.

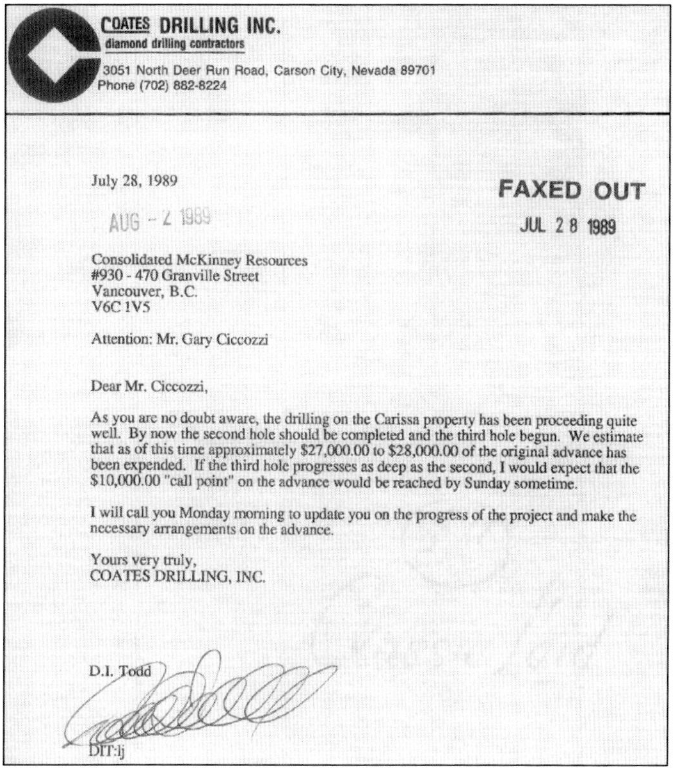

COATES DRILLING INC.
diamond drilling contractors
3051 North Deer Run Road, Carson City, Nevada 89701
Phone (702) 882-8224

July 28, 1989

AUG - 2 1989

FAXED OUT
JUL 28 1989

Consolidated McKinney Resources
#930 - 470 Granville Street
Vancouver, B.C.
V6C 1V5

Attention: Mr. Gary Ciccozzi

Dear Mr. Ciccozzi,

As you are no doubt aware, the drilling on the Carissa property has been proceeding quite well. By now the second hole should be completed and the third hole begun. We estimate that as of this time approximately $27,000.00 to $28,000.00 of the original advance has been expended. If the third hole progresses as deep as the second, I would expect that the $10,000.00 "call point" on the advance would be reached by Sunday sometime.

I will call you Monday morning to update you on the progress of the project and make the necessary arrangements on the advance.

Yours very truly,
COATES DRILLING, INC.

D.I. Todd

DIT:lj

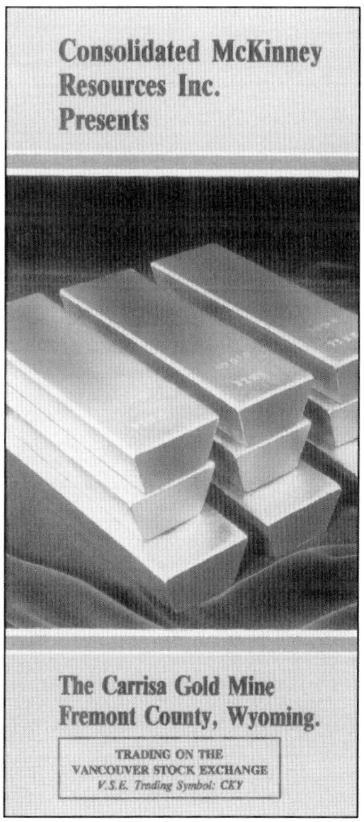

Modern Mine Promotion. A handful of companies reviewed the Carissa in the 1970s, 1980s, and 1990s. Consolidated McKinney Resources, Inc., produced full-color brochures, a detailed prospectus, and a VHS cassette tape for potential investors to review. Gold mining during this period became an increasingly global enterprise, dominated by a handful of multinational conglomerates that focused mainly on open pit mining.

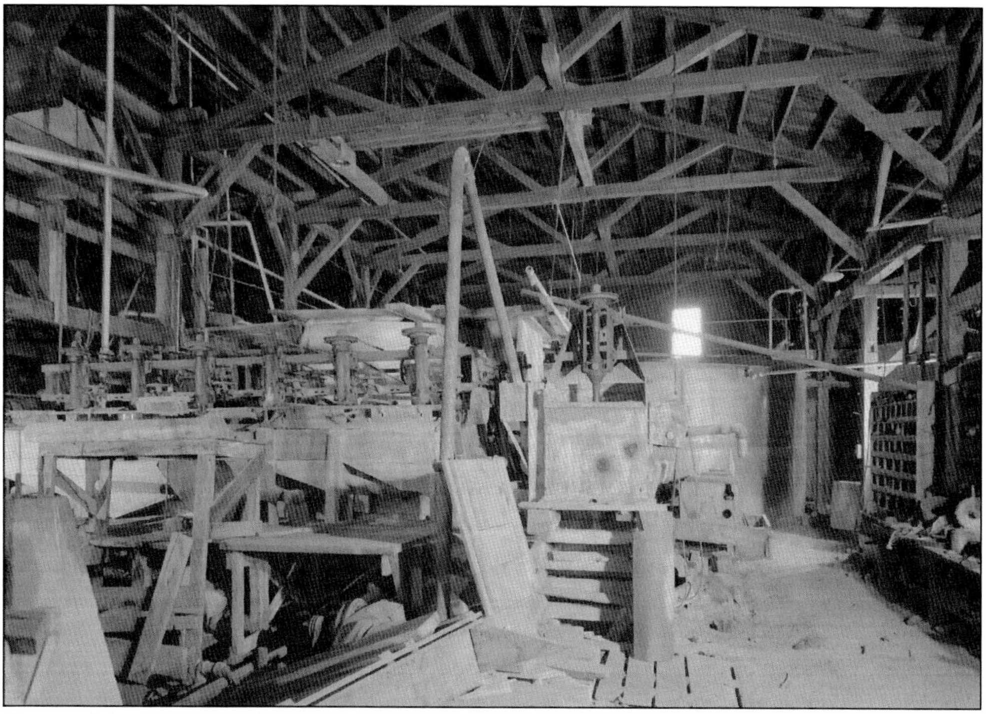

CARISSA MILL INTERIOR. The Historic American Buildings Survey documented the Carissa Mill in 1974, after two decades of disuse. Much of the original equipment remained in place, although some was already missing.

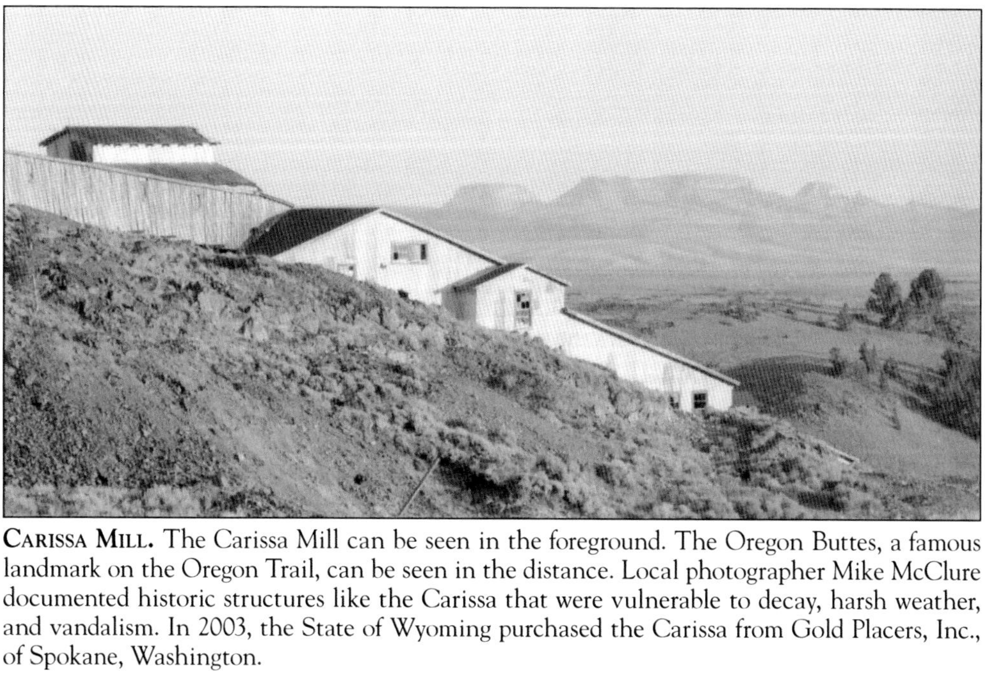

CARISSA MILL. The Carissa Mill can be seen in the foreground. The Oregon Buttes, a famous landmark on the Oregon Trail, can be seen in the distance. Local photographer Mike McClure documented historic structures like the Carissa that were vulnerable to decay, harsh weather, and vandalism. In 2003, the State of Wyoming purchased the Carissa from Gold Placers, Inc., of Spokane, Washington.

Four

Atlantic City

Atlantic City was established on Rock Creek in the spring of 1868. While the quick wealth may have been found in placer mining the creeks and gulches, hard rock miners attacked exposed quartz veins with vigor as well. The power of Rock Creek was harnessed by several mills and arrastras that were erected to pulverize the ore. Support industries like freighting, timber cutting, and blacksmithing also took root in the community. For a time, Atlantic City could boast that it was home to all the frills of a long-established town.

With the bust of the early 1870s, the town quickly dropped from several hundred residents to only several dozen. Those remaining took over abandoned hard rock mines and claims on local creeks, content to augment their ordinary income with any proceeds from mining gold, rather than rely exclusively on fortune. By the late 1880s, Frenchman Emile Granier revived the area with a massive hydraulic mining operation that yielded less gold than hoped, but delivered a temporary reprieve for local business and industry. The next gold boom arrived with the Dexter Mining and Development Company of Rochester, New York, in the early 20th century. The firm bought up claims, hired men, and erected a massive new mill. Results were disappointing and operations ceased, returning Atlantic City to a quiet existence once more. Paradoxically, the true 20th-century gold boom in Atlantic City arrived during the years of the Great Depression when a dredge worked Rock Creek near town. As a nation languished economically, Atlantic City hummed with steady activity and optimism.

In the late 1950s, corporate giant United States Steel began development just outside of Atlantic City. Within a handful of years, the Atlantic City iron ore mine was Fremont County's largest employer, and yet another wave of newcomers arrived. The face of the former gold town changed once more. When US Steel closed down in the early 1980s, Atlantic City's new arrivals fled the area as quickly as they had come, leaving the area distinctly different from what they had found upon their arrival.

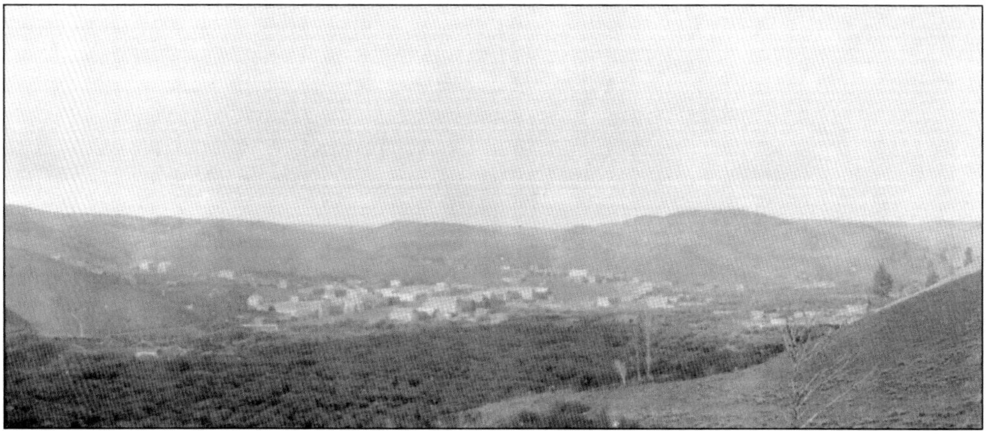

Atlantic City, 1869. Famed photographer William Henry Jackson captured this image of the boomtown during a visit to the newly-opened region. The community featured one of Wyoming Territory's first public schools and its first brewery. Perhaps as many as 800 citizens called the town their home.

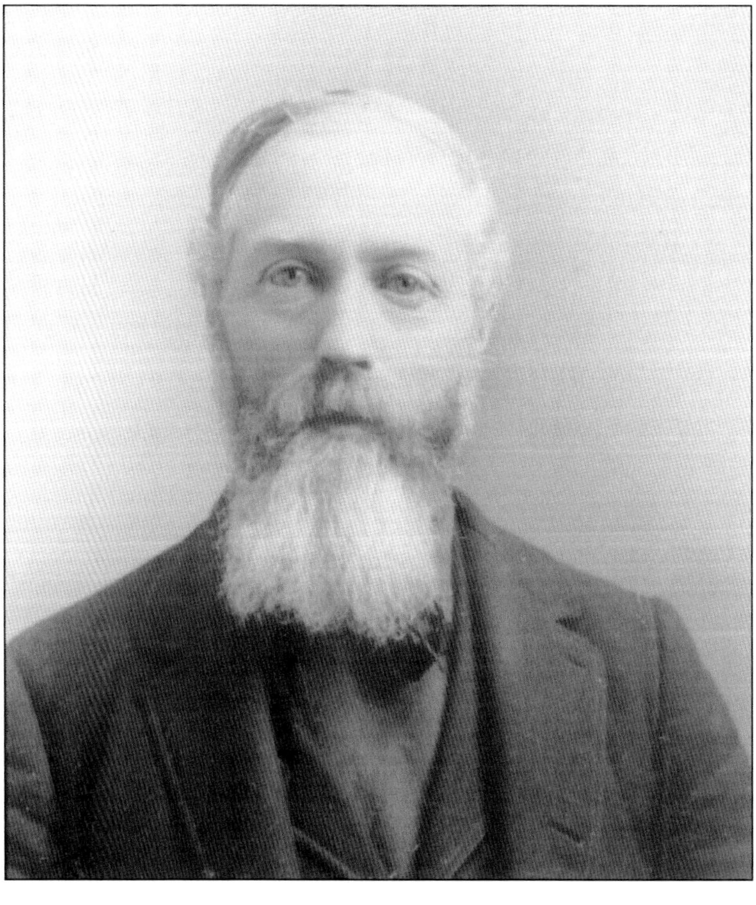

Samuel L. Spangler. Born on November 16, 1849, in Muskingum County, Ohio, Spangler trekked to Cheyenne and Fort Bridger in 1874. His work as a freighter introduced him to the Sweetwater Mines, then in decline. Spangler worked the Red Canyon gold placers between Miners Delight and Lander. Later, Spangler took up the Orient Lode claim near Atlantic City, renaming it the Ground Hog.

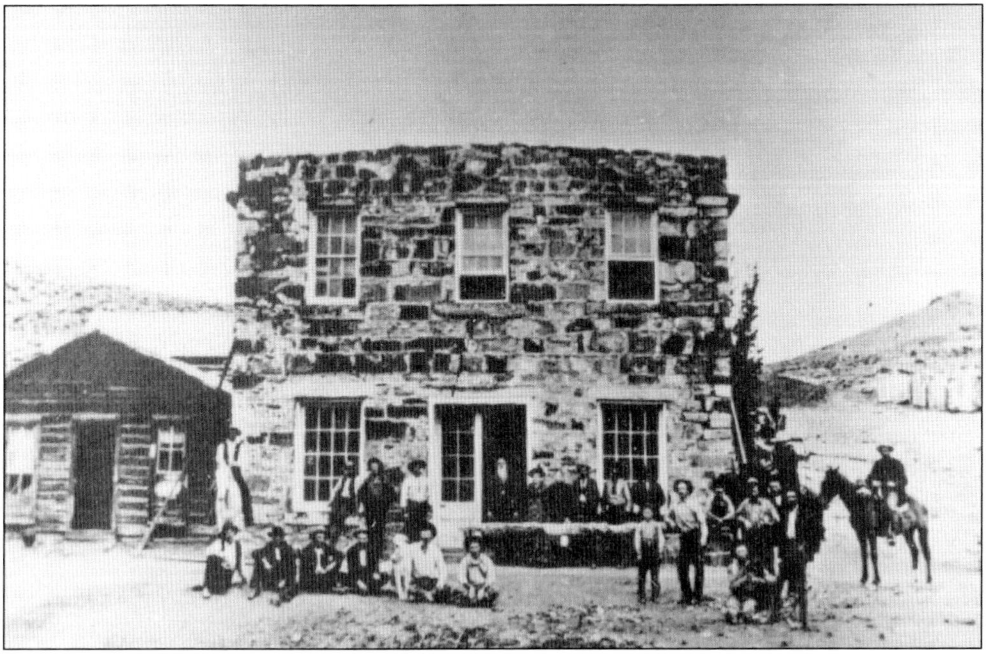

McAuley's General Store and Dance Hall, 1893. Constructed in 1869 by John Anthony, it is the largest masonry structure in the area, the stone having come from the Beaver Creek area. The building housed gaming tables, a saloon, and a post office during the town's heyday. An earthquake weakened the sandstone structure in the early 1900s, necessitating the removal of the upper story. In later years, Tom Hyde operated the smaller structure as a dance hall and community building.

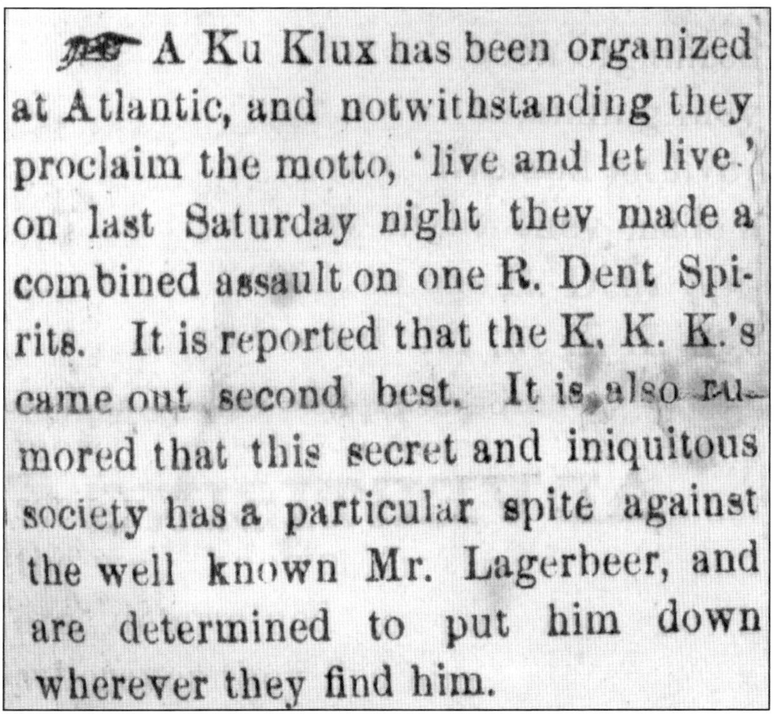

A Ku Klux has been organized at Atlantic, and notwithstanding they proclaim the motto, 'live and let live.' on last Saturday night they made a combined assault on one R. Dent Spirits. It is reported that the K. K. K.'s came out second best. It is also rumored that this secret and iniquitous society has a particular spite against the well known Mr. Lagerbeer, and are determined to put him down wherever they find him.

South Pass News, June 28, 1871. The area boasted two newspapers during the gold rush: the *South Pass News* and the *Sweetwater Mines*. Surviving copies speak optimistically of the area's bright future and report local events in an entertaining manner, despite dealing with sometimes "iniquitous" subject matter.

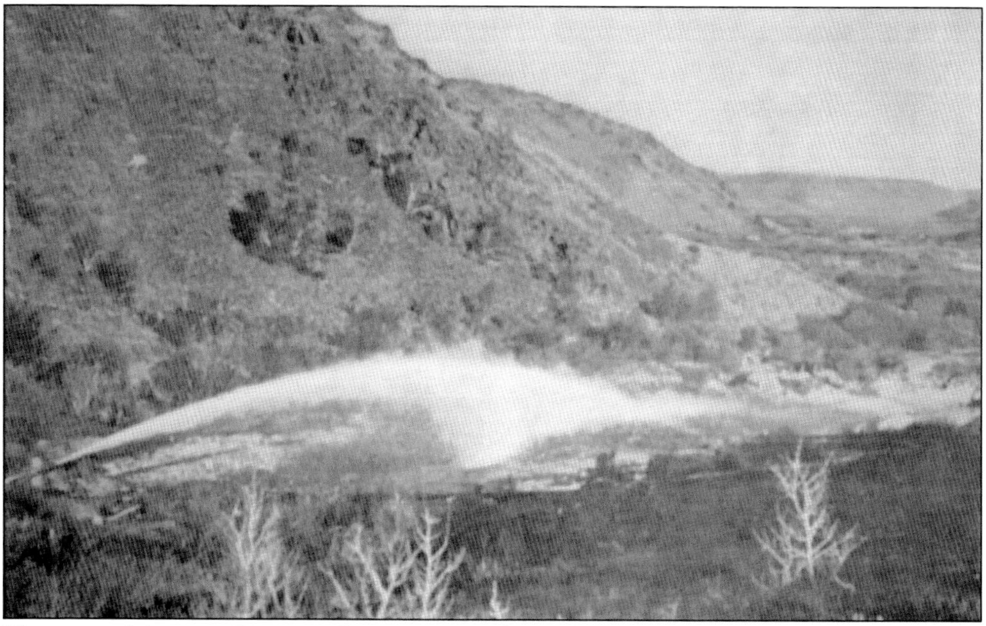

Hydraulic Monitor Washing Gravel. Water from Christina Lake traveled by way of earthen ditches and wooden flumes to Atlantic City, losing 2,250 feet in elevation. The falling water created immense energy when funneled through the nozzle of the monitor. Miners intended to use the water to blast gold-bearing gravels into sluices for easy recovery. The gravel deposits of Rock Creek frustrated the miners' work, despite the engineering marvel.

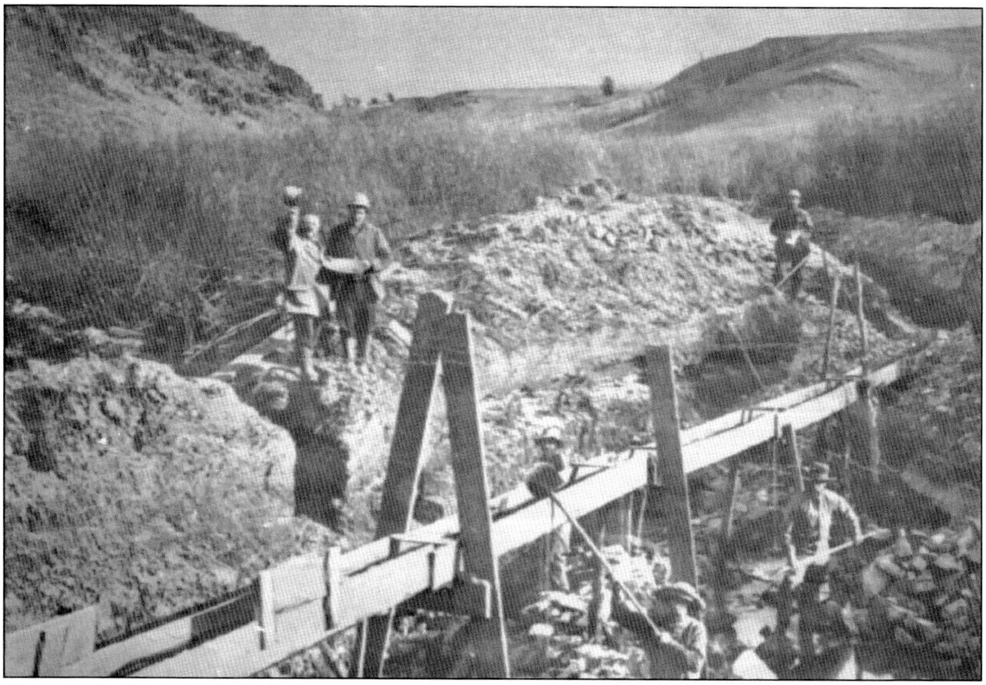

Granier's Ditch. At left, Emile Granier, a French financier, intended to take California's successful hydraulic mining methods and apply them to the gravels of Rock Creek. While his first cleanup in 1891 yielded 6,720 ounces of gold, the venture ended in failure.

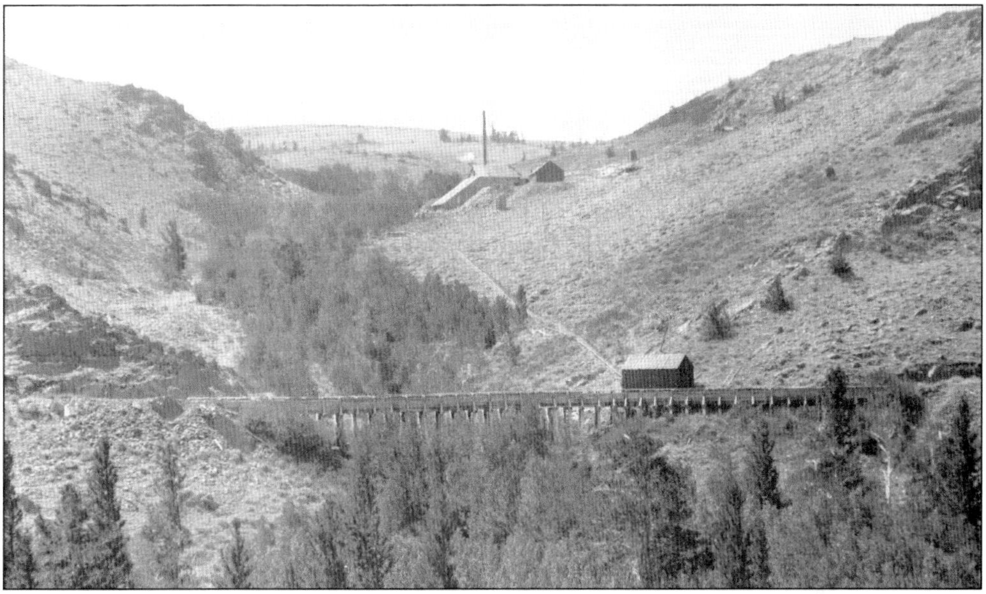

Tabor Grand Mine and Mill. Located just outside Atlantic City, the mine was named for the Tabor Grand Hotel of Leadville, Colorado. The mill structure at the center of the image burned to the ground as the result of careless thawing of frozen dynamite. The wooden flume in the foreground is one of 29 that carried water the 25 miles from Christina Lake to Emile Granier's hydraulic mining venture below Atlantic City.

Ten Stamp Mill. Stamp milling has its origins in medieval Europe, when technology was little advanced from that of ancient Rome. A number of stamp mills were located at the Sweetwater Mines from 1869 to 1935. Stamps in the district were powered by either waterwheels or steam. Ore was fed into screened battery boxes below the heavy hammer-headed rods held vertically in the timber frame. As the drive wheel turned, each rod assembly rose and fell onto ore below, breaking free the fine gold from the rock. Water was fed to the box, with the fine particles flowing through the screen and onto mercury-coated copper tables where the gold was captured in the mercury.

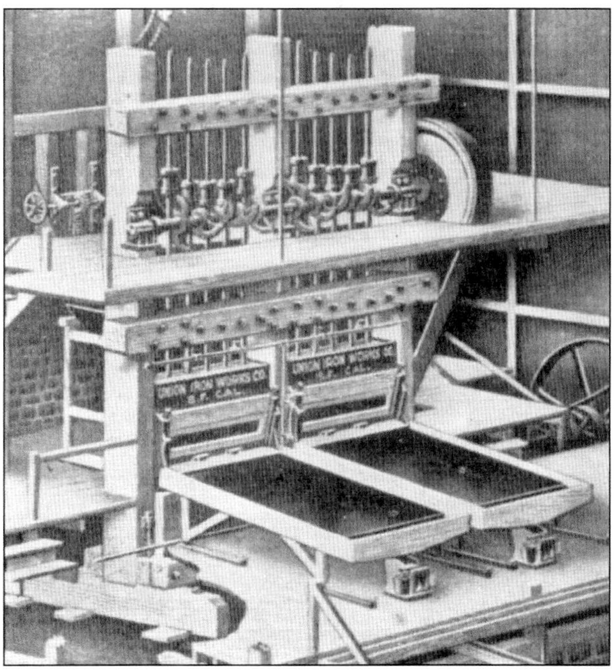

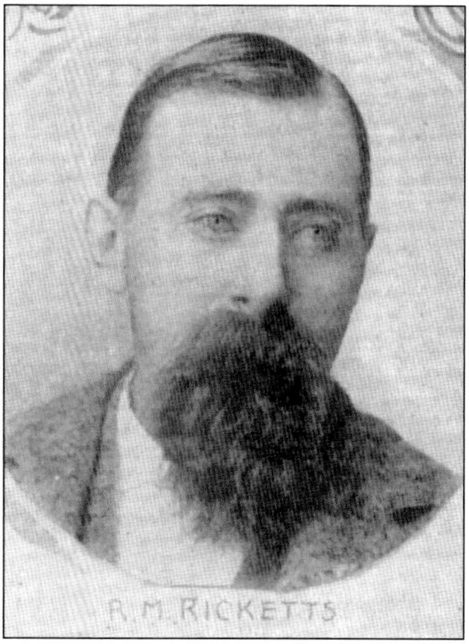

Rufus Ricketts. Nineteen-year-old Ricketts came to the gold camps in 1869 from Tennessee. He was a miner, freighter, and helped construct Camp Stambaugh. Ricketts owned the Mary Ellen Mine and Rustler Mine in the late 1890s. In 1897, he was getting .25 ounces of gold per ton from the Rustler outside Atlantic City. Ricketts began to wind up his local business matters by 1900. He then moved to Roswell, New Mexico, before traveling to Denver, Colorado, where he died in 1904.

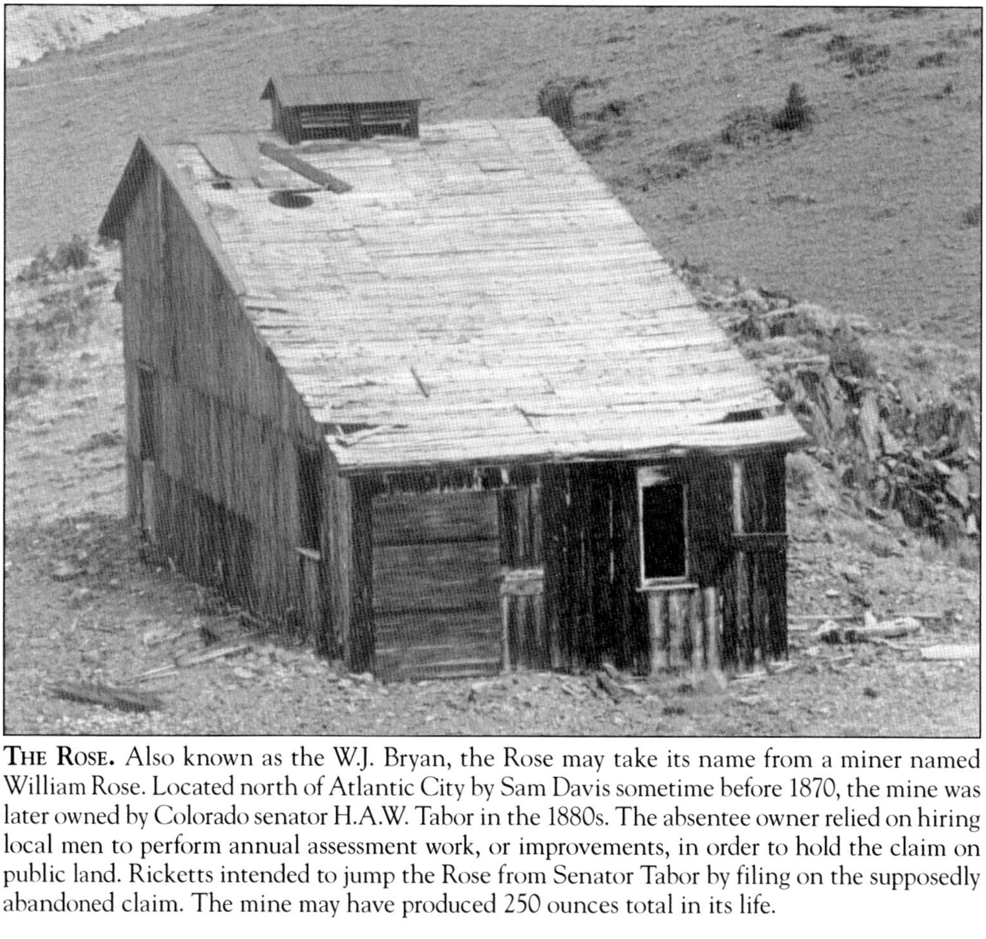

The Rose. Also known as the W.J. Bryan, the Rose may take its name from a miner named William Rose. Located north of Atlantic City by Sam Davis sometime before 1870, the mine was later owned by Colorado senator H.A.W. Tabor in the 1880s. The absentee owner relied on hiring local men to perform annual assessment work, or improvements, in order to hold the claim on public land. Ricketts intended to jump the Rose from Senator Tabor by filing on the supposedly abandoned claim. The mine may have produced 250 ounces total in its life.

BEN'S HEAD.

Rufus M. Rickets Works on It With a Winchester.

Mr. Ben Evans, of Atlantic City, received word from the Tabor Mines and Mills Company, of Denver, to resume work upon their property in that mining district, the Tabor Grand and the Rose mines, and continue until two hundred dollars in work had been done upon each claim, this would be the annual representation expenditure necessary to hold the claims until January 1, 1898. Mr. Evans, as soon as he received the notification from Denver went immediately to the Rose lead and began work thereon, when R. M. Ricketts, who had previously posted a notice on this property came to Evans and ordered him to desist from the work, as he proposed to take the property. Evans replied that the property was not jumpable, even if no work were done until after 1896 had passed, so that his notice was clearly a "bulldozing" scheme, and as he was authorized to do the work and had begun in time the property was legally in the possession, through him, of the Tabor Mines and Mills Company, and he should most certainly fulfill the trust placed in him and hold the property. Upon this Mr. Ricketts struck him over the head with a Winchester rifle, knocking him senseless and cutting a long, deep gash across the top of his head. Mr. Evans lay senseless for some time and when he came to he saw Rickets hurrying away in the distance.

A warrant was obtained and Ricketts arrested and brought to Lander by Deputy Sheriff Tom Brady. He was arraigned in Judge Wallace's court Monday morning where he plead not guilty to the charge of "Assault with intent to kill," and asked to have the case postponed for twenty-four hours, which was granted, and at the time set he was examined, and the judge deeming the evidence sufficient to hold him to appear at the next term of the district court in the sum of $500, which amount of bail was furnished and all concerned have returned to the mines.

CLAIM JUMPING. Mining was serious business—a person's livelihood. The incident reported in the *Lander Clipper* on January 8, 1897, between Evans and Ricketts, was played out more quietly in other local mines as well. Ricketts later pleaded guilty to assault and battery, for which he paid a $25 fine, about the value of one ounce of gold at the time.

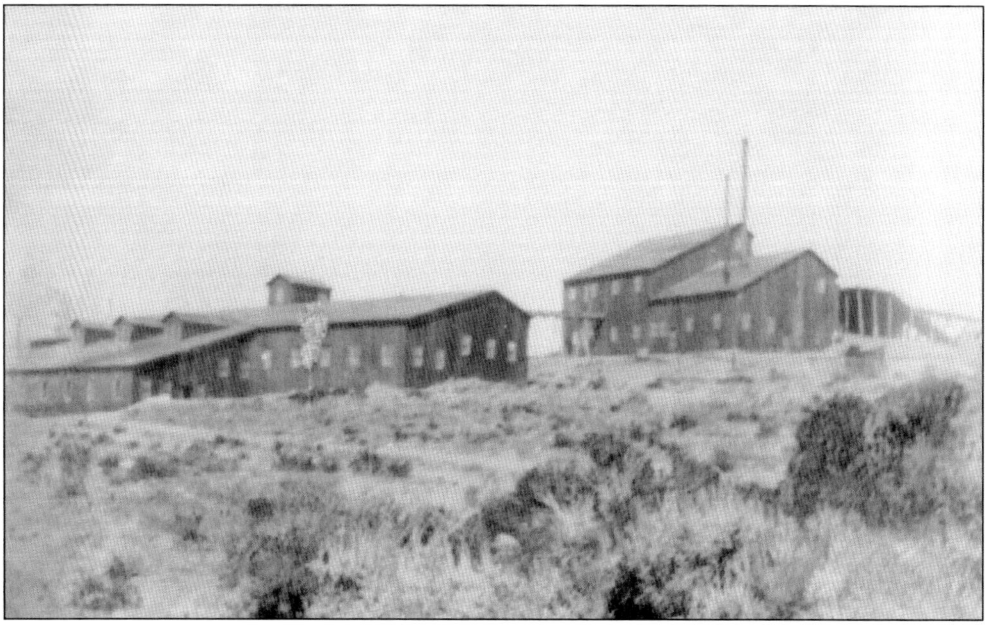

DEXTER MILL, 1905. Dexter Cahoon of Rochester, New York, promised to successfully process the ore produced by local mines. Milling at the Dexter relied on mercury-based amalgamation and cyanide to recover gold values. Pulverized ore was flushed by water over mercury-coated copper plates where the dense gold particles became trapped in the quicksilver, while lightweight wastes passed by. Cyanide dissolves gold for later recovery.

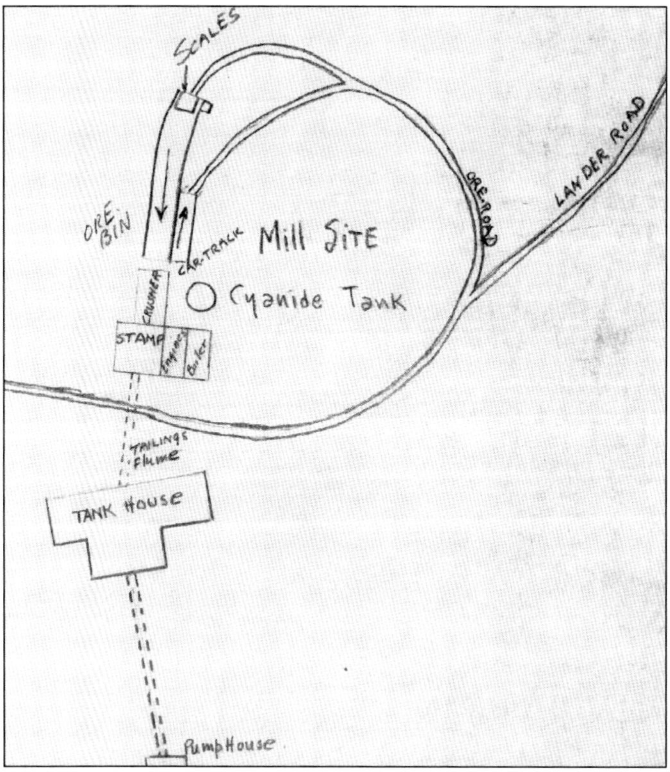

PLAN OF DEXTER MILL SITE, 1905. Incoming ore was weighed at the scales and dumped into bins prior to initial breaking done by a No. 3 Gates gyratory crusher. Twenty stamps, weighing 1,050 pounds each, pulverized the ore into fine grains, freeing the gold for recovery. Tailings from the stamps were then treated with a cyanide solution. Power was provided by several boilers and steam engines. Water for processing came from Rock Creek. Dismal gold recovery rates quickly doomed the venture.

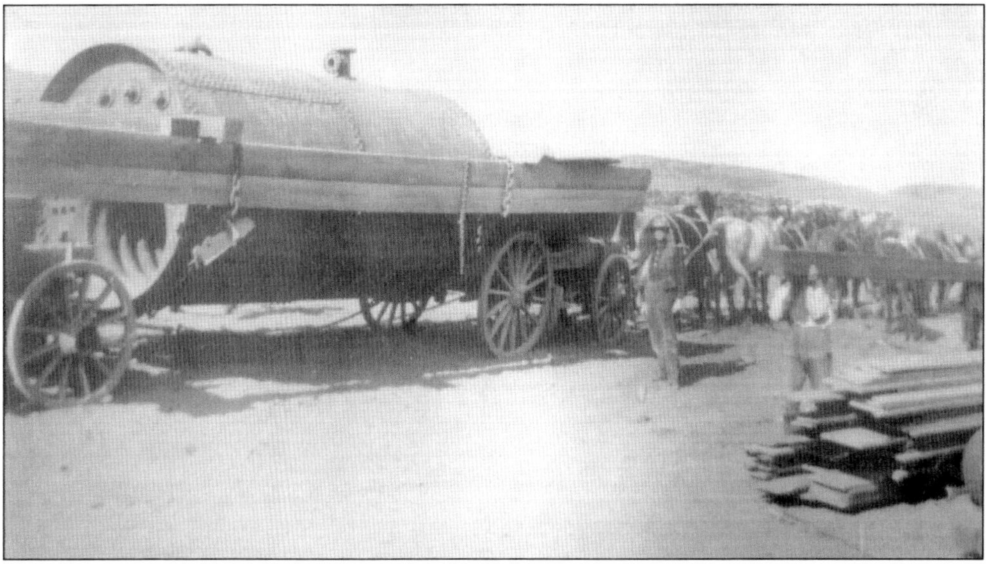

Freighting in the Dexter Mill's Boiler, 1904. The Dexter generated the power required to operate the stamps by burning cordwood to create steam. The energy of the steam was converted to motion through the use of engines. Freighting of equipment from the Union Pacific stations at Point of Rocks and Rocks Springs was a specialty occupation that demanded experienced teamsters, horses, and wagons.

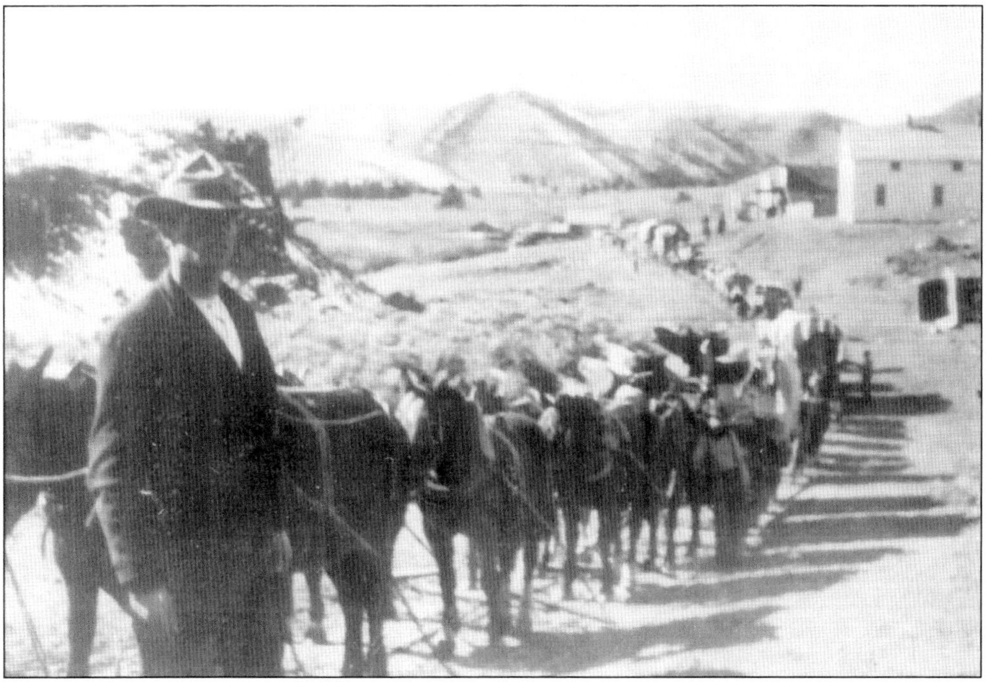

John McGetrick, Freighting Quartz, 1904. The Iowa native moved to the area in 1896 by way of Colorado with his wife and the first seven of their eight total children. McGetrick was a local miner who made use of the processing available at the Dexter Mill. State geologist Henry Beeler reported in 1908 that the mill had a capacity of 150 tons per day. The mill recovered little gold from local ore, and miners soon renounced the Dexter.

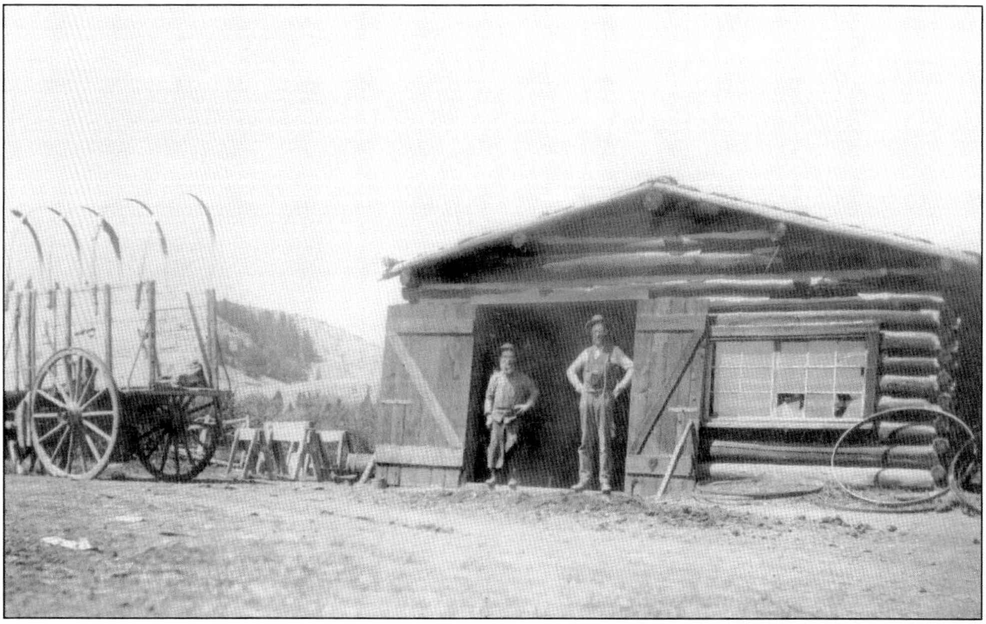

HARSCH BLACKSMITH SHOP. Pictured here are Phil Harsch (left) and Tom Brady. Harsch, born in Luxembourg, and his son Henry ran this blacksmith shop until the 1920s. When the E.T. Fisher Dredge went along Rock Creek in the 1930s, the shop was torn down. Brady was elected Constable for Atlantic City in November 1896. During his career as a lawman, Brady also served as deputy game and fish warden for Fremont County and city marshal for Lander.

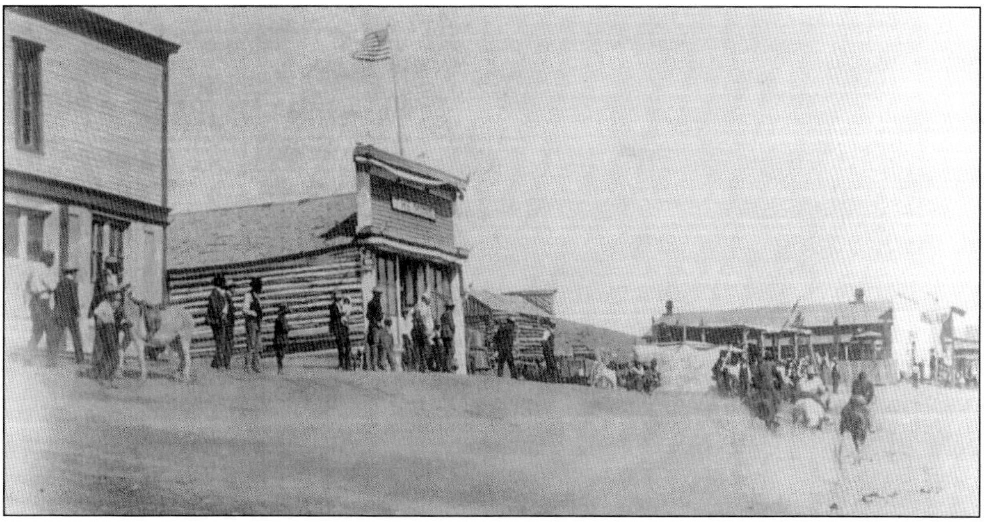

LABOR DAY, 1905. A federally recognized holiday since 1894, the day was an occasion for the citizens of Atlantic City to gather for public speeches, horse racing on Main Street, and celebrate the unofficial end of summer. Flag flying saloons like The Mint helped locals to cope with the dust kicked up by the brisk wind and racing horses. Labor Day may also have been an occasion for the local chapter of the Western Federation of Miners to congregate.

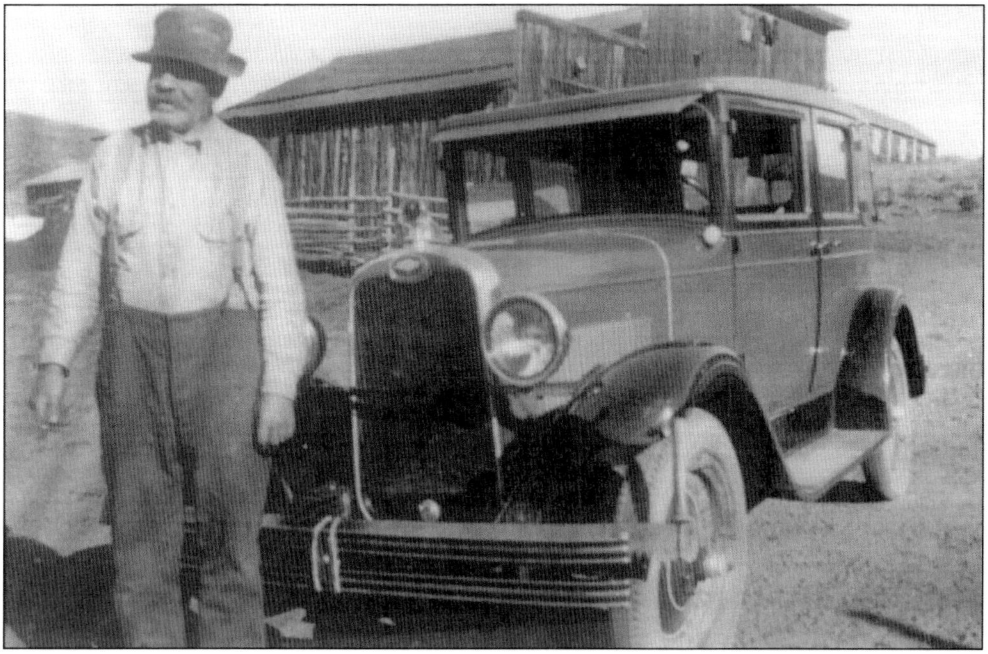

Lawrence L. Giessler, Late 1920s. The longtime Atlantic City merchant, postmaster, justice of the peace, and freighter was born in Baden, Germany, in 1855. He ranched south of Atlantic City, keeping about 100 head of cattle. For years, the Giessler Store was a fixture on Main Street until closing a handful of years after Giessler's death in 1929.

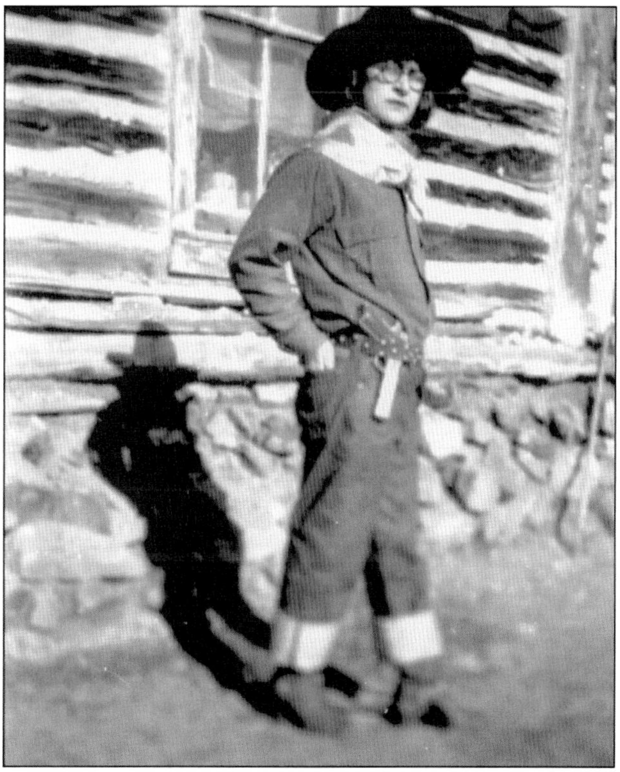

Zoe Green, 1929. While her three siblings were all born in Atlantic City with the assistance of midwife, Hannah Swabes, Zoe was born in Rock Springs. In 1929, Zoe was part of the crew that moved the Dexter Mill from Atlantic City to South Pass City, where it became Midwest Mines' new Carissa Mill. For $5 a day, Zoe drove a White's truck with 21 forward gears and 7 reverse gears. Half of the time, the brakes did not work. Later, Zoe was a caretaker at the Carissa and helped keep the workings pumped out.

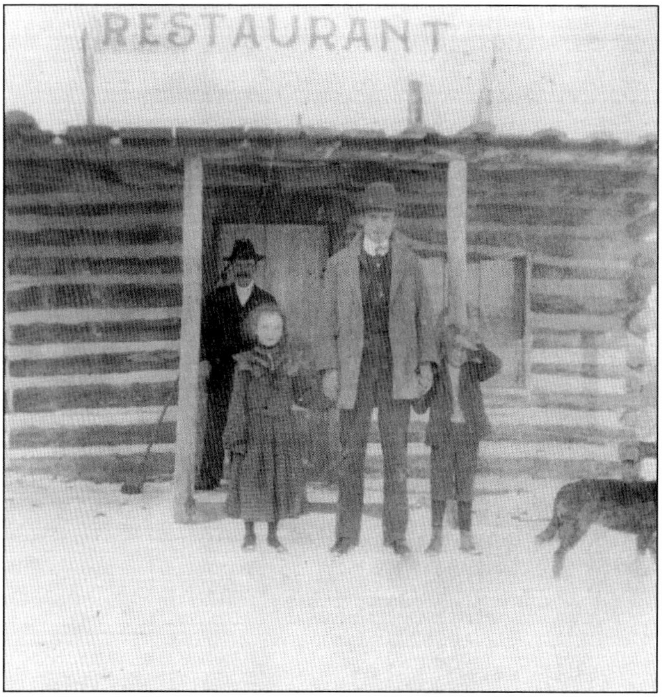

Carpenter Restaurant, 1903. From left to right are Clarence Emmett Carpenter, Hazel Carpenter, Casey Llewellyn, and Clarence Emmett Carpenter Jr. Clarence Emmett Carpenter and his wife, Nellie, moved to Atlantic City in 1890. By 1903, Nellie remodeled an abandoned 1868 gold rush building to board miners. The couple divorced in 1907, with Clarence leaving for Nevada and Nellie remaining in Atlantic City to support their eight children. At this time, according to *The Miner*, published in Hudson, Wyoming, Llewellyn was watchman at the Mary Ellen.

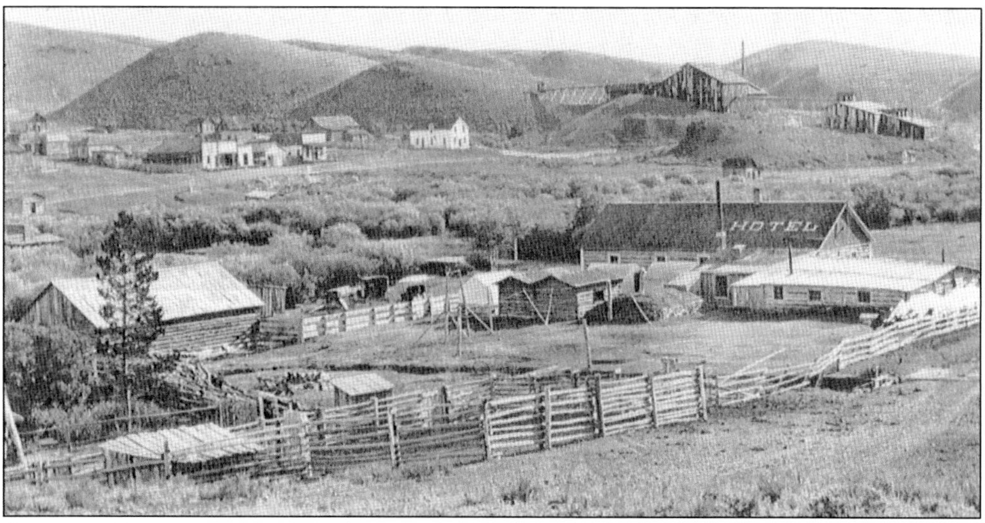

Atlantic City, 1920s. Prior to the 1930s boom when the Fisher Dredge came to town, Atlantic City was dominated by the massive, but shuttered, Dexter Mill in the distance. The white-sided Sypes House stands in the center distance. The Red Cloud Saloon and Giessler Store round out the main business district. The Carpenter Hotel is in the foreground.

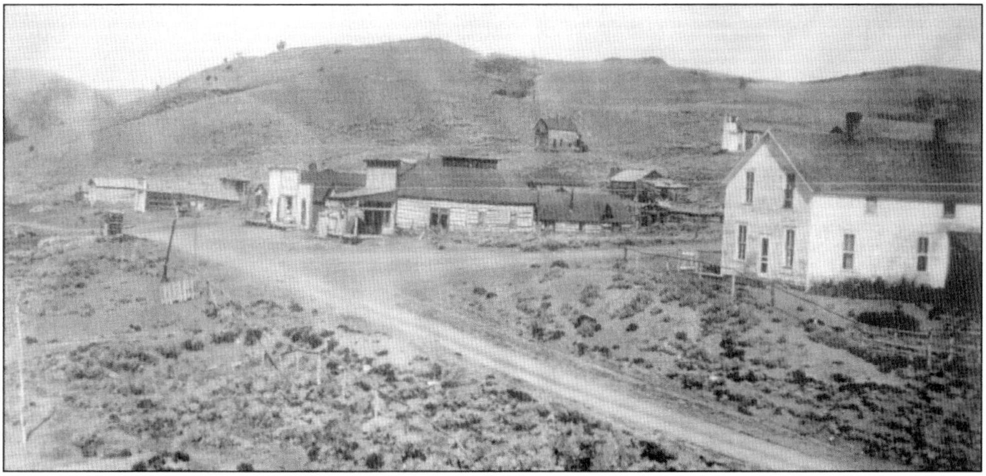

Atlantic City Main Street, 1920. The white clapboard-sided Sypes House featured six bedrooms and two bathrooms. Charles Sypes was a bookkeeper for the Dexter Company until it went under. When the Tim Ba Bah Company assumed control of Dexter's property, Sypes stayed on as their resident agent. His wife, Elizabeth, was a trained singer, spoke French and Italian, and displayed a dress and manner that marked her as aloof. She died in 1926. Charles died in 1936 from carbon monoxide poisoning after struggling with financial strain and depression.

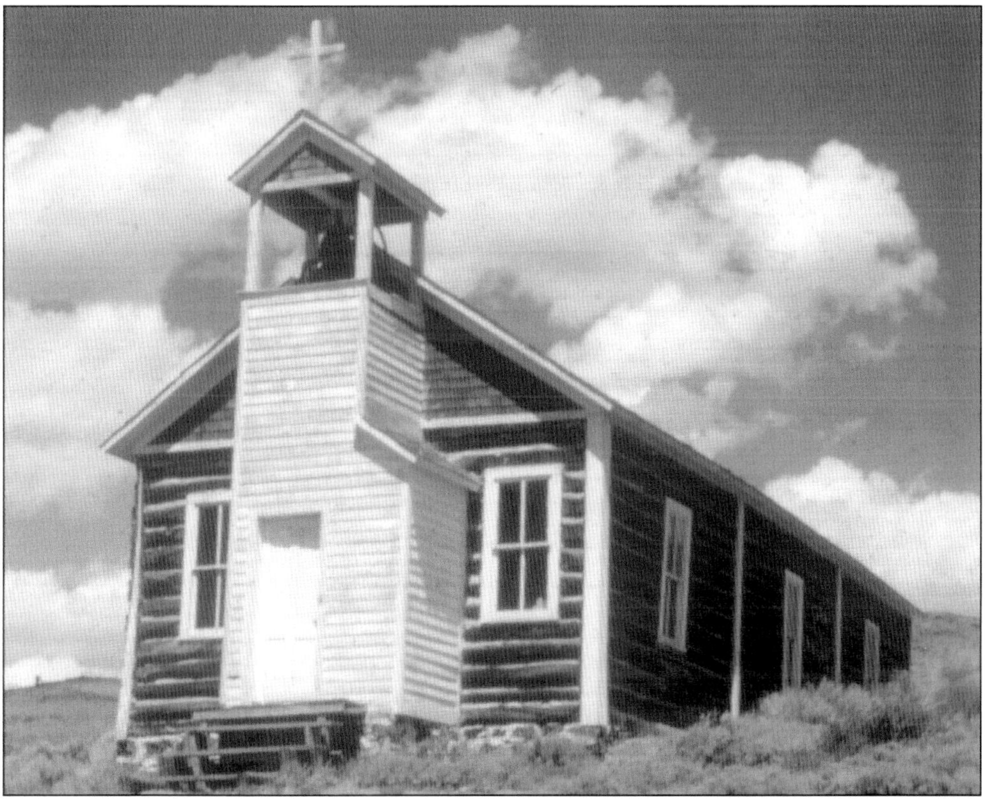

St. Andrew's Episcopal Church. Local residents, especially Ellen Carpenter, were involved in organizing the construction. Dances and plays were held to raise money. The church was consecrated in 1913. Worship services, weddings, and funerals are still held.

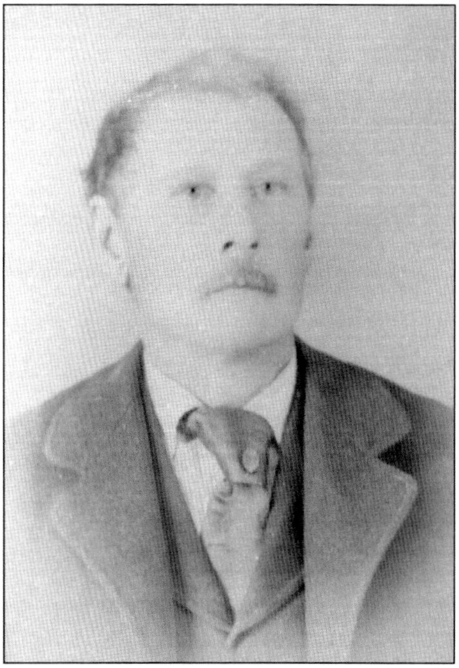

JOHN "JACK" HUFF. Huff was born in 1842 in Waterloo, New York. Anxious to see new country, Huff worked for the Chicago, Burlington & Quincy Railroad. He saw service with the Union at the siege of Vicksburg, Mississippi, and later returned to railroad work, this time with the Chicago & Northwestern. Huff helped construct Fort Carlin near Cheyenne, and then participated in the rush to the Sweetwater Mines. The *Fremont Clipper* stated that on March 29, 1895, Huff had taken over the management of the Garfield Mine and Mill outside Atlantic City. In later years, Huff moved to Southern California for its climate.

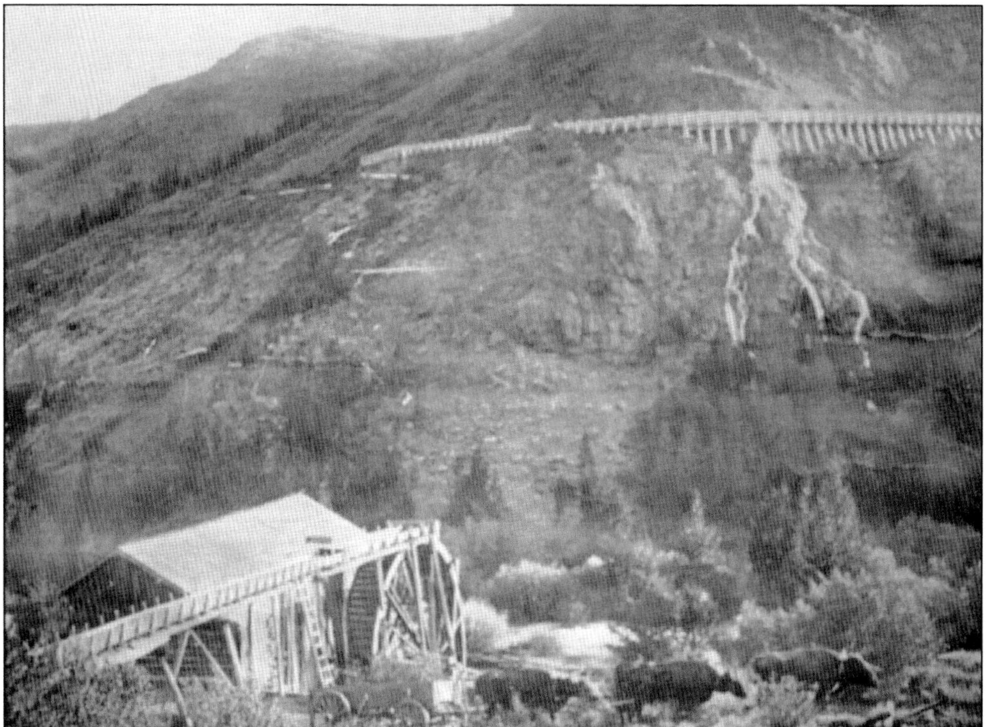

HUFF MILL. A team of oxen delivers a load of ore to the Huff Mill located on Rock Creek above Atlantic City around 1894. The water-powered mill featured 10 stamps and amalgamation recovery. In the background, a long stretch of wooden flume of Granier's Ditch can be seen leaking water down the steep hillside.

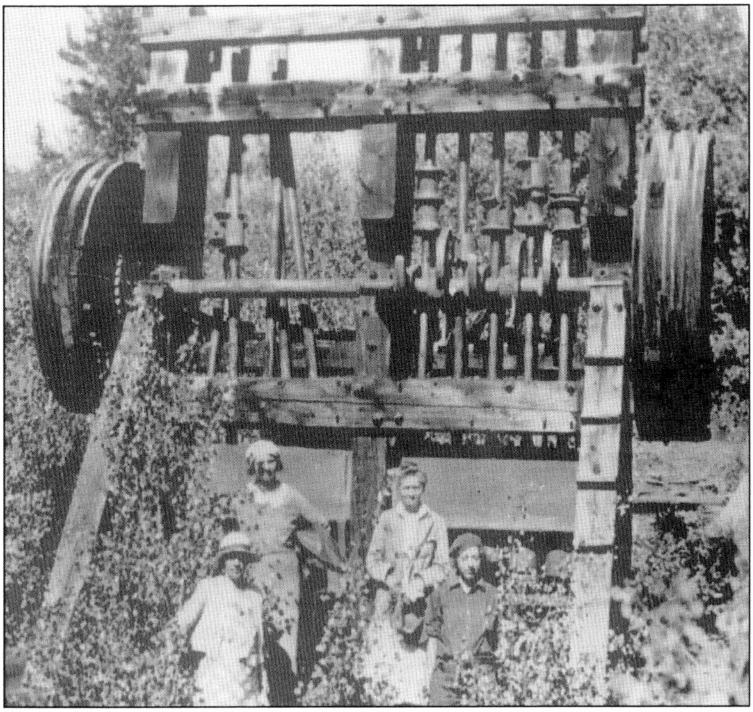

HUFF MILL, 1934. From left to right are Anne Carpenter, Maude Lee, Ellen Carpenter, and Janet Robinson. With the wooden housing presumably salvaged in order to construct other local buildings, only the massive timber and iron stamp mill components remain intact. Long out of service, the stamps appear nearly overgrown. World War II scrap drives soon claimed even these final remnants.

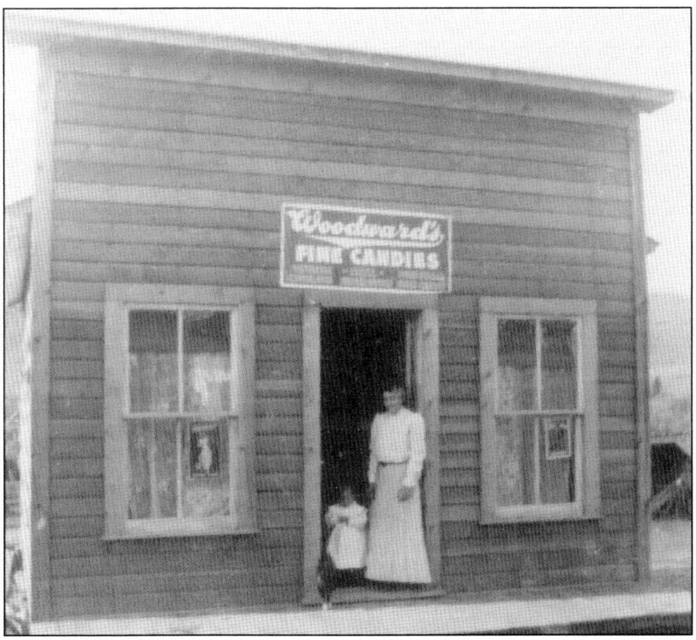

HUFF SISTERS' CANDY AND NOTION SHOP. Viola Huff (right) is seen standing with an unknown child. Around the turn of the 20th century, outside capital again flowed into the quiet town. In addition to the Dexter Mill venture, smaller construction projects, like this small store, put up around 1903, helped reinvigorate the town. Viola Huff married Dexter Cahoon's brother Walter.

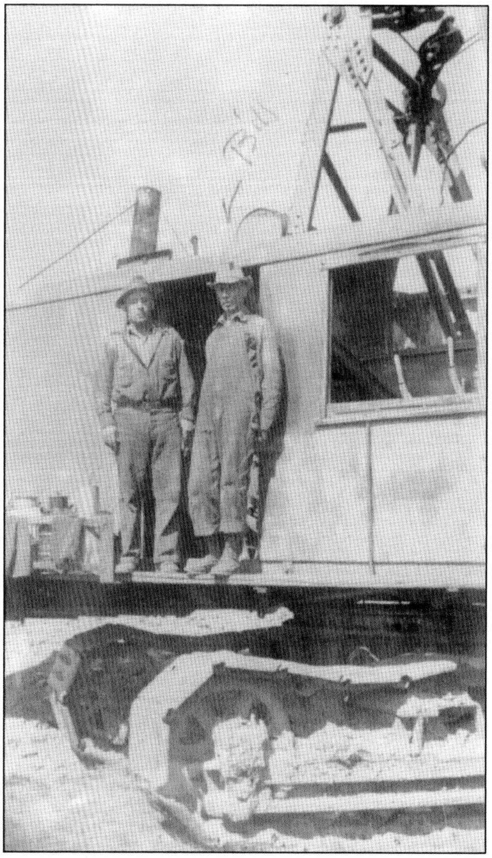

E.T. Fisher Company Dredge, 1936. Pictured here are Roy Spiva (left) and Bill Kempf. Mining operations at the E.T. Fisher Co. dredge began on May 20, 1933, and required a diverse workforce. The men stand atop the firm's gasoline-powered dragline shovel that is capable of moving 2,800 cubic yards of gold-bearing gravel into the wash plant every day. The secondhand dragline shovel cost the firm $14,000 and after being off-loaded by the Union Pacific Rail Road in Rock Springs, it walked to Atlantic City on its caterpillar tracks in just 12 days.

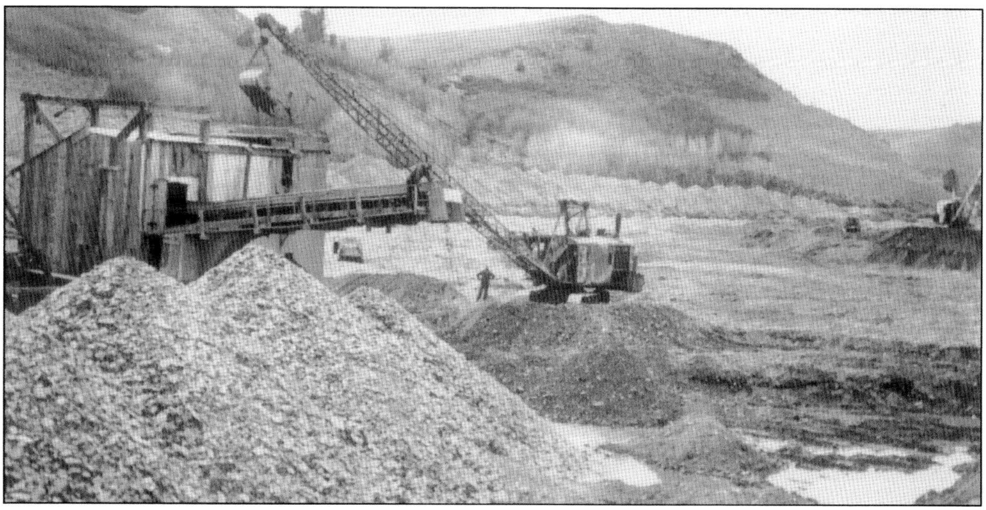

Wash Plant and Dragline. The shovel on the Fisher Dredge emptied into the wash plant some 27 feet above ground. A trommel (a rotating, inclined cylindrical screen with wash jets) helped to free the fine gold from the gravel, sand, and clay. The slurry then flowed over sluices with riffles, or small ridges, inside. The heavy gold tended to drop and get caught in the riffles, while the wastes flowed by with the water. Nearly 100 pounds of mercury in the riffles enhanced gold recovery.

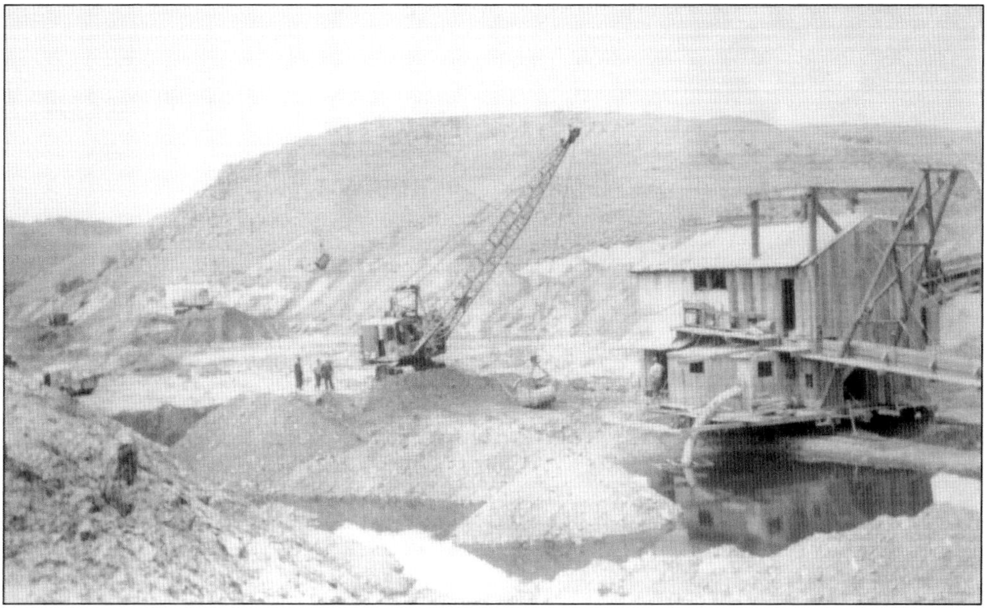

Fisher Dredge, Mid-1930s. Six men worked the day and afternoon shifts, and five men worked at night. The cost of labor, fuel, and supplies totaled about $150 per day.

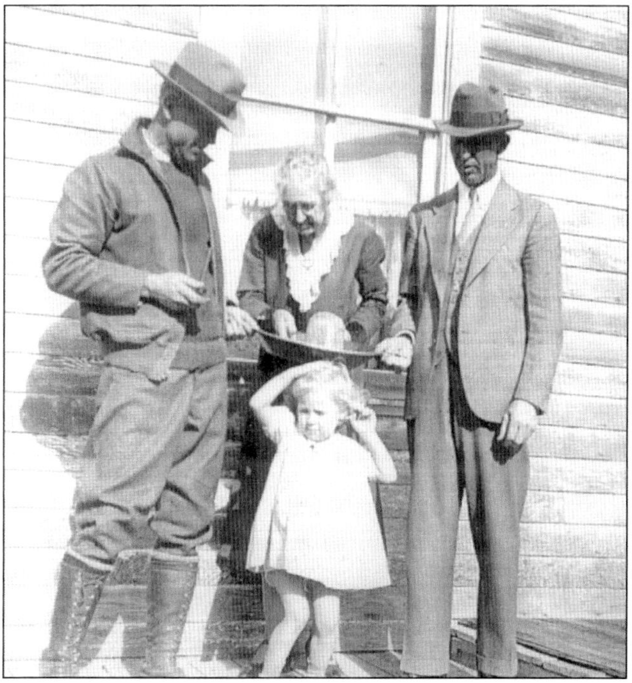

The Crawfords. Sons Win and Charlie Crawford with their mother, and Win's daughter, Nancy are pictured here. The Crawfords were partners in the dredge, with sizeable experience and wealth in Seattle, Washington, mining and lumber ventures, as well as in Alaska's gold fields. They also had experience in dredging Idaho's waterways. The adults hold a gold pan with a large gold retort from a recent cleanup. The venture officially reported recovering 11,500 ounces of gold, although speculation suggests that they quietly collected three times that amount. The dredge may have been the single most successful gold mining operation in the area's history.

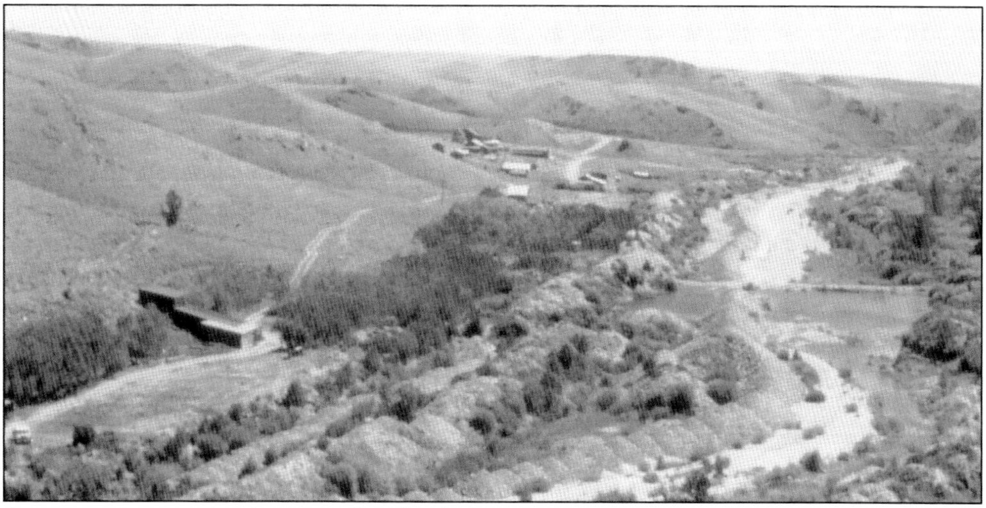

ATLANTIC CITY, 1951. Ten years after the dredging operations ceased, the main channel of Rock Creek is still dominated by piles of tailings. Frank Lemley's mill building stands idle on the left. The Lemley Mill featured two small Huntington mills and mercury-based recovery of the fine gold particles.

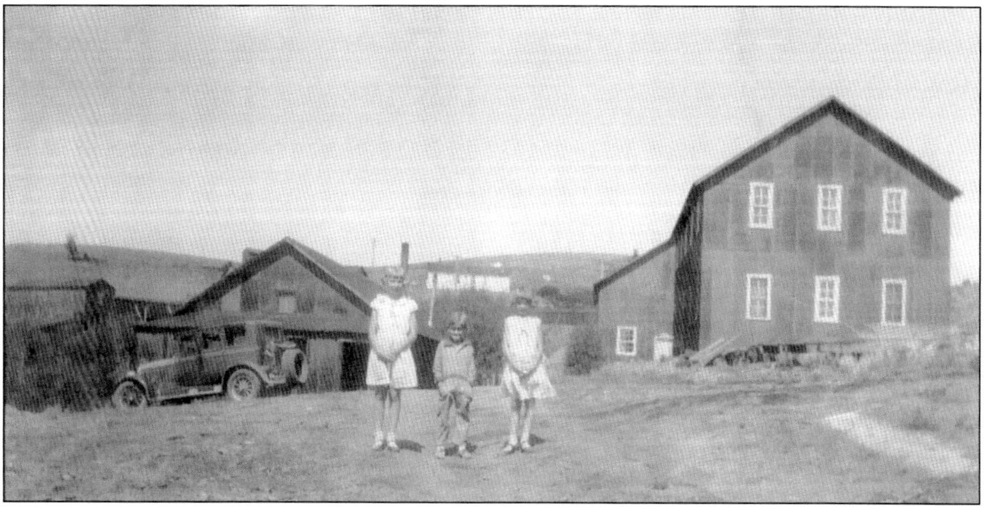

MIDAS MINE, 1930S. From left to right are Marguerite, Wally, and Betty Carpenter. Patented in 1900 by James McAvoy, Rufus Ricketts, and John Huff as the Diana Lode, the mine was renamed by the Quealy family of Kemmerer, Wyoming, when they acquired the property from John R. Boardman. Two-dozen men were employed in the mine and mill, including Jim Carpenter, the father of the children in the photograph. Carl Pfaff Sr. of Kemmerer, Wyoming, was the superintendent. The cookhouse is at left, the white Quealy residence in the center background, and the employee bunkhouse stands at right. Around 1941 with operations halted, the buildings were disassembled and moved to Montana. Total production for the property is estimated at 500 ounces of gold.

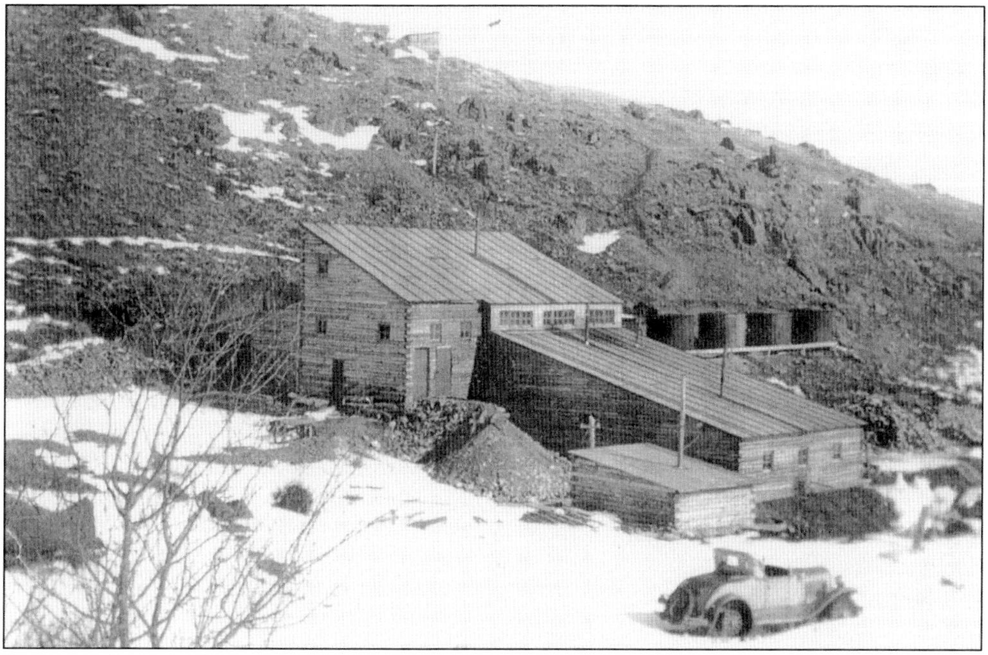

CONNELLY MILL ON BIG ATLANTIC GULCH, 1937–1938. Father and son, Bert and Warren Connelly, took up gold claims on Big Atlantic Gulch outside Atlantic City and lived there year-round. Their effort at stock selling seems to have gathered them enough capital to build this mill. It is not known to have run much ore. Locals recall how the Connelly's place provided a nice stopover in the winter for those skiing or snowshoeing to and from Atlantic City.

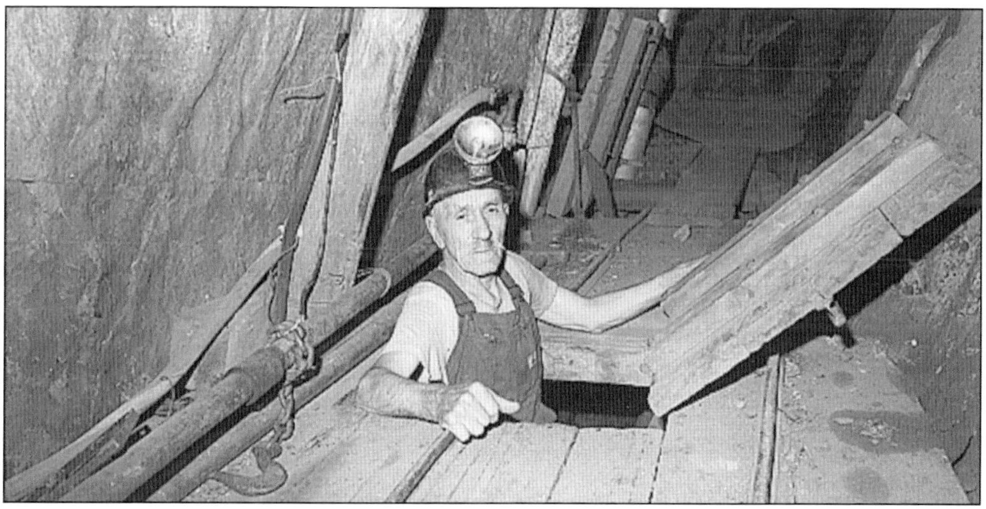

ROBERT "SHORTY" HADDENHAM AT THE ST. LOUIS MINE. Located late in 1868 as the Jim Dyer Lode by a party of men including Jim Dyer, the claim was later known as the St. Louis. The *Fremont Clipper* of March 29, 1895, states that Robert McAuley had the mine and was sinking a new shaft. Before moving to Atlantic City in 1868 and patenting the mine in 1902, Lydia McAuley had fought Indians alongside her husband, Robert, at their stage station in 1866 near Julesburg, Colorado. She gave the mine to their six-foot, four-inch son "Timberline" Bob McAuley. The young McAuley was a crack rifle shot and rustled more than a few cattle in his youth. Here, recent owner Haddenham is shown near air, water, and electrical lines.

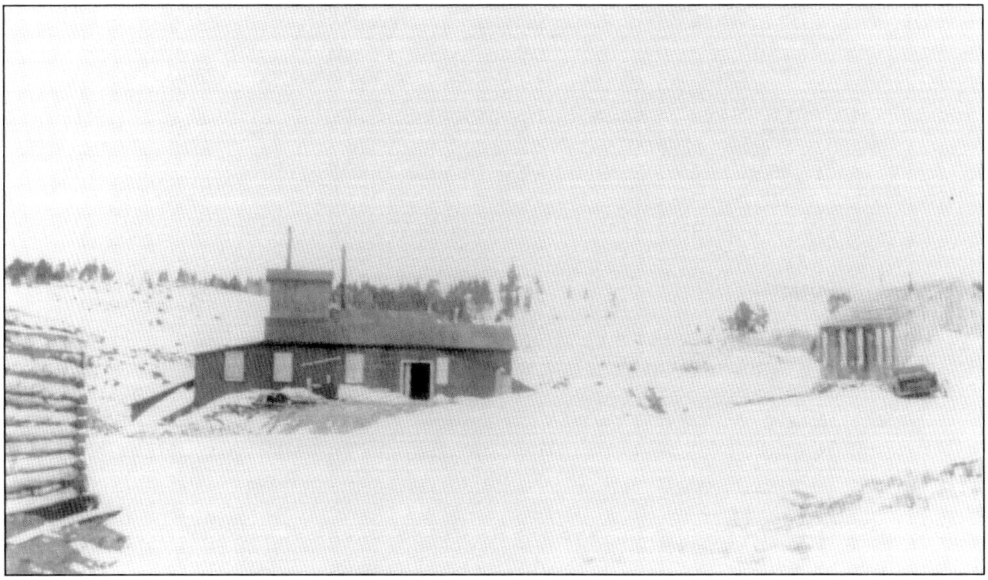

MARY ELLEN MINE & MILL, C. 1900. C.G. Coutant's *History of Wyoming* says the location of the mine was made in 1869 by Pease, Frye, and Perkins. According to the granddaughter of Perkins, the mine took its name from her grandmother Mary Perkins and her sister Ellen King's combined names. The *Salt Lake Tribune* reported on January 2, 1900, that the property was to start up soon with a mill building that was moved in from the defunct Diamond Development Company on Beaver Creek, near Miners Delight. The *Salt Lake Tribune* stated that on August 13, 1900, the mill was up and running. John P. Ibson of Denver, Colorado, served as manager.

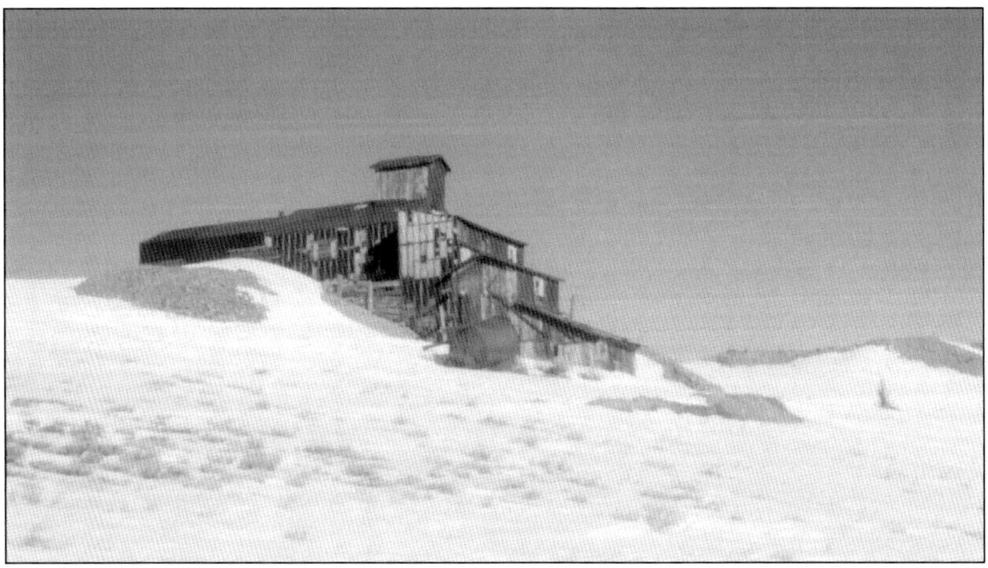

MARY ELLEN, 1951. Little changed since it was erected half a century earlier, the mill building stands amid mine dumps. The Mary Ellen is credited with a production of 6,050 ounces in Wyoming state geologist C.E. Jamison's 1911 report on the area.

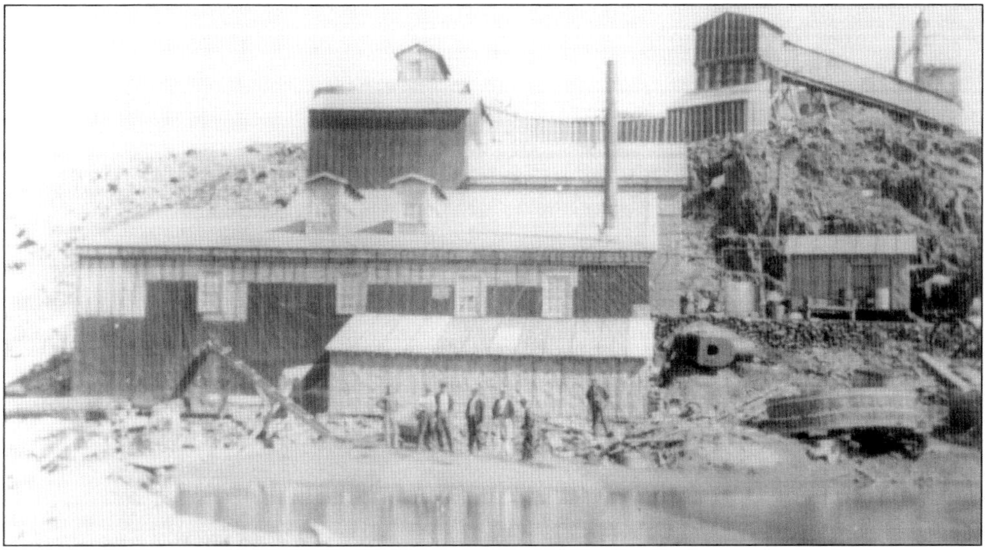

DUNCAN MINE & MILL, 1935. The ore was hoisted from the shaft at the upper right corner of the image and proceeded through the mill building's crushing and recovery machinery below. The Duncan featured 1,050-pound Nissen stamps and mercury recovery of gold values. The mill later tried flotation and cyanide to recover more gold, but rampant high grading of rich ore helped to close the mine again in 1935.

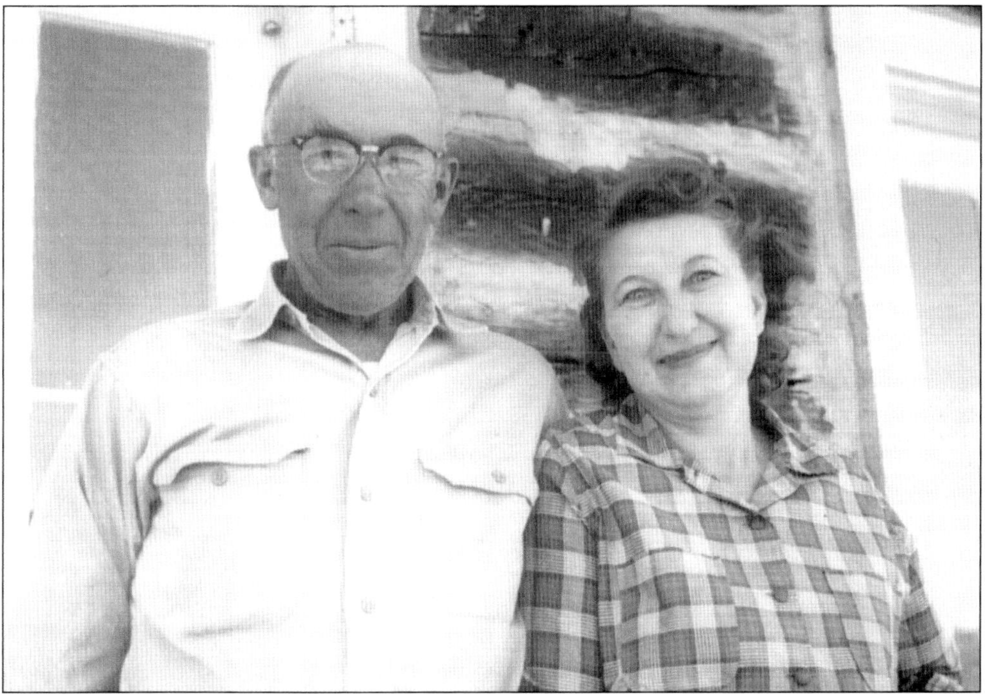

WALTER "RAY" AND GLADYS "BOBBY" JENKS. Married in 1931 in their native Colorado Springs, Colorado, Ray and Bobby spent six years in New Mexico's zinc and copper camps during World War II. Ray was later a partner in the Elayer Company based in Silver City, New Mexico, when a friend introduced him to the Duncan in 1949. He restarted the mine, making doré deposits at the Denver Mint from March 1950 through July 1958. By September 1964, Elayer was bankrupt.

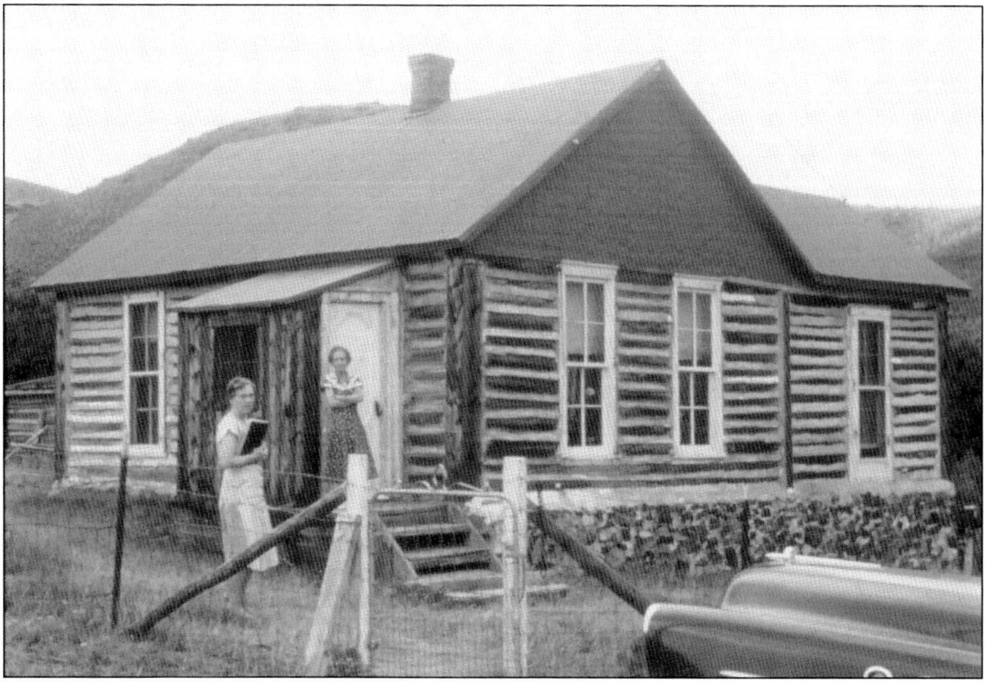

HELEN HENDERSON AND MARTHA GUSTAFSEN, 1958. Gustafsen (right), the daughter of Phil and Martha Harsch, visits with Helen Henderson (left), of Bridgeport, Nebraska, during one of the Henderson's research trips. Martha married a Norwegian man named Pete Gustafsen in 1912.

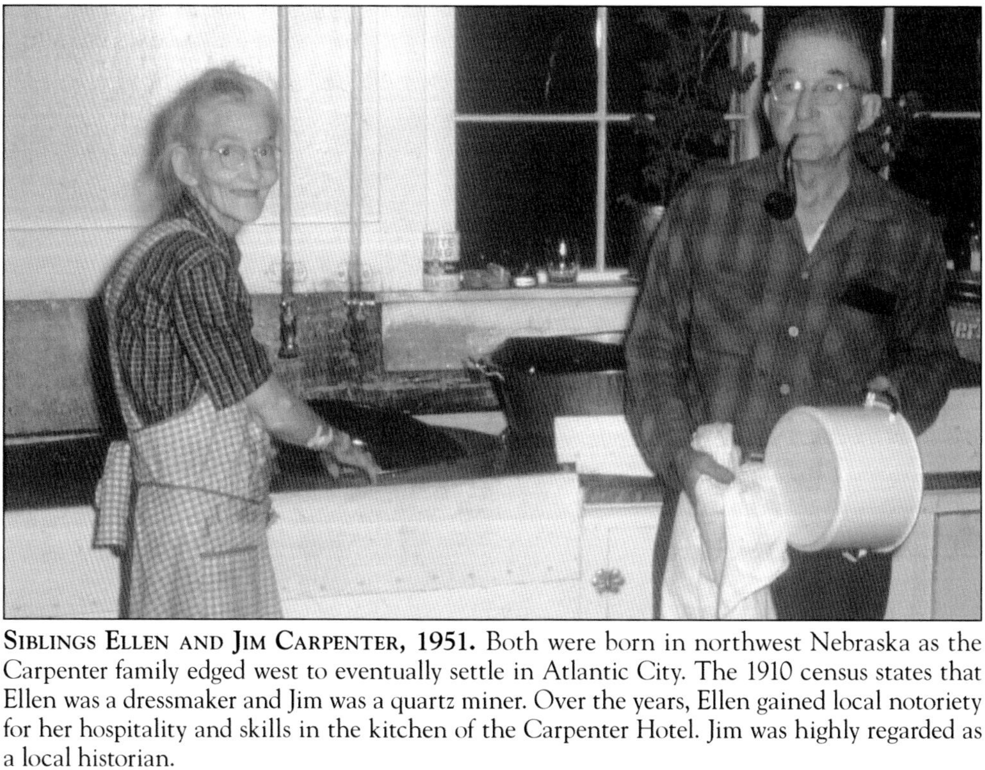

SIBLINGS ELLEN AND JIM CARPENTER, 1951. Both were born in northwest Nebraska as the Carpenter family edged west to eventually settle in Atlantic City. The 1910 census states that Ellen was a dressmaker and Jim was a quartz miner. Over the years, Ellen gained local notoriety for her hospitality and skills in the kitchen of the Carpenter Hotel. Jim was highly regarded as a local historian.

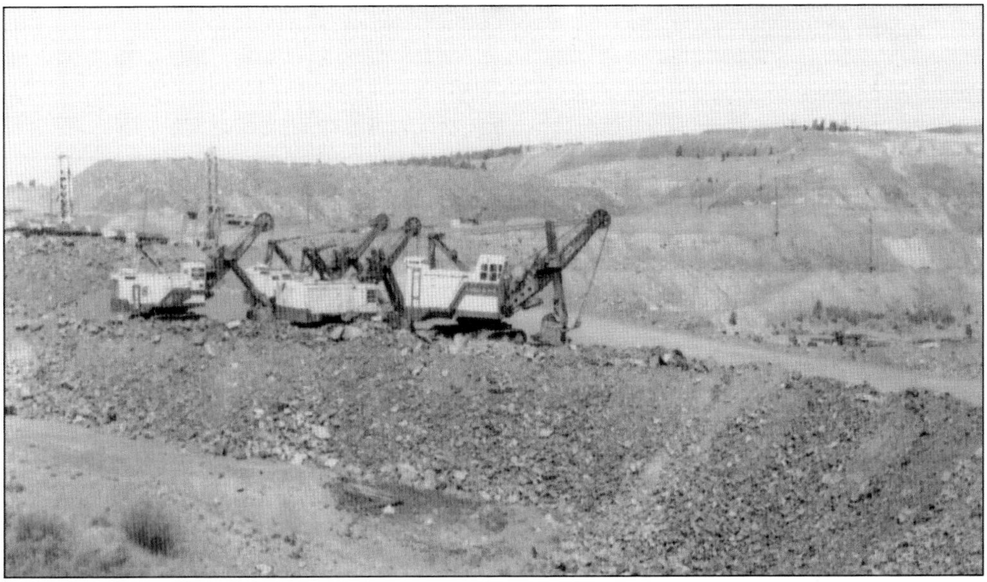

Iron Ore Boom. Planning for the open pit iron mine began in 1954, with construction on the property beginning in 1960. The P&H blast hole drills in the left background created vertical boreholes to be filled with explosives. Electric-powered shovels loaded six cubic yards of rock at a time into 45-ton diesel dump trucks for transport to the crushing and screening buildings. Final grinding took place at the mill. US Steel was once Fremont County's largest employer. Upon closing, the county experienced yet one more mining bust.

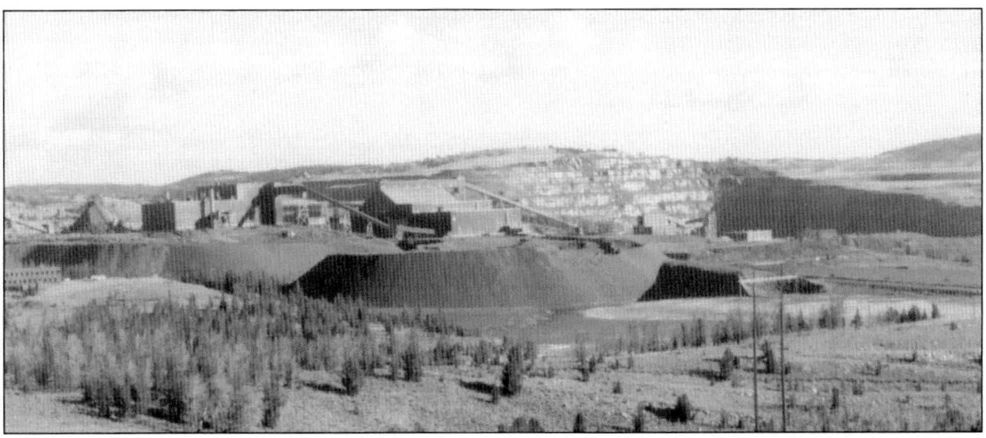

Atlantic City Ore Operations of US Steel Corp. The complex once included some of the largest buildings in the entire state of Wyoming. The raw ore was pulverized and mixed with water. The fine iron particles were drawn away from the wastes by magnets. The iron was mixed with bentonite clay as a binding agent and rolled into marble-sized balls for rail transport. It was 279 miles to the blast furnaces of the Geneva Works in Provo, Utah. Each train was generally composed of 94 hopper cars capable of carrying 90 tons each.

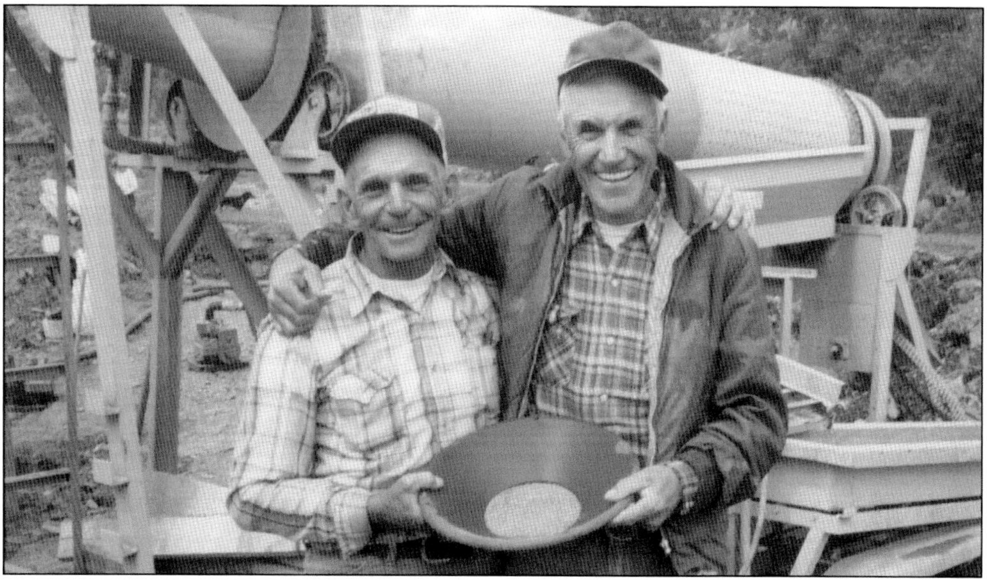

Buddy Presgrove and Hank Hudspeth, 1985. Placer miners still attempt to recover gold from overlooked stretches of gulches and creek bottoms throughout the Sweetwater Mines area. Above, the two men display 16 ounces of fine gold recovered in three days' work. Below, a backhoe excavates gravel down to bedrock and empties it into a small wash plant where the heavy gold will be recovered. The tools in many instances have improved, but the working conditions still demand miners willing to get dirty, wet, and brave the dangers attendant to mining.

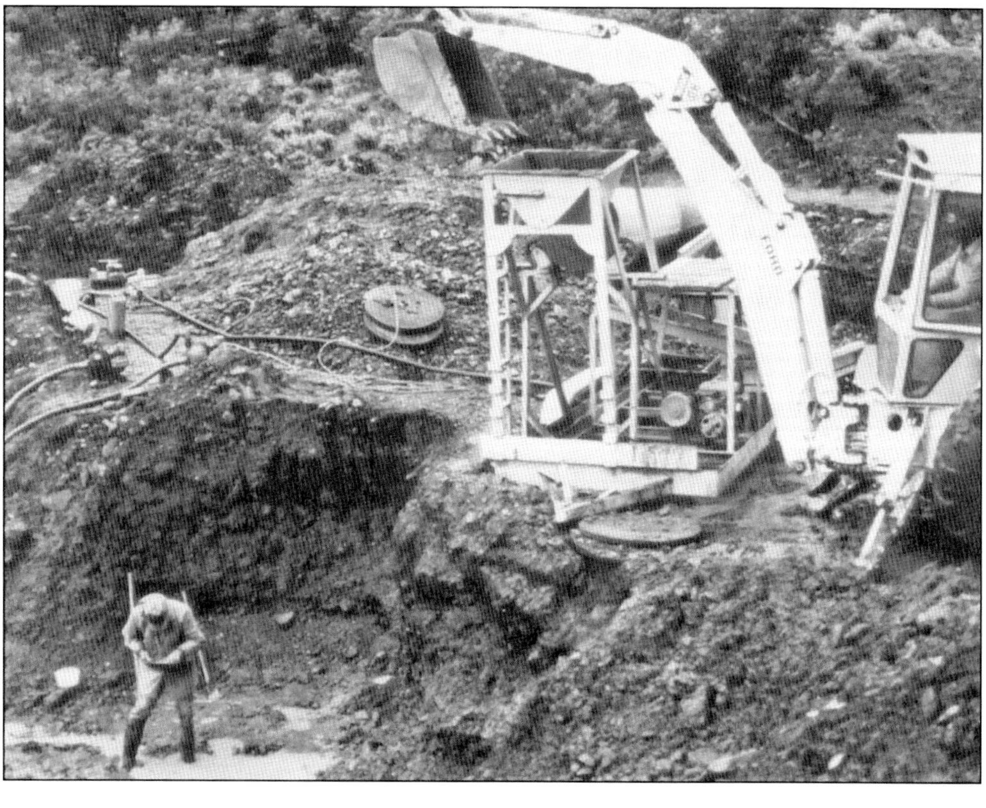

Five

Camp Stambaugh, Miners Delight, and Lewiston

Two seasons of mining at the Sweetwater Mines resulted in the deaths of prospectors, woodcutters, freighters, and even children at the hands of Native war parties. Nationally, both the gold rush and the local Indian problems received coverage by newspapers like *The New York Times*. Wyoming Territory Gov. John Campbell knew that once spring weather permitted Arapaho, Cheyenne, and Sioux mounted warriors would visit the Mines again. Camp Stambaugh was established on June 20, 1870, and staffed with two companies of the 2nd Cavalry and one company of the 14th Infantry. The bust of the early 1870s made the post largely obsolete once it was completed. The Plains Wars geared up, but most engagements took place far from the area. Once tribes were pacified and placed on reservations, Camp Stambaugh was ordered closed on May 9, 1878. Nothing remains of the post.

Miners Delight was established as Hamilton City in the gold rush season of 1868. Placer miners scoured local gulches for placer gold, but there was a single big hard rock mine in the area—the Miners Delight. The Miners Delight was recorded on September 13, 1867, by a party comprised in part by Francis McGovern, John Holbrook, and Jonathan Pugh. The men made regular deposits at South Pass City's Exchange Bank from 1870 to 1872. The federal census conducted on June 17, 1870, identified Hamilton City as a town of 75 inhabitants. With the collapse of much of the local mining in the early 1870s, the name of the settlement gradually shifted to that of the only major employer, the Miners Delight. The mine was run by Hub Gold Mining Company from 1881 to 1882 with discouraging results. The mining season in 1907 saw the arrival and departure of the Miners Delight Mining Company without actually mining any ore. The Great Depression saw a resurgence of interest in local placer mining for the hard cash that it could provide. Some locals remained, but by the 1970s, Miners Delight had become a true ghost town.

Gold discoveries were made on Strawberry Creek as early as the 1840s, but not followed up until some years later. James L. Sherlock assigned the origin of Lewiston to a placer miner by the name of Lewis. Ore deposits were located by A.T. Burr, H.G. Nickerson, and others. Boom and bust ensued. While the town is now gone, rich ore may yet remain.

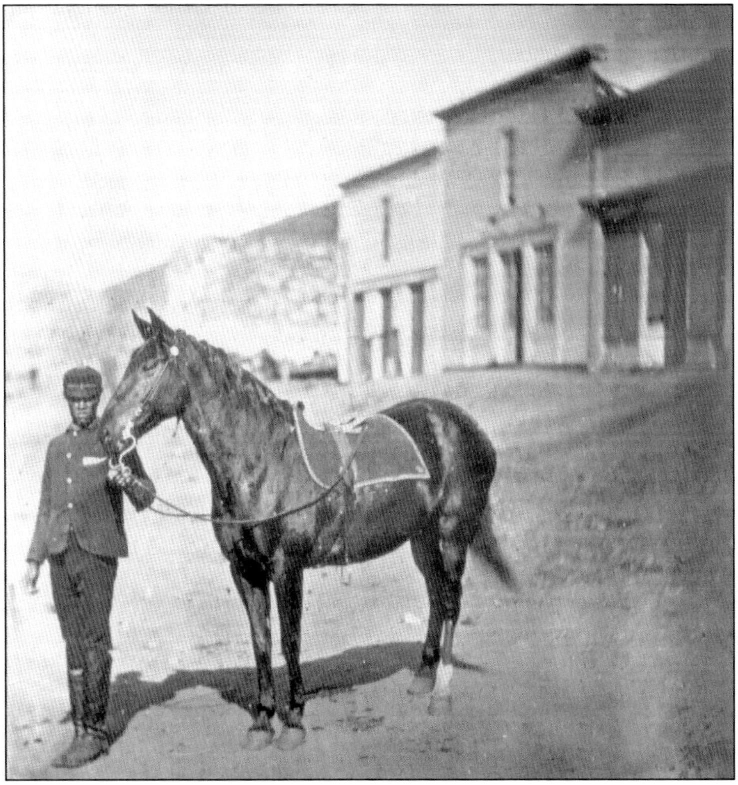

Unidentified Groom with Cavalry Horse from Camp Stambaugh, 1869. The image was taken on Atlantic City's early Main Street and is credited to frontier photographer William Henry Jackson. The building on the right is The Mint Saloon, standing from the gold rush through the late 1920s.

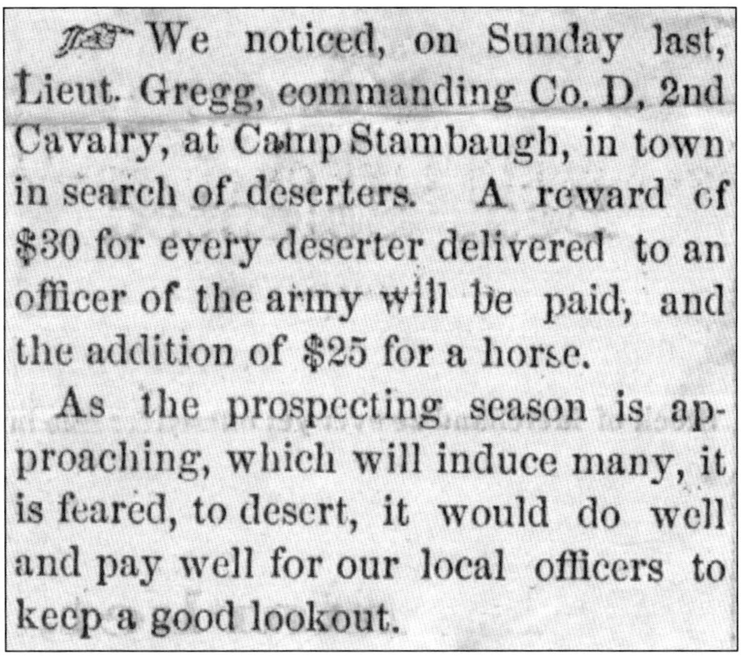

☞ We noticed, on Sunday last, Lieut. Gregg, commanding Co. D, 2nd Cavalry, at Camp Stambaugh, in town in search of deserters. A reward of $30 for every deserter delivered to an officer of the army will be paid, and the addition of $25 for a horse.

As the prospecting season is approaching, which will induce many, it is feared, to desert, it would do well and pay well for our local officers to keep a good lookout.

***South Pass News*, April 5, 1871.** Notices like this one were commonplace in regions that hosted both military posts and deposits of precious metals. During the winter of 1870 and 1871, one private was shot dead in an Atlantic City saloon and another suffered frostbite that required amputation of his toes. The next winter, another froze to death on the route to Atlantic City.

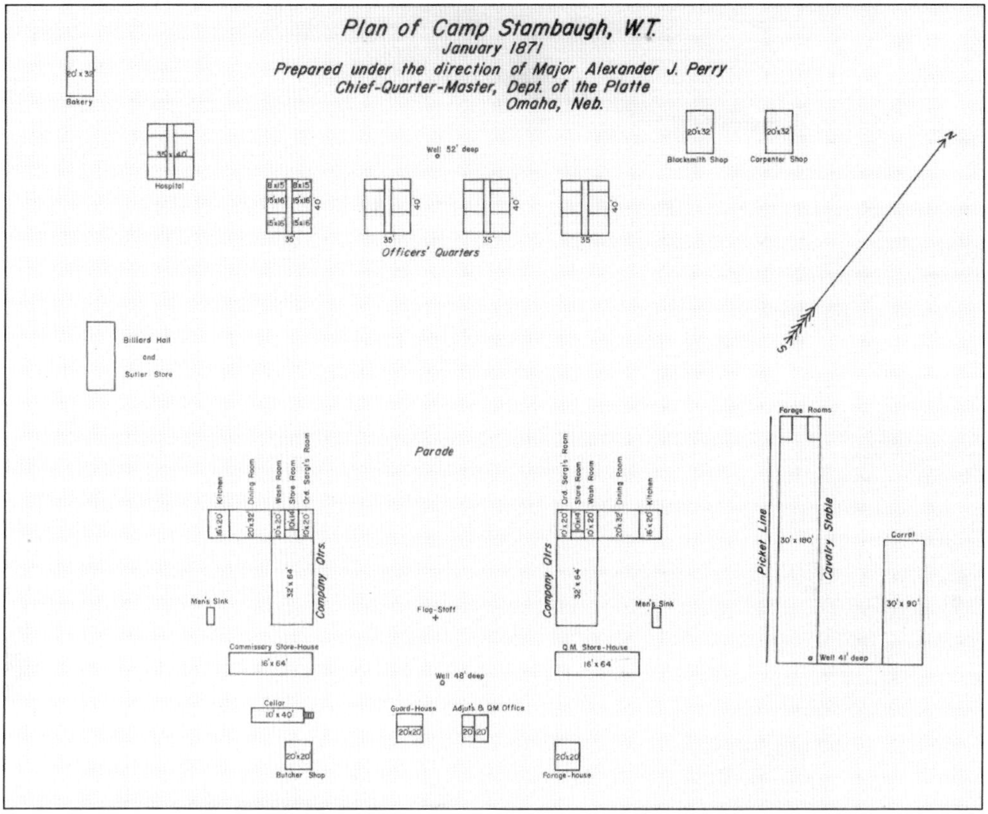

Plan of Camp Stambaugh, 1871. Named for Lt. Charles B. Stambaugh, who was killed while pursuing Indians in nearby hills, the post consisted of two cavalry companies and one infantry company. The Army reserved the title of "fort" for permanent military establishments like Fort Laramie or Fort Washakie. Camps were often established for temporary operations and relied on forts for their supplies, personnel, and command.

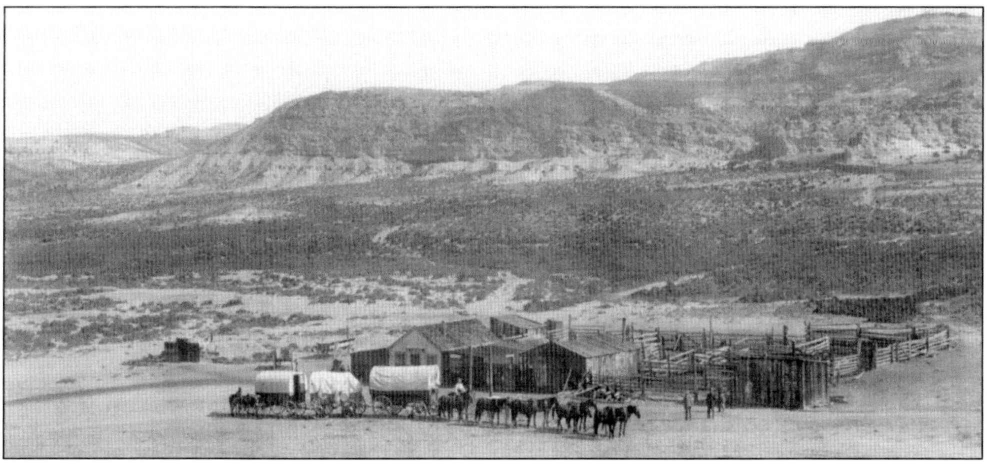

Halter and Flick Store, Point of Rocks. The railroad station at Point of Rocks was the closest to the Sweetwater Mines and, as a result, was a major commercial crossroads for the area. For a time, the station was assigned a United States Post Office under the name "Almond." Local freighters like L.L. Giessler and Tom Brady picked up supplies and equipment at Point of Rocks.

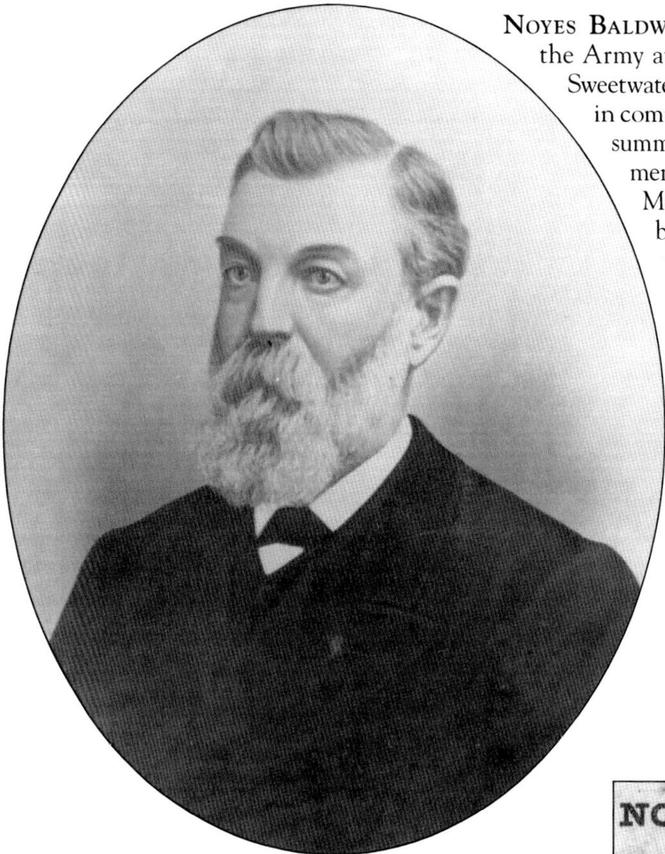

NOYES BALDWIN. Baldwin was serving in the Army at Fort Bridger when rumors of Sweetwater gold began. Major Baldwin was in command of Fort Bridger during the summer of 1865 and took a force of 40 men to reconnoiter the Wind River Mountains. Baldwin was pleased by the indications of gold, and when he was discharged from the military the next year, he relocated to the Popo Agie River as a trader licensed to deal with the Shoshone. Increased Indian conflicts caused him to move back to the safety of Fort Bridger in 1867.

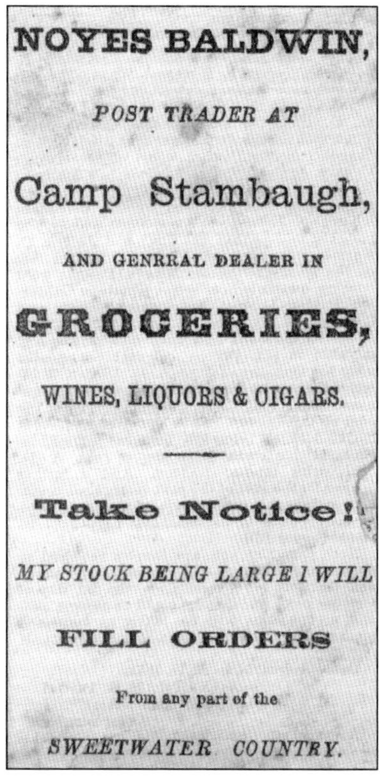

NOYES BALDWIN,

POST TRADER AT

Camp Stambaugh,

AND GENRRAL DEALER IN

GROCERIES,

WINES, LIQUORS & CIGARS.

Take Notice!

MY STOCK BEING LARGE I WILL

FILL ORDERS

From any part of the

SWEETWATER COUNTRY.

SOUTH PASS NEWS, AUGUST 31, 1871. In 1866, Baldwin built his first trading post near present-day Hudson, Wyoming, and in his first season, Baldwin secured 3,700 skins from local Indians. In 1869, Baldwin relocated to the mining camps on South Pass City's Dakota Street. In late 1870, Baldwin established himself at Camp Stambaugh as the sutler, or post trader.

PROSPECTING A LOCAL CREEK, C. 1900. Pictured here are William Green (left) and Anthony William. An unidentified man is seen in the back. Following the gold rush, locals staked claims on public ground as it became available. Placer mining required simple tools, was relatively safe and easy to learn, and could be combined into regular travel or work activities. A dollar or two of gold dust from a day's work provided much needed spending money in the cash-starved local economy.

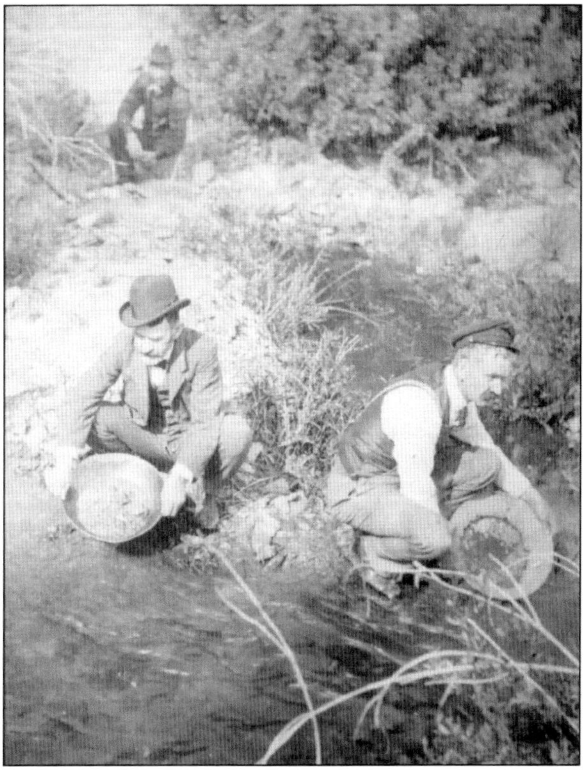

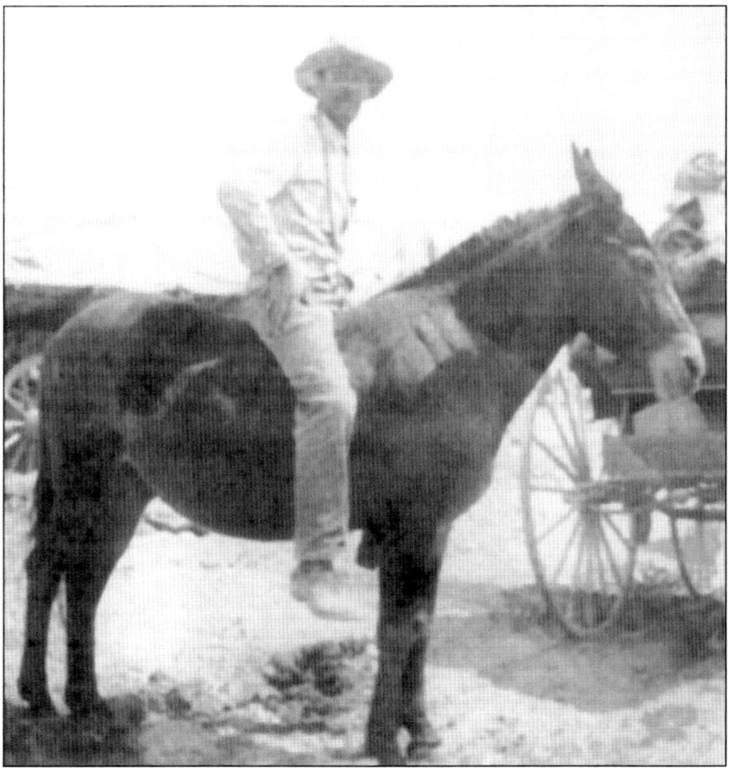

JAMES "CHRIS" STAGEMAN MOUNTED ON SATAN, 1905. Born in 1867 in Council Bluffs, Iowa, Chris came to Wyoming in 1890, arriving at Point of Rocks. He spent 17 years mining and freighting in Wyoming, mainly near Atlantic City, Miners Delight, and Pacific Springs. From June to November 1895, Chris and his two partners took about 40 ounces of gold from McAuley Gulch near the Oregon Buttes.

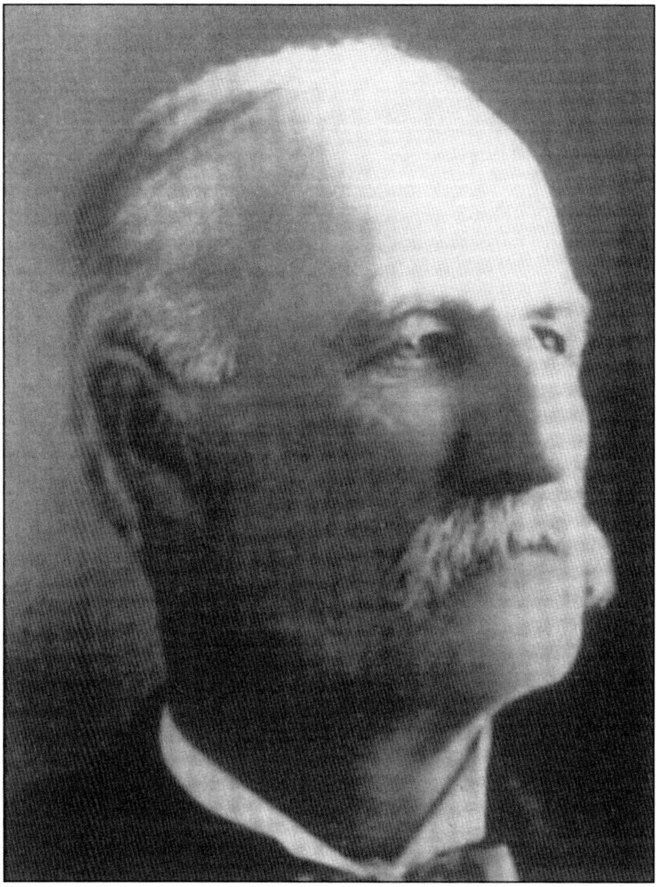

HERMAN G. NICKERSON. Born in 1841 in Litchfield, Modena County, Ohio, Nickerson entered the Union Army in 1861, where he became captain of Company I of the 168th Ohio Infantry. After the war, he began to study law but went to Montana in 1866. The rush to the Sweetwater Mines in 1868 included Nickerson. He worked as a miner at Miners Delight, but was also civically active. A Republican, Nickerson ran for the first territorial legislature in 1869, losing to Democrat William Bright. In 1870, "Cap" Nickerson was the local superintendent of schools. Nickerson moved to Lander, becoming a justice of the peace, state legislator, and signer of the Wyoming State Constitution.

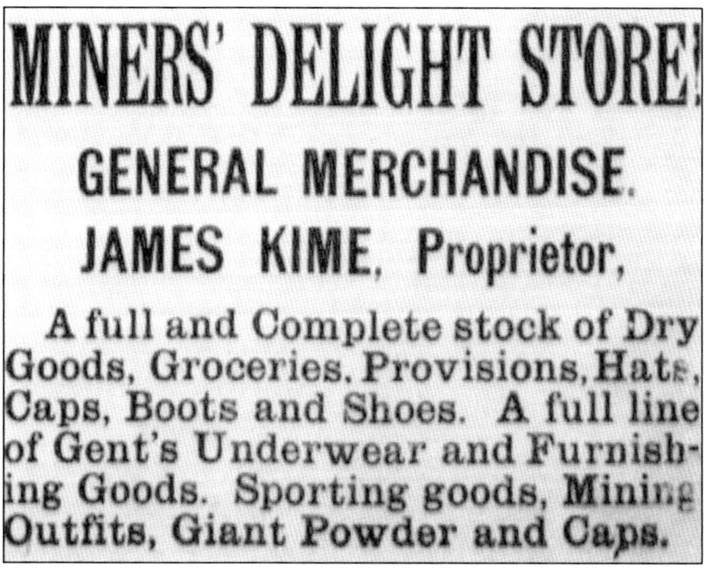

JAMES KIME. Wyoming historian Charles G. Coutant states that Kime moved to Atlantic City by the fall of 1869. The Pennsylvania-born teamster had previously helped found Cheyenne in 1867. By 1870, Kime had established himself in Miners Delight, becoming the postmaster in 1872. He operated his mercantile in a portion of the same building for decades. Kime, a Democrat, was elected to the state senate in 1893.

MINERS DELIGHT , 1907. The lode was filed on September 13, 1867, by a party including John Holbrook, Francis McGovern, and Jonathan Pugh. One of the district's heaviest producers, it last yielded ore in 1895. Those who reaped rewards in the boom paid a price in later years. McGovern is said to have had killed two men in gunfights; one each in Atlantic City and South Pass City. He tried his hand in the great Black Hills gold rush in 1876 before returning to the Sweetwater Mines and being kicked to death in a Rock Springs saloon in the 1880s. Holbrook became an invalid and retired to California. Pugh was taken by alcoholism. The map is by Dan Hausel.

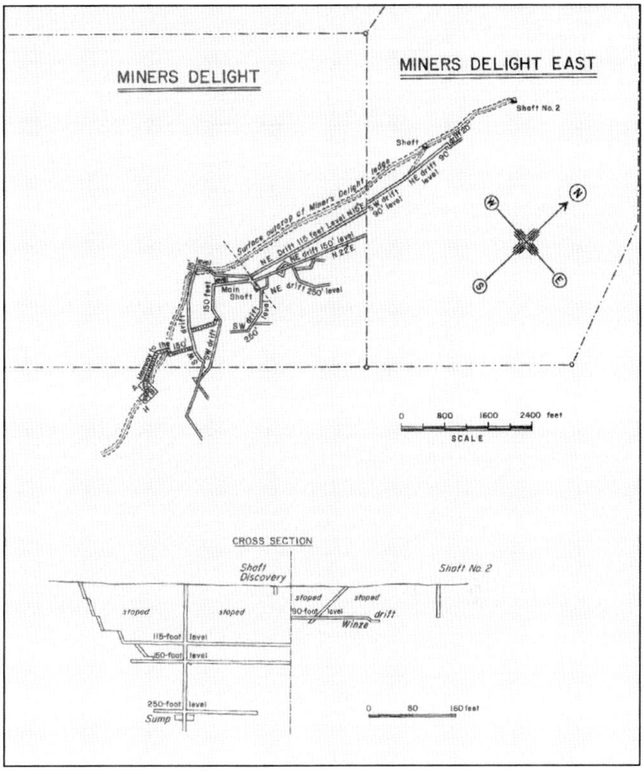

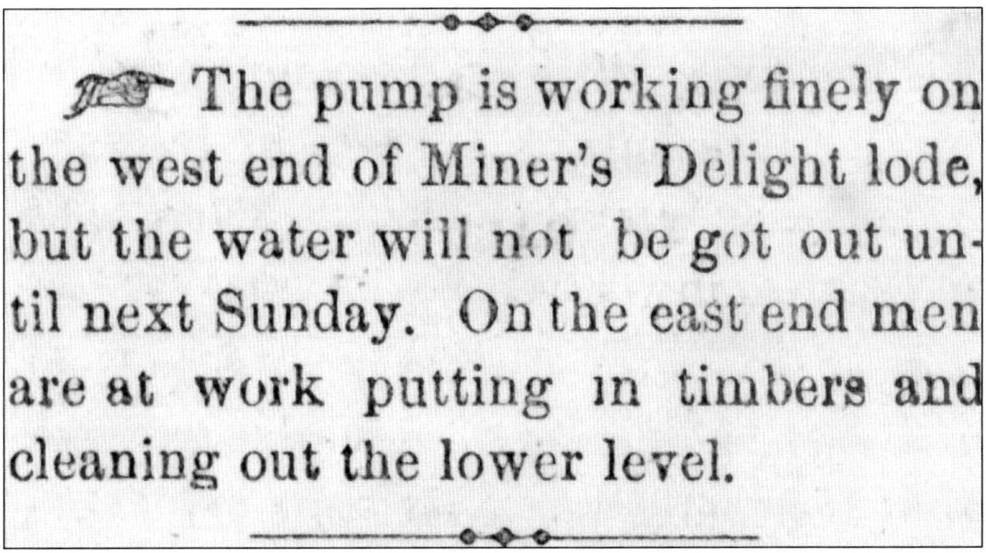

The pump is working finely on the west end of Miner's Delight lode, but the water will not be got out until next Sunday. On the east end men are at work putting in timbers and cleaning out the lower level.

SOUTH PASS NEWS, AUGUST 31, 1871. The Miners Delight was like most of the mines in the area below a fairly shallow depth—wet. Shrewd investors demanded to see the ore in place and sample it personally. A sale could not be made with flooded mine workings.

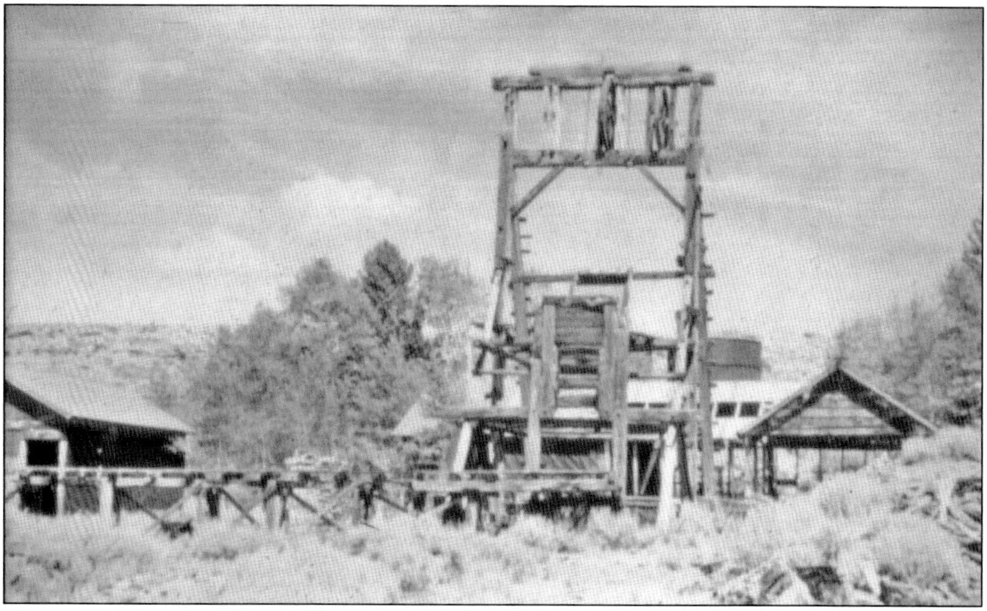

Miners Delight. Two-post gallows-style headframes are an iconic image of early Western mines. Easy to assemble and made of local materials, they were top choices for outfits concerned with turning small, relatively undeveloped prospects into larger, paying operations. A hoist cable ran from the winch mechanism over the sheave (pulley) wheel to a bucket below.

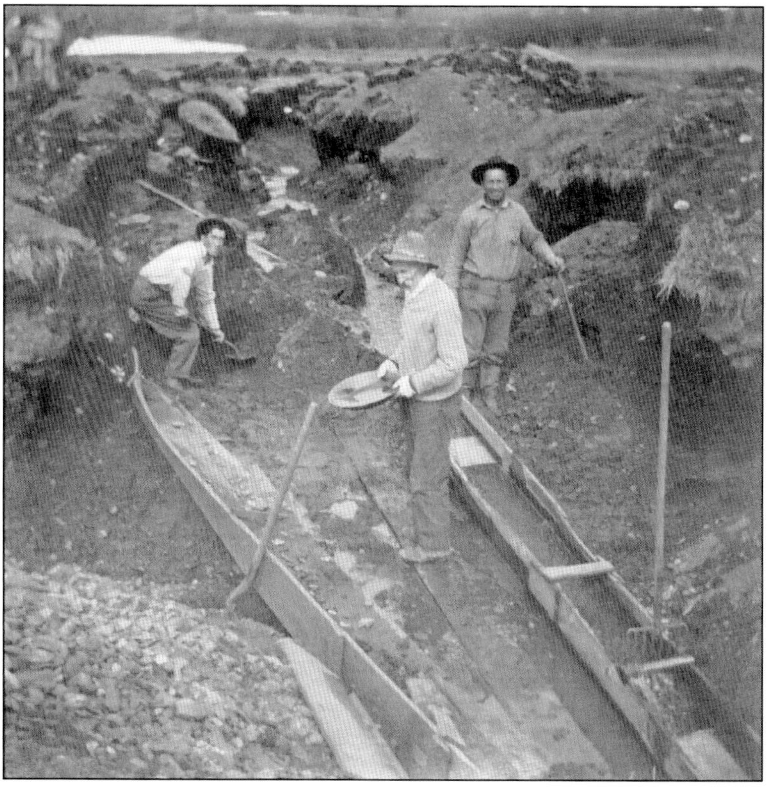

Placer Mining in Meadow Gulch. Henry Swabes (center) and two unidentified assistants test the gravels near the Miners Delight Mine. Placer miners targeted gold deposits that had been eroded by water and moved away from their original source. Placer miners depended on a reliable water flow to flush the light clays, sands, and gravels from their sluices, leaving the heavy gold behind.

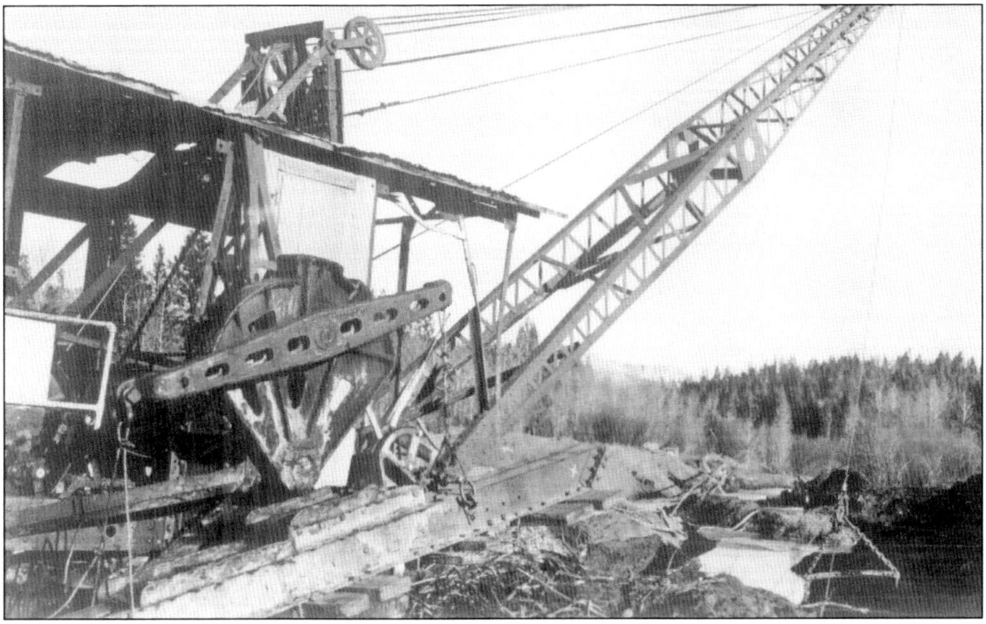

SWABES DREDGE ON MEADOW GULCH. Dredges rely on powerful shovels to quickly strip huge swaths of gold-bearing gravel clear down to bedrock. The bucket is emptied into a wash plant where water and agitation are used to separate gold particles from waste material. Gold production of Meadow Gulch, near Miners Delight, is cited as 50,000 ounces.

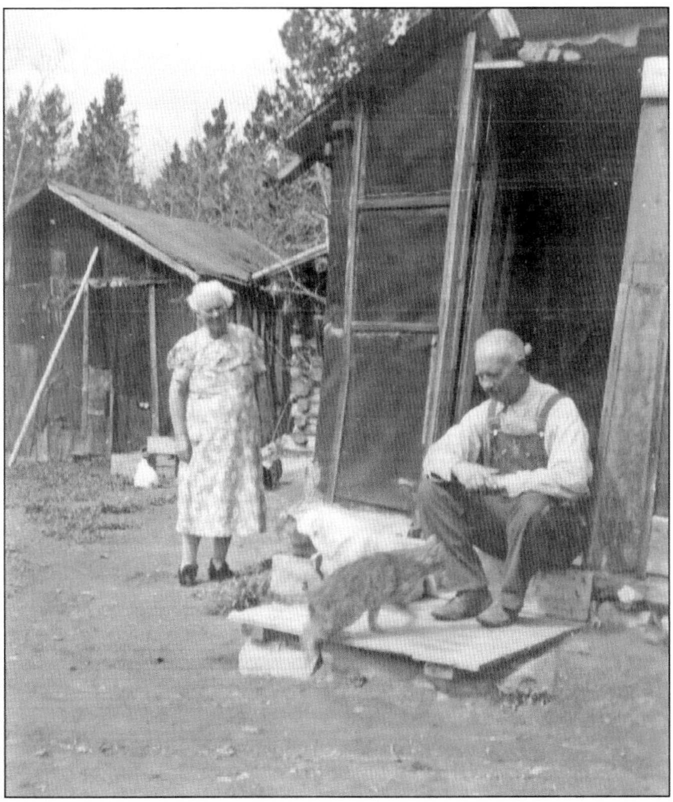

HANNAH AND HER SON REYNOLD "RENE" SWABES. Henry and Hannah Swabes had four children when they moved to Atlantic City in the 1890s. Their fifth child, and third daughter, Jessie, was the only one still living with them in 1910. The Swabes' cabin in Miners Delight was a regular stop for locals who could smell Rene's baking in the simple cabin.

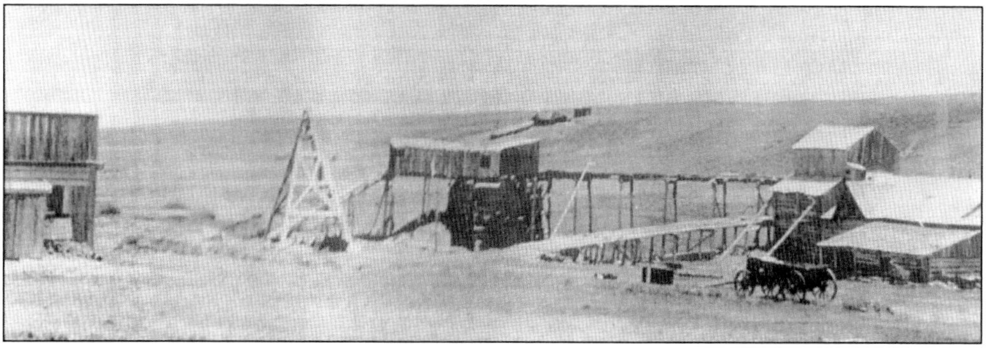

LEWISTON, 1894. Bullion Mine is seen in the foreground and Helen G Mill is in the background. The Bullion was located almost on top of the Oregon-California-Mormon-Pony Express Trail along the north side of Strawberry Creek. The main shaft, located under the derrick at left center, was 70 feet deep, with 500 feet of drifts following the vein. Its production is unknown. The Helen G Mill was part of the 1893 Chicago World's Fair before it was erected at Lewiston.

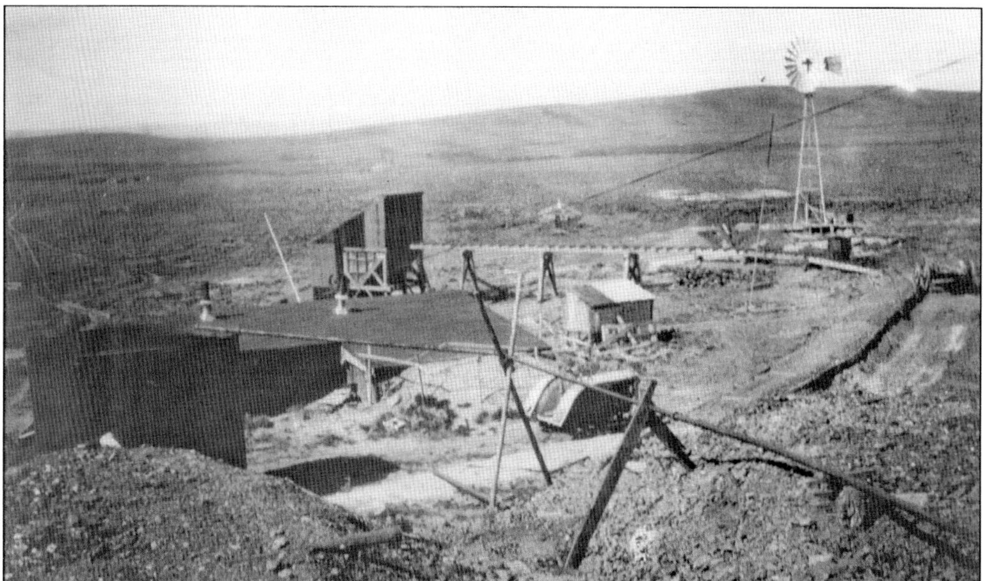

HIDDEN HAND MINE. At first, the property was called The Mikado after the Gilbert and Sullivan production, but was renamed by new ownership in the 1890s. The Hidden Hand was known as a mine with extremely rich high-grade ore shoots interspersed amongst lower-grade material. The mine was plagued by high-grading and ore theft took place both by the handful and the ton.

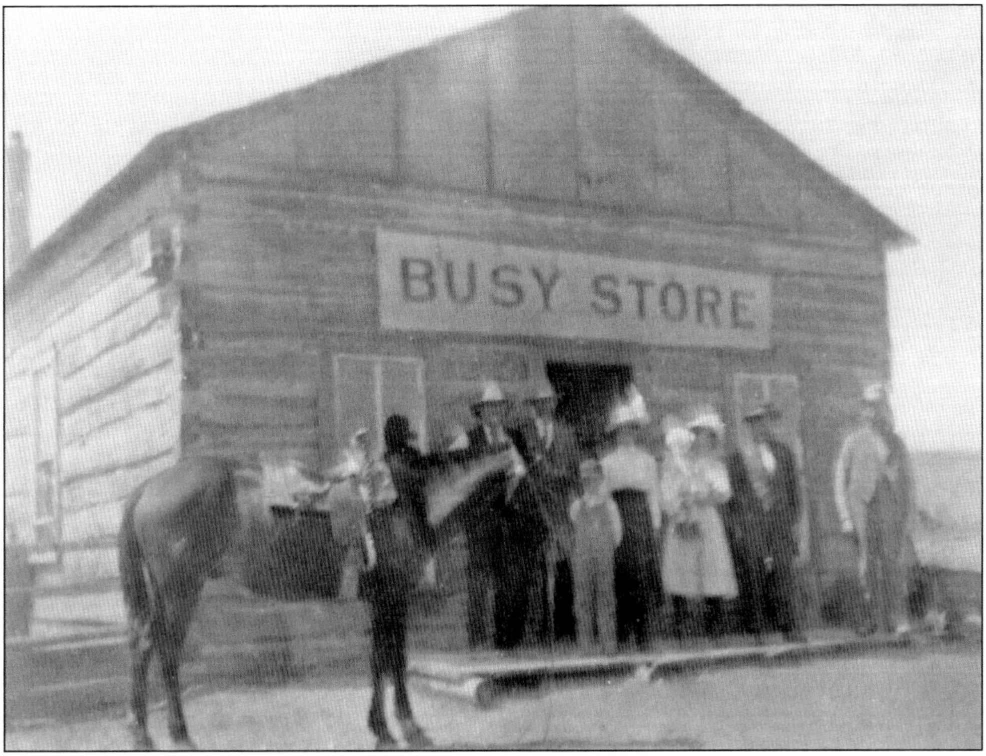

Gustin Store, Lewiston. Around 1894, Edward A. Gustin Sr. bought this building and began a post office and mercantile business. The large Gustin family moved to the Lander area in 1900, but the post office remained open until April 1906.

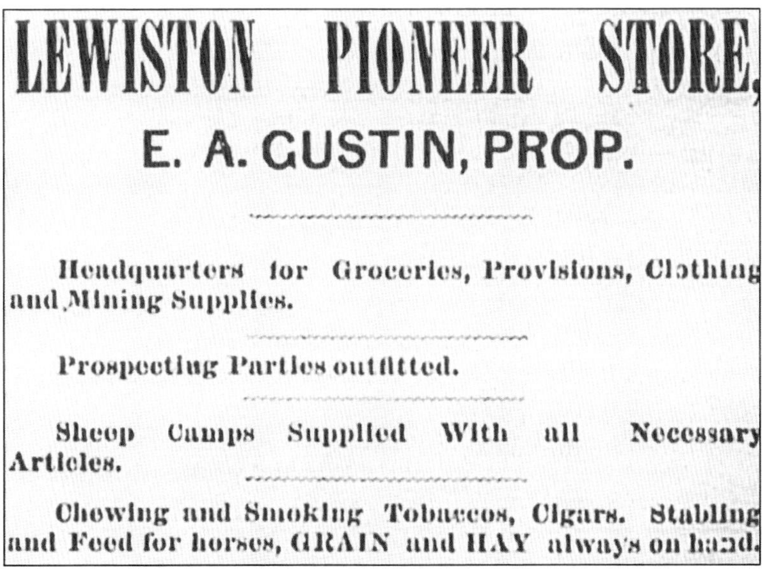

LEWISTON PIONEER STORE,

E. A. GUSTIN, PROP.

Headquarters for Groceries, Provisions, Clothing and Mining Supplies.

Prospecting Parties outfitted.

Sheep Camps Supplied With all Necessary Articles.

Chewing and Smoking Tobaccos, Cigars. Stabling and Feed for horses, GRAIN and HAY always on hand.

***Fremont Clipper*, December 21, 1894.** Rural stores were a lifeline to local residents and passersby alike. They were post offices, social crossroads, and served to promote commerce.

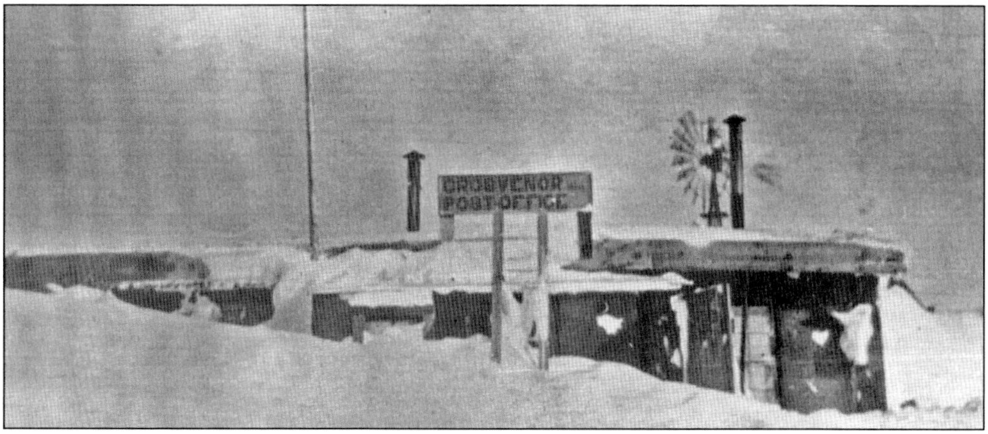

GROSVENOR POST OFFICE. Wallace Grosvenor's father had amassed a fortune in an array of business ventures including farmland in Casselton, North Dakota, Washington State timber and sawmills, and mines like the Hidden Hand at Lewiston. Mine manager George P. Paine was named postmaster in October 1912 for the six miners and their families at the mine. Rampant high-grading of rich ore caused the mine and post office to shut in March 1915.

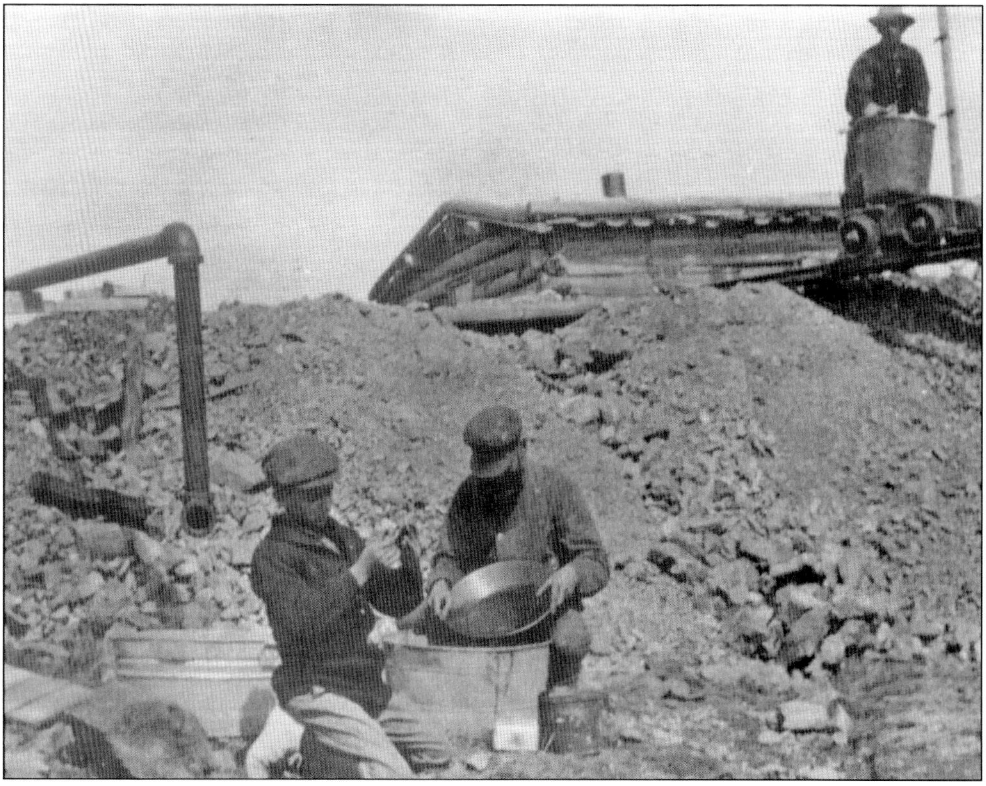

WALLACE GROSVENOR, JAMES F. ANDERSON, AND EARL SARTWELL. Soon after his father's death, Grosvenor embarked on the adventure of visiting the family's holdings with his uncle George P. Paine. About 10 years old at the time, Grosvenor immediately developed a keen interest in the property. He returned in 1927 to restart the operation, but his partner's financing, in the form of a rich widow, failed. Grosvenor leased the mine a number of times, but the terms of the lease required methodical mining, not the wild "gophering" employed by those seeking quick money.

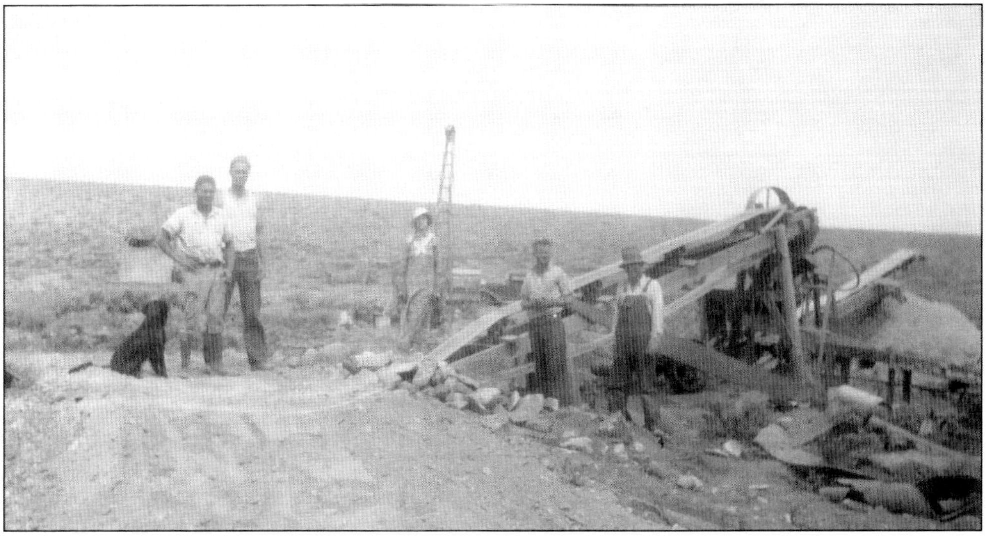

Sarah Gillespie and Crew Near Lewiston. Gillespie (center) first attempted to promote her property as the Mother Lode Claim at Copper City and then later as Radium Springs. Her daughter Eutha lived with her at their remote homestead. One worker, who charged his room and board with Sarah Gillespie against his summer wages, found that at the end of his term of service, he owed more than the wages totaled.

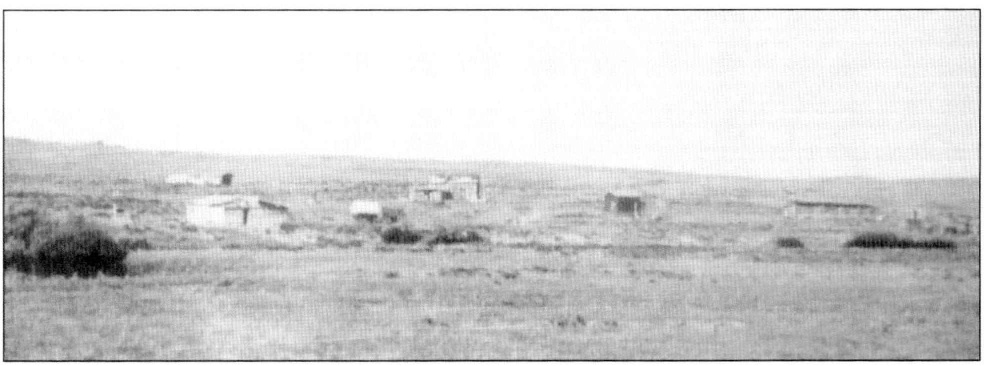

Lewiston, 1930. Wallace Grosvenor recalled that Lewiston was comprised of at least 25 buildings. Most of the structures were miners' residences, but Jenny Boylan also had a restaurant in town. Mines included the Hidden Hand, Iron Duke, Mint, Bobtail, Burr, and other properties.

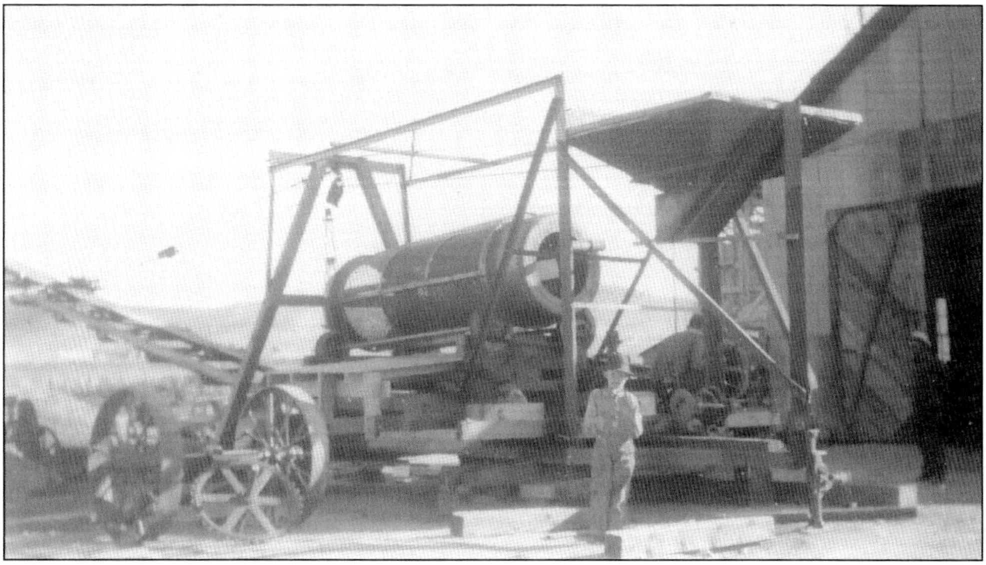

Alfred "Apple" Bramwell and John E. Whisenand's Wash Plant. Sweetwater County, Wyoming, sand and gravel plant owner John Whisenand freighted in a wash plant from Illinois in 1939, and hired a crew of Union Pacific Railroad machinists and welders, including Alfred's father, William, to erect it. Whisenand's idea was to dredge the Sweetwater River in the Wilson Bar area, site of earlier strikes.

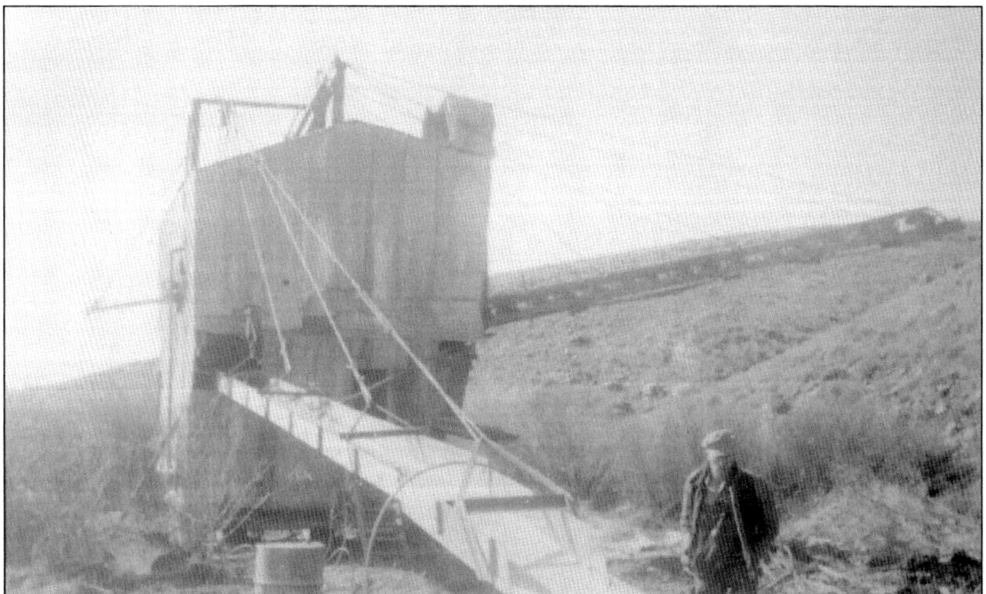

Whisenand's Wash Plant at Wilson Bar. Oversized material was directed by conveyors to the right, while fine sand and gravel tailings were discharged by the center chute. Gold was recovered from riffles lined with quicksilver inside the wash plant. Whisenand's operation, like others, suffered from having too many hands in the sluice boxes.

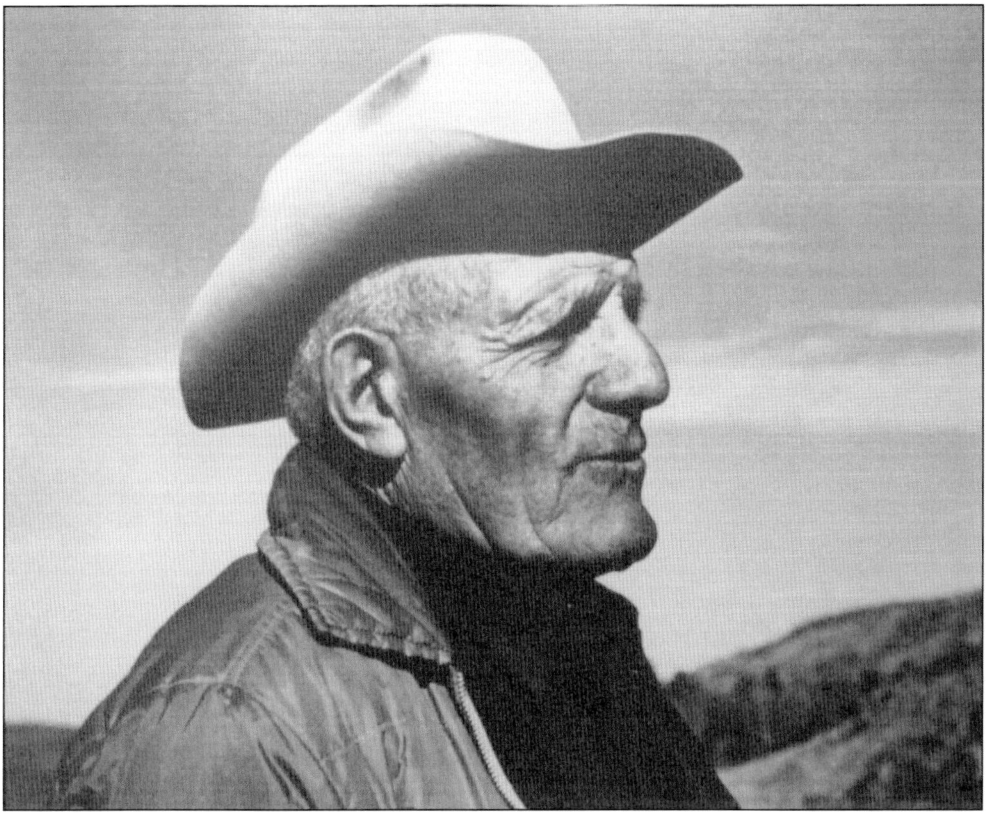

SAM VJESTIC. A native of Yugoslavia, Vjestic was hired by Carl Pfaff Sr. to work on the Iron Duke at Lewiston in 1937 as an underground miner. During the late 1940s, Vjestic worked at the Carissa as a miner, drilling, loading, and firing his own rounds. He was considered the best underground miner at the Carissa. In the mid- to late 1950s, Vjestic worked at the Duncan. During a brief lease on the Hidden Hand, Vjestic may have taken out as much as $30,000.

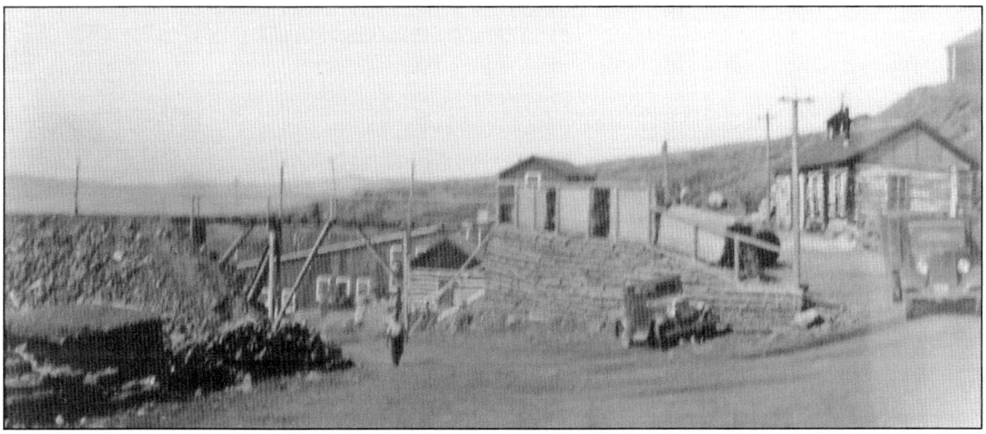

GOLD DOLLAR. Isaac G. Burton, Burt Lambert, Bill Matheson, and Tom McGrath located the claim in 1890, calling it the Pay Rock. Their work included sinking a 110-foot shaft and blasting out 500 feet of drifts. McGrath hired Jim Carpenter to help him put up the structures in 1908. By 1935, McGrath was the sole owner. He sold to Lewis Flader and the mine became known as the Gold Dollar. Flader operated the property for about three years, disappointing investors.

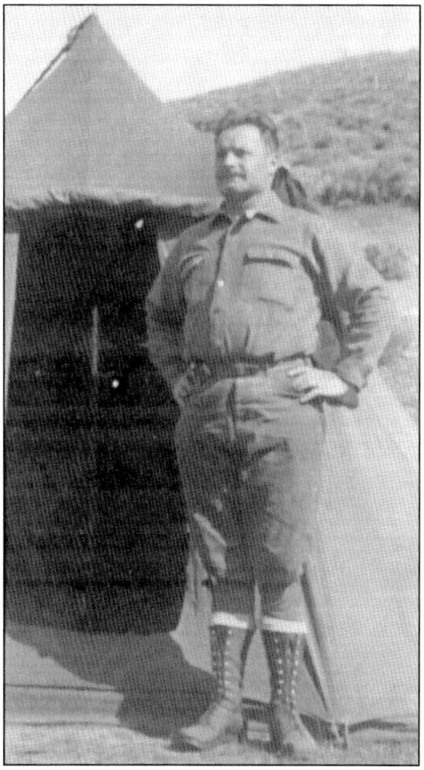

Lewis Flader. The promoter from Denver, Colorado, had a substantial hand in the revival of the Sweetwater Mines beginning with his lease of the Miners Delight in 1927. Whatever his designs on that property were, nothing came of them. In 1928, Flader leased the Diana Mine from Tom McGrath, a native of Pennsylvania who had come west and turned to mining activities around Atlantic City. Flader's attentions soon turned from the Diana to McGrath's other property, the Pay Rock group.

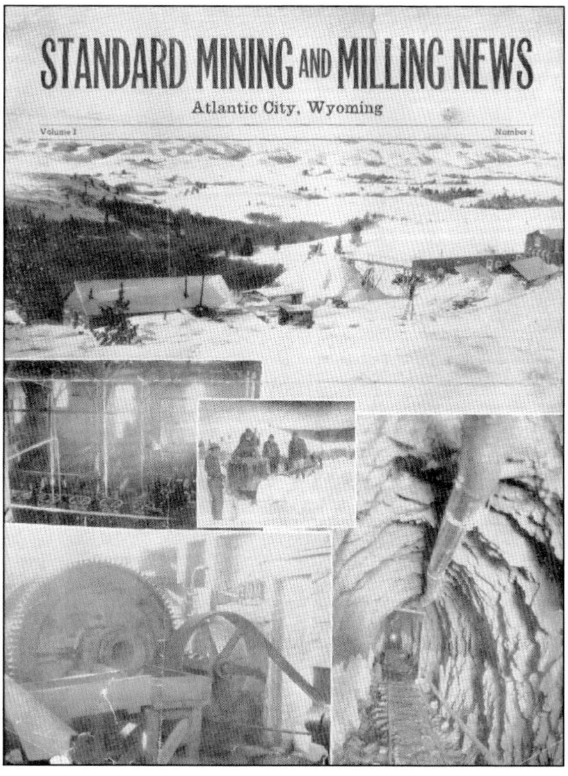

Mining Promotion, 1930s. The job of attracting investors to area mining properties proved difficult, even during the gold rush of the late 1860s. Hard rock, or underground, gold mining was an entirely different venture than panning and prospecting on the surface. Hard rock mines required expensive machinery, fuel supplies, and knowledgeable mining men to get up and running. Promoters raised cash through public stock sales to equip mines and mills and pay wages to the miners. Mark Twain once cautioned that a gold mine is a hole in the ground owned by a liar.

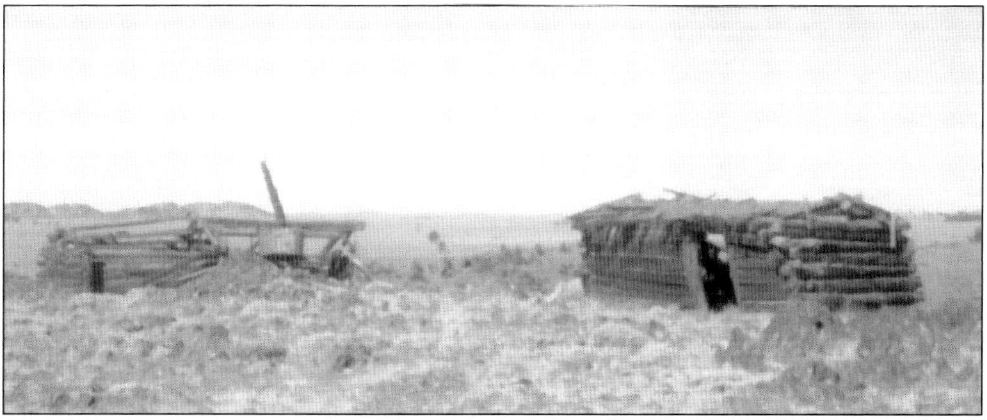

The Carrie Shields. Capt. A.G. Turner discovered the gold-bearing quartz vein in September 1867. Turner was originally from Alabama, but gold called him to California in its boom days. Turner followed the lure of another boom, this time settling in Centerville, Boise County, Idaho, in 1862. Turner was among the experienced miners from Idaho and Montana to investigate the earliest reports of gold along the Sweetwater River.

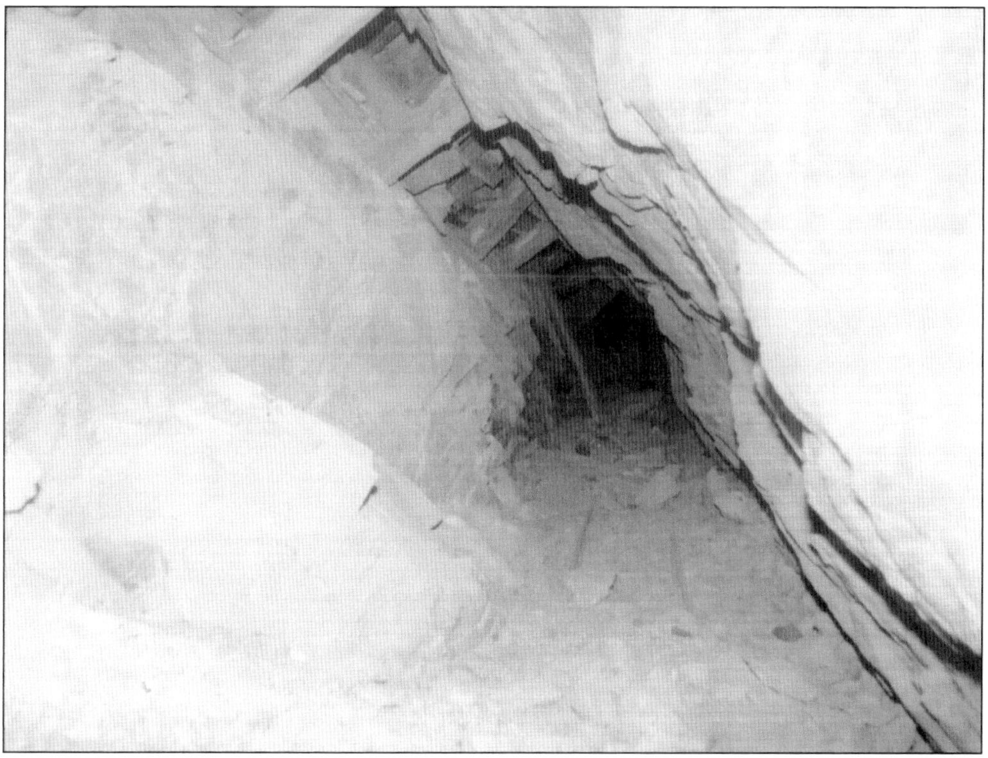

Mine Drift and Open Stope. The vein at the Carrie Shields was explored with an incline shaft from the surface and two adits below. An adit is a drift, or mine tunnel, that connects with the surface. The vein at the Carrie Shields is angled at about 50 degrees, with the hanging wall above the vein and the footwall below. Miners drilled the gold-bearing quartz with blast holes and removed ore and waste rock with cars that rolled on narrow tracks. Before they renewed their drilling efforts, the hanging wall was supported with timbers to prevent cave-in. Early gold production is estimated to have been 1,750 ounces of gold.

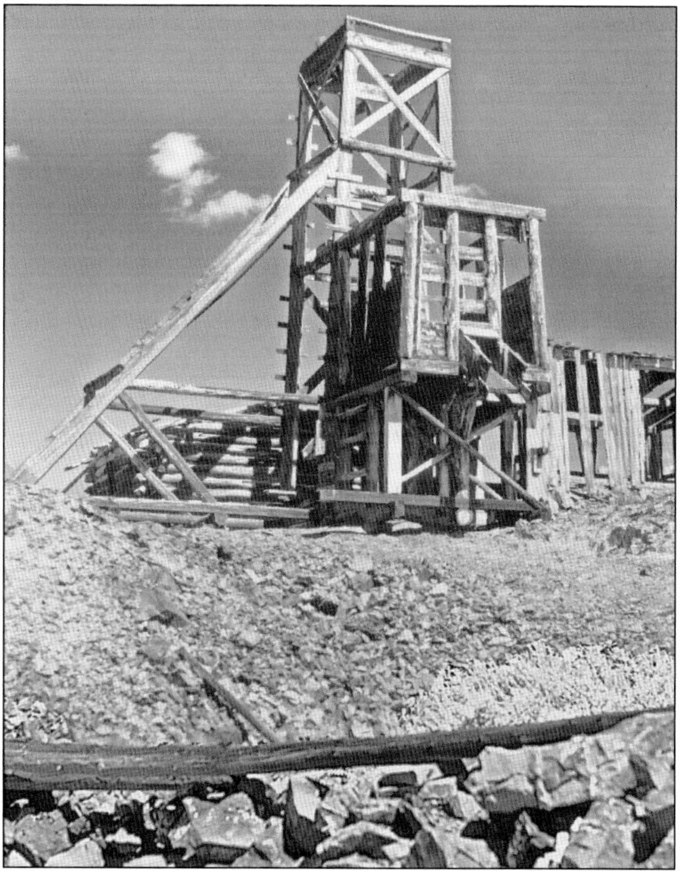

B and H Mine. The strike was located on April 24, 1868, by F.P. Sandborn and others as the Empire State. Martin Collins relocated the property around 1890. In 1923, J.J. Marrin briefly had the mine before selling out to John Bane's B&H Gold Mining Company in 1926. Bane worked to improve the surface facilities, including moving Marrin's 10 stamp mill from South Pass City to nearby Palmetto Gulch. Total lifetime production of the mine is given as 450 ounces by Frank Armstrong in his 1948 US Geologic Survey report. It is the only mine in the area that carries significant silver with the gold.

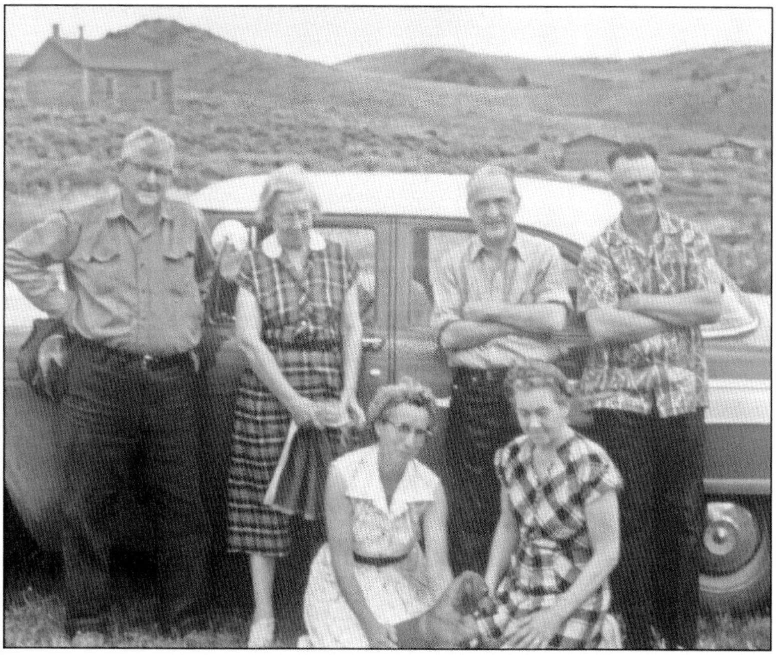

August 1956. From left to right are John Bane, Leola, Helen Helfrick, Peter Decker, Helen Henderson, and Fred Stratton Jr. In addition to his involvement in mining, Bane was widely recognized as a source of information on the immediate area. At times, he was the only person living in South Pass City year-round.

Six

Education, Leisure, and Travel

Daily life in the immediate area required substantial effort and planning to provide for even a basic existence. However, residents of the district learned to emphasize the enrichment that could be found in education, outdoors activities, and travel to distant destinations. School in the immediate area was a basic affair, usually taking place in the winter months when outdoor activities were suspended. Teachers and their level of preparation regularly varied. Schoolhouses also changed over the years. Students' attention centered mainly on basic skills, but was matched with an array of new readings, songs, and experiences.

Historically, residents of the South Pass area were also afforded a wide variety of outdoor leisure activities. Even seasonal chores like cutting firewood or putting up hay were coupled with picnic lunches in memorable settings. Locals explored their surroundings in order to better inform themselves as to the natural resources to be found in each drainage, every meadow, and the many miles of winding game trails. Residents soon learned the best spots to catch fish, trap valuable furbearers, and harvest big game. The balance of work and leisure harmonized with the regular change of the seasons.

Whether they were born in the area or had resettled from elsewhere, residents of the immediate area often enjoyed the opportunity to travel to visit family, inspect work opportunities, and see new country. Locals regularly traveled to nearby destinations in Fremont and Sweetwater counties, but longer journeys ranged from those intended to seek advanced medical treatment to those centered on the celebration of weddings and births. South Pass residents could take pride in their preparation to claim even a temporary place in the larger world. Families and communities awaited travelers' return to homes and lives that richly rewarded them for their toil and fidelity.

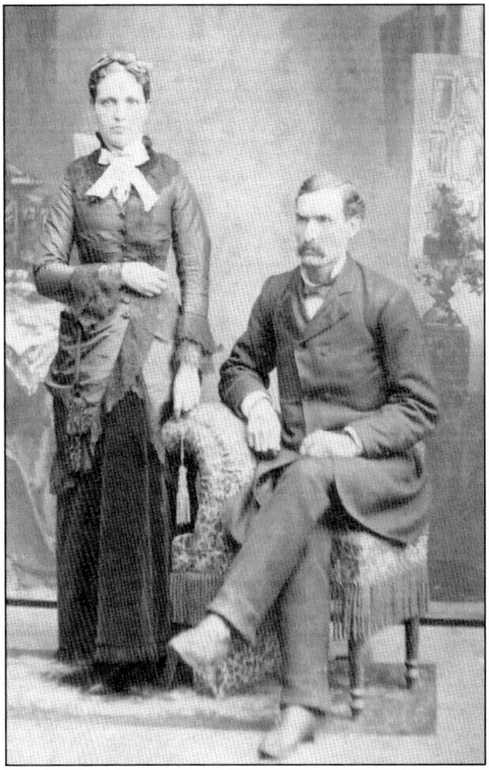

Laurena and Dr. Walter Lovejoy. Lovejoy, from Old Rippey, Iowa, first attempted to make a living off the land by hunting and trapping with his brother Fred. The two took up some gold claims in the area and worked to improve them. A graduate of medical schools in Keokuk, Iowa, and Chicago, Illinois, Dr. Lovejoy was a welcome addition to the remote communities. His surviving diaries speak of teaching school, tending to his patients, and making a living off the land.

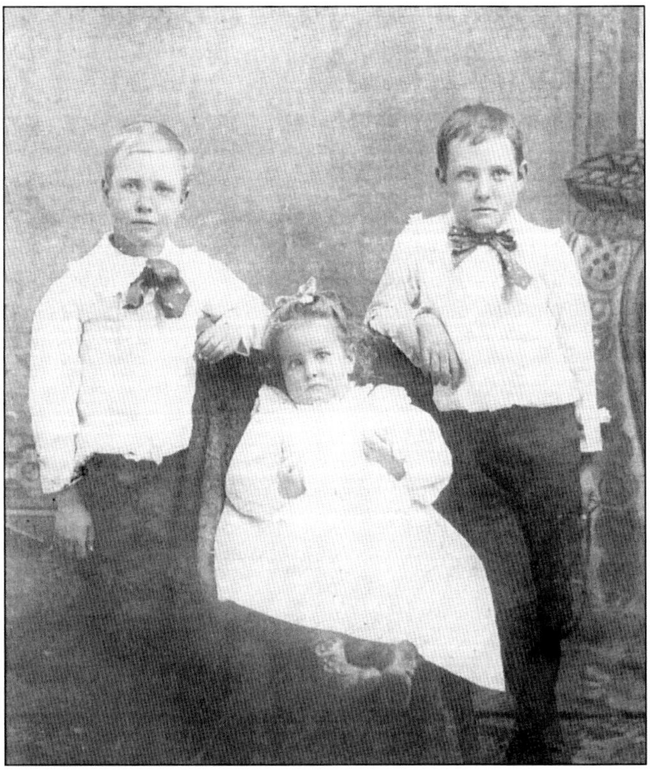

Addison, Maude, and James Lovejoy. The three children of Dr. Lovejoy and his wife were all born in either Atlantic City or South Pass City. After leaving South Pass City for Kemmerer, the children soon lost their mother to an extended illness. Maude returned to Iowa to be raised by family, while the boys followed their father to the Baker City, Oregon, gold mining district.

Dr. Walter Lovejoy, Schoolmaster. The residents of South Pass City encouraged the education of their children, starting their informal schooling at home and then continuing with formal education as the availability of suitable teachers allowed. Over the years, students were instructed in improvised schoolhouses, including the abandoned jail and the White Swan, a former saloon. The children of South Pass City have successfully competed at such diverse institutions of higher learning as Creighton in Omaha, Nebraska, and the United States Naval Academy at Annapolis, Maryland. These school documents are signed by Dr. Walter Lovejoy.

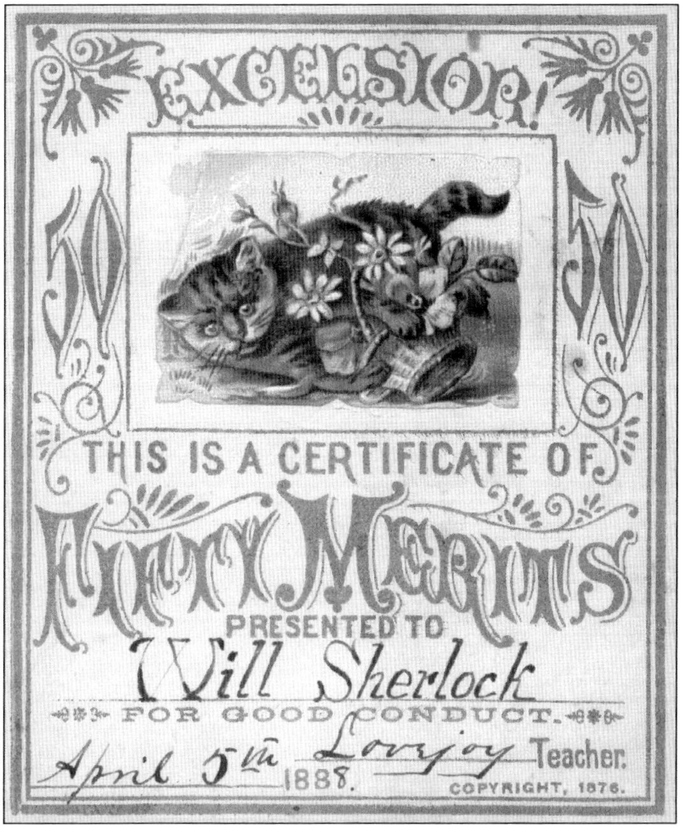

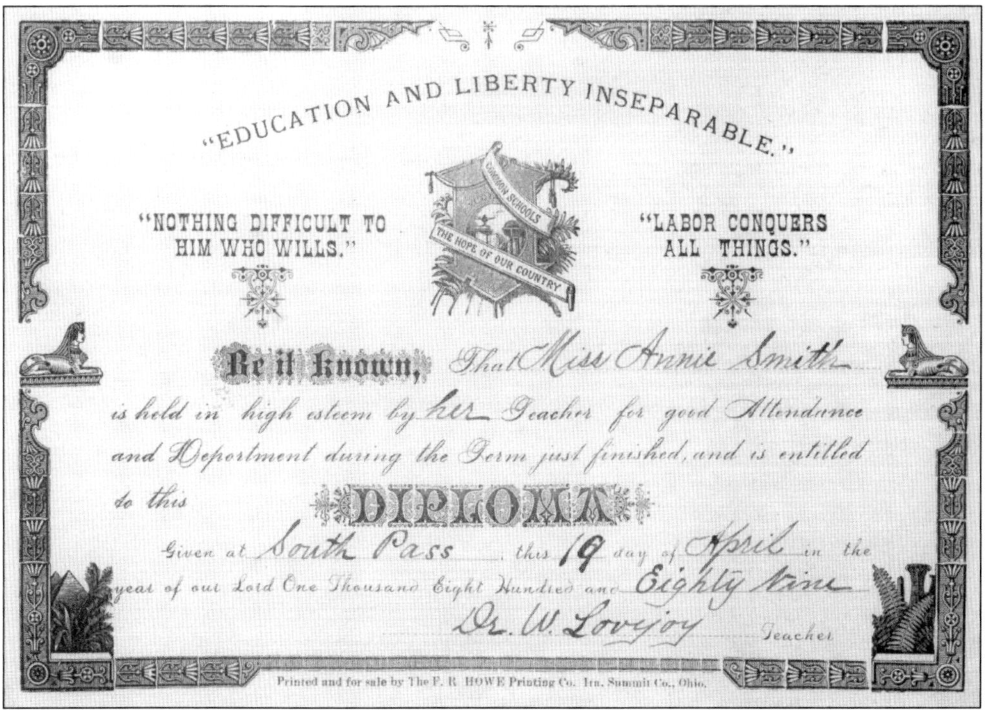

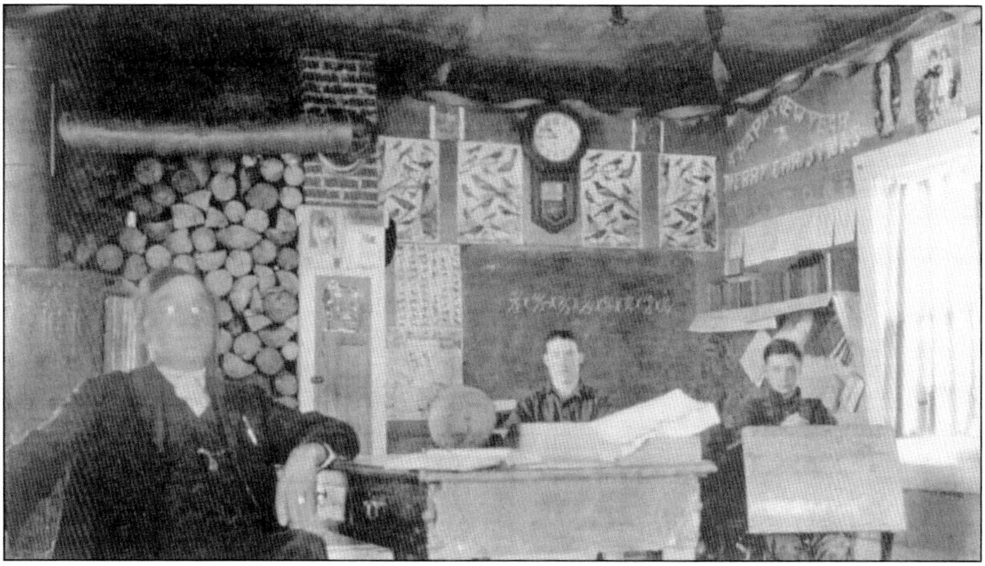

SOUTH PASS CITY SCHOOL. Pictured here is teacher Mr. Mowrer (left) with students William and John McOmie in 1925. Like much of the nation, one-room schools were common until recently. The teacher undoubtedly had the full attention of his two students. Conversely, from the state of the classroom, the students also had the full attention of the teacher. Crepe paper streamers hang in the window, posters depict all manner of birds, and a festive holiday banner hangs on the wall. The woodpile near the stove is a reminder of the time of year and the climate of South Pass.

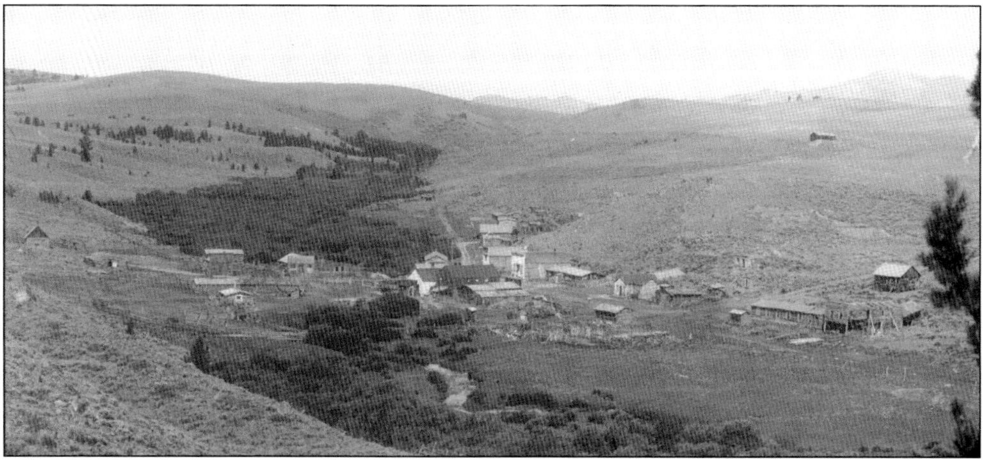

SOUTH PASS CITY, 1915. With large-scale mining ventures on hold again, the community shifted once more to raising livestock, cutting hay, and limited commercial enterprises. Janet Sherlock-Smith, her children, and their families owned almost the entire town. The school building is obscured in this image by the tree branch at right. Four years earlier, it had stood at the center background of the image, but was removed to higher ground to protect it from flooding.

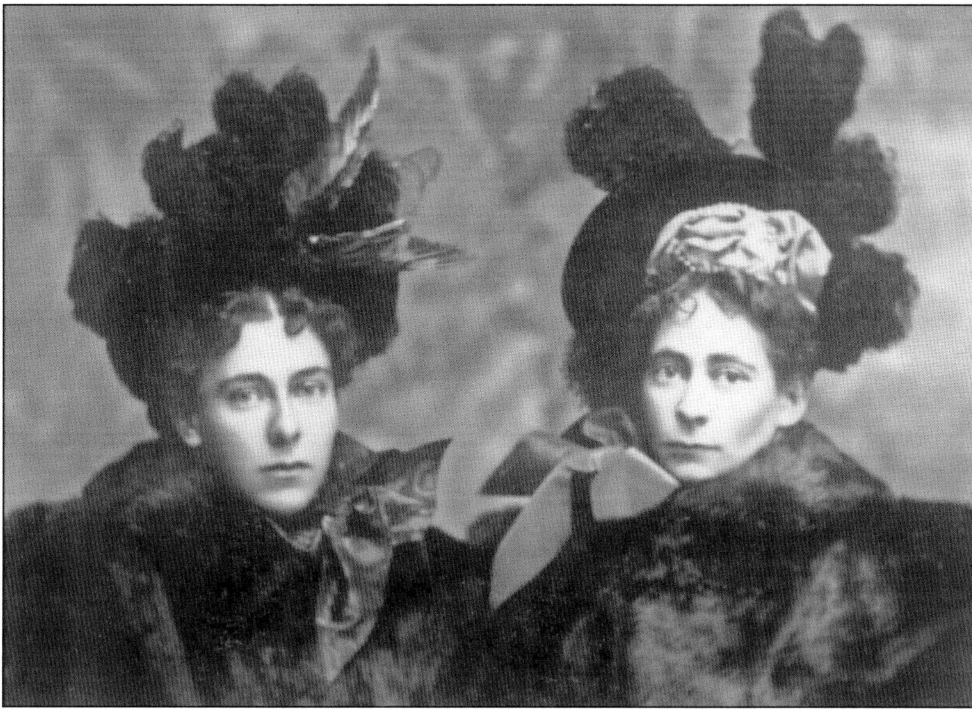

FASHION AND FUNCTION. Anna Smith and her half sister Jennie Sherlock pose in stylish and warm apparel. Regular dances, parties, and special occasions kept locals occupied, but also bundled up for the travel required between Atlantic City and South Pass City.

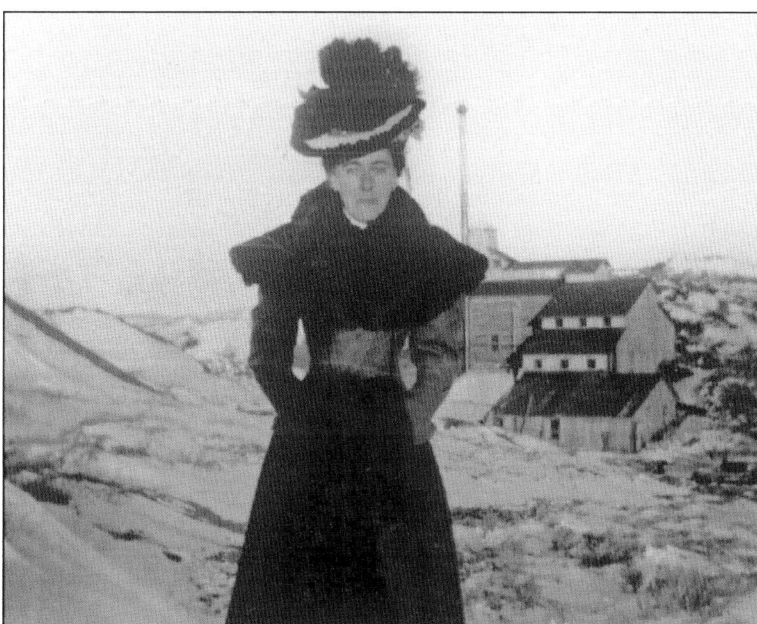

NEWLYWED BRIDE. Anna Smith-Tibbals visits the Carissa Mine outside South Pass City a week after her November 1899 marriage to mine manager Barney Tibbals.

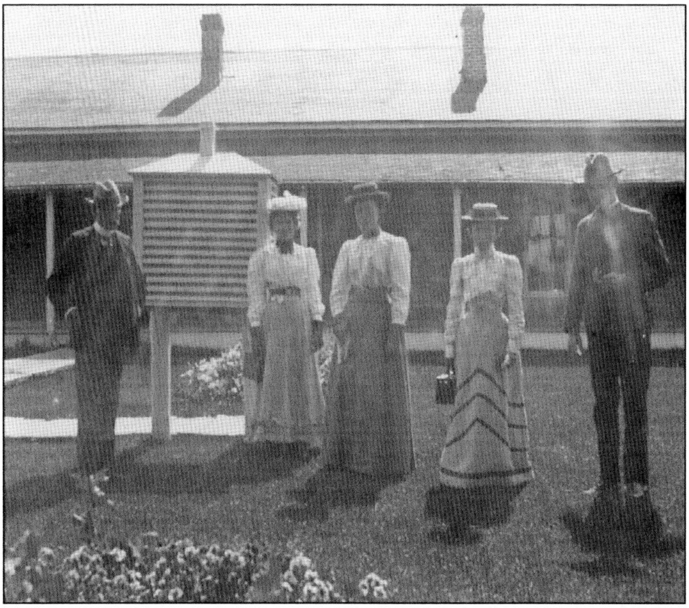

Fort Washakie, August 1899. From left to right are William Sherlock, Miss Knott, Mame Crowley, Anna Smith, and Dr. Godfrey visiting the fort grounds. Fort Washakie, 45 miles north of South Pass City, served as a military post from 1869 until 1909. Efforts to acculturate the Shoshone and Arapaho residents of the reservation centered on boarding schools and compulsory courses in English language, agricultural practices, and fostering a mainstream cultural identity.

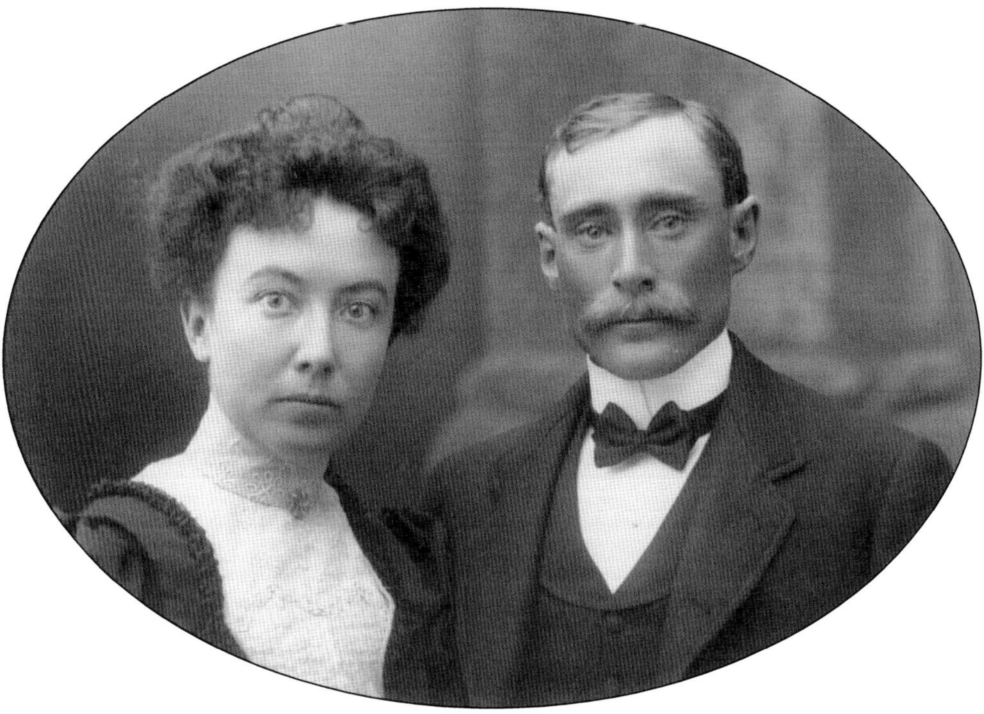

Mame and Will Sherlock. The fifth child of Richard and Janet Sherlock, Will was born at South Pass in 1871. Will married Mame Crowley on November 8, 1901, at her parents' home in Lander. The Sherlocks held diverse business interests beyond South Pass City, including sheep ranching. Their numerous flocks wintered on Muskrat Creek, some 70 miles from South Pass City.

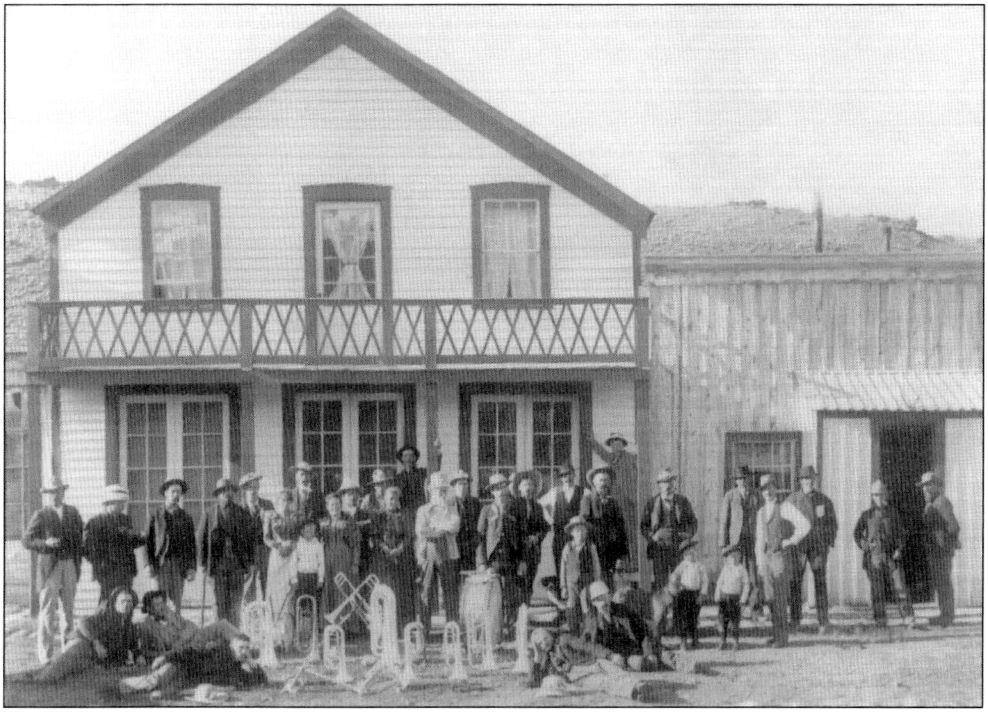

ROCK SPRINGS MARCHING BAND IN SOUTH PASS CITY, 1893. Local citizens gather with the visiting musicians during a tour of the mining district intended to raise interest in properties that had seen little work in nearly 20 years. By 1897, the Carissa and South Pass City were booming.

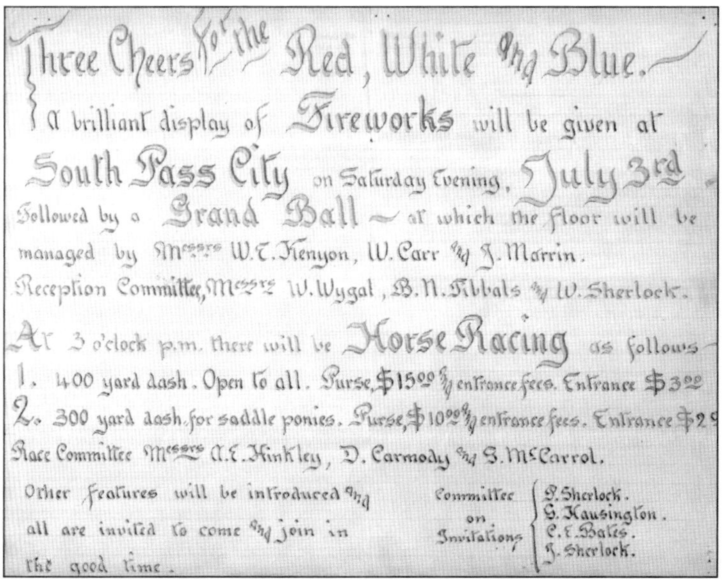

Three Cheers for the Red, White and Blue.
A brilliant display of Fireworks will be given at
South Pass City on Saturday Evening, July 3rd
Followed by a Grand Ball — at which the floor will be
managed by Messrs W.E. Kenyon, W. Carr and J. Marrin.
Reception Committee, Messrs W. Wygal, B.N. Tibbals and W. Sherlock.
At 3 o'clock p.m. there will be Horse Racing as follows
1. 400 yard dash. Open to all. Purse, $15.00 & entrance fees. Entrance $3.00
2. 300 yard dash, for saddle ponies. Purse, $10.00 & entrance fees. Entrance $2
Race Committee Messrs A.E. Hinkley, D. Carmody and S. McCarrol.
Other features will be introduced and all are invited to come and join in the good time.
Committee on Invitations: P. Sherlock. S. Hausington. C.E. Bates. J. Sherlock.

CELEBRATING INDEPENDENCE. In 1897, South Pass City celebrated in memorable fashion with attractions including fireworks and horse racing. Those involved in the preparations constitute a who's who of the town at the turn of the century, with miners, saloon owners, ranchers, and merchants. The winners' purses nearly equal the value of one ounce of fine gold.

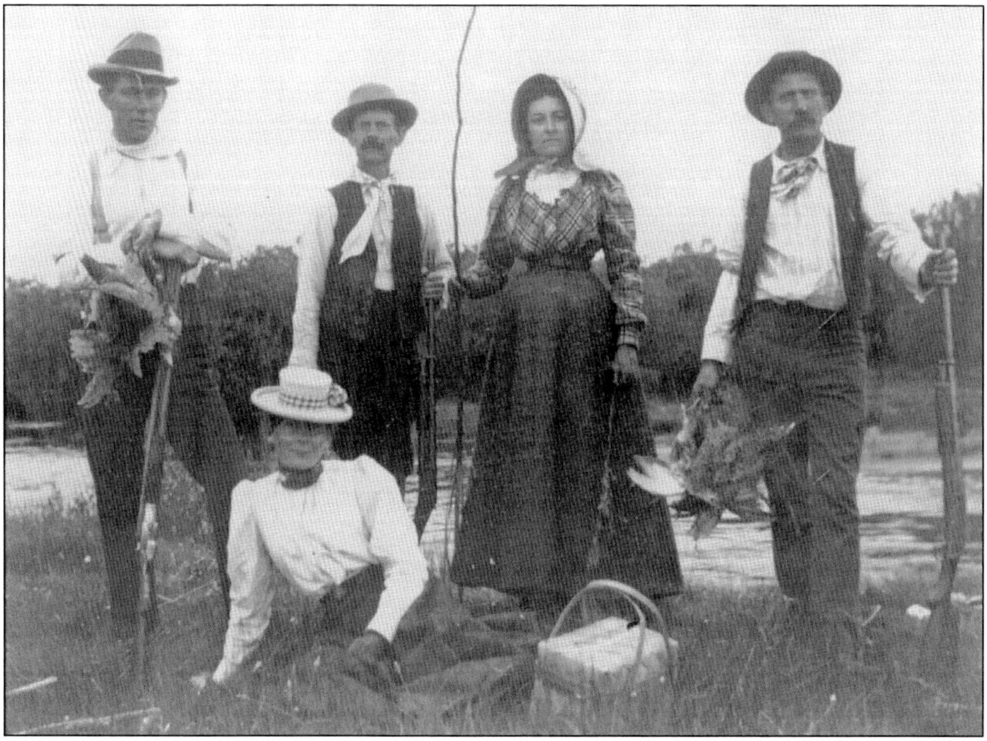

SUMMER FUN ON THE SWEETWATER, 1899. Standing are, from left to right, James Ernest Smith, Barney Tibbals, Anna Rottgen, Maurice Llewellyn, and Jennie Sherlock (seated). Late August and early September were once considered the best times to hunt sage grouse before the young-of-the-year birds had reached their full size and their distinctive full flavor. Fishing poles and picnic baskets round out an enjoyable day trip.

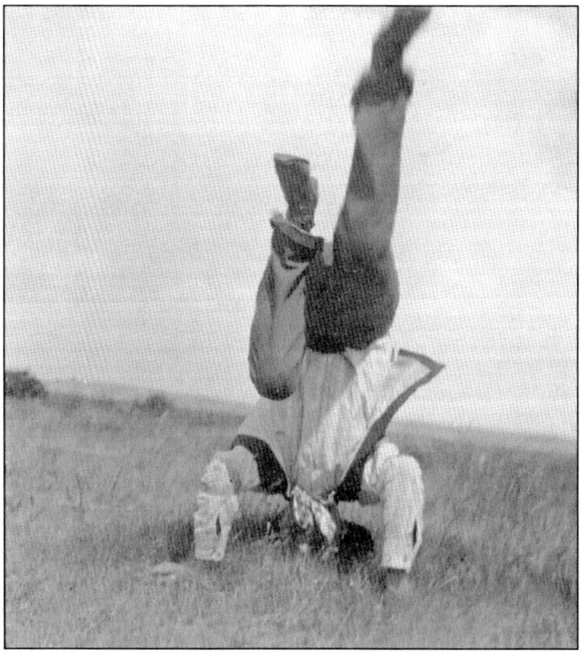

MAURICE LLEWELLYN. Locals knew the longtime area mine and mill operator at Atlantic City's Mary Ellen Mine as "Casey." He was born in Pennsylvania in 1860, perhaps becoming acquainted with underground mining there. Here, Llewellyn shows off for the camera and his companions.

OUTING IN THE SOUTHERN WIND RIVER RANGE, 1903. Susie Moore, Barney Tibbals, and Leon appear to take a break at a patch of blown down timber. Whether on a picnic or out for a ride, they are not dressed for a day's work clearing trees. The small caliber single-shot rifle and ax are part of the regular kit kept in the wagon.

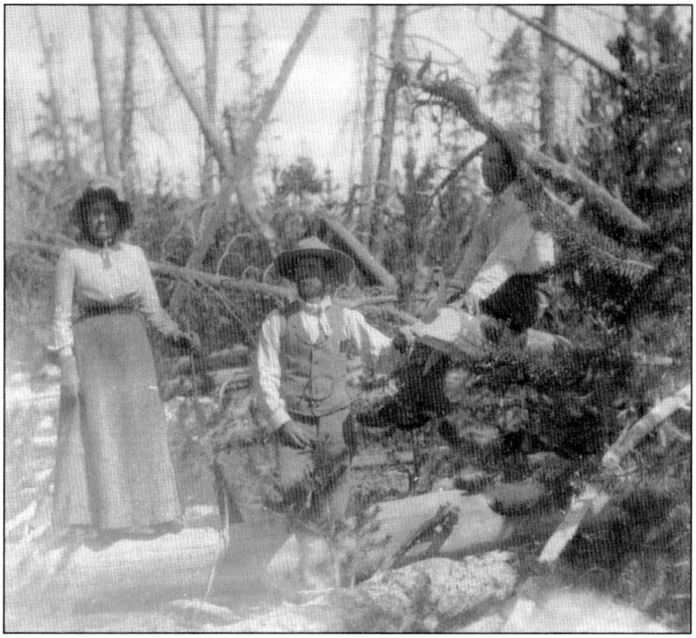

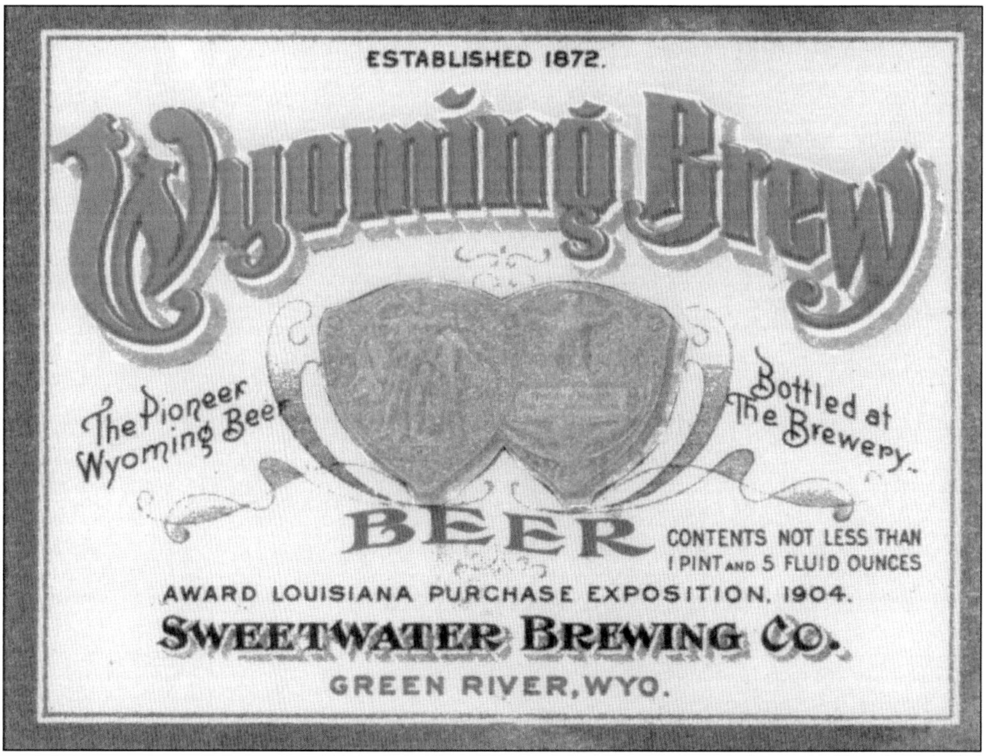

REFRESHMENTS TO GO. Bottled beers, like the Sweetwater Brewing Company's Wyoming Brew, made it possible for locals to take smaller quantities of beer along on short trips into the surrounding countryside. The bottles were heavy and fragile, but well worth the effort. So popular was bottled beer among local outdoors enthusiasts that, after scaling an as yet unnamed local summit near South Pass City, amateur mountaineers labeled it Pabst Peak.

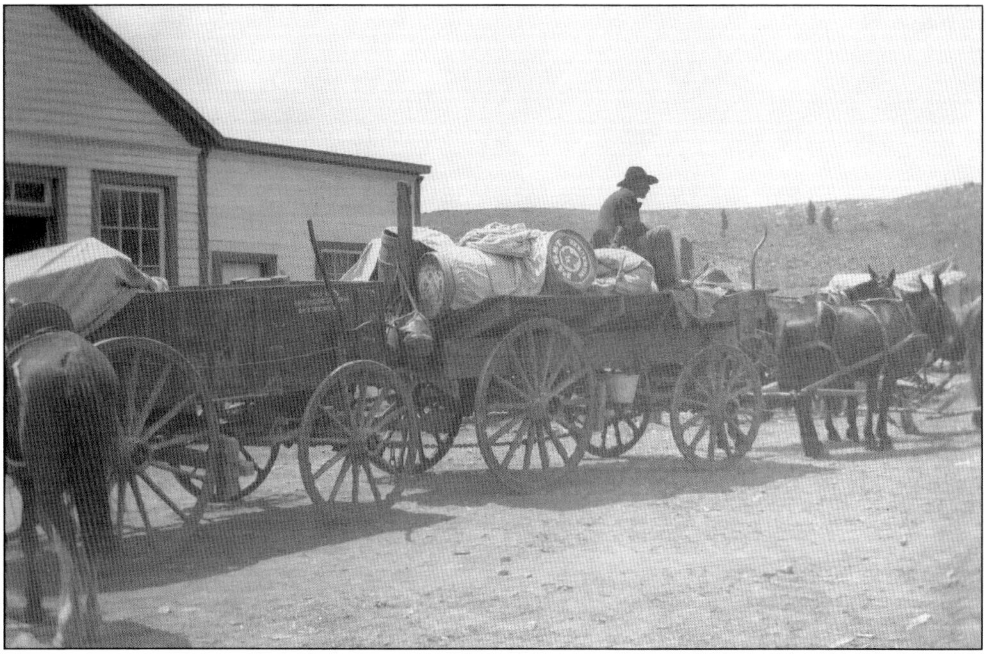

FREIGHT WAGON ON SOUTH PASS AVENUE, 1900. During the height of the 1868 gold rush, the town had boasted two breweries. By 1900, the town's saloons relied on freighters to supply what was considered a basic necessity. The beer keg here was from Pabst Brewing Co. in Milwaukee, Wisconsin.

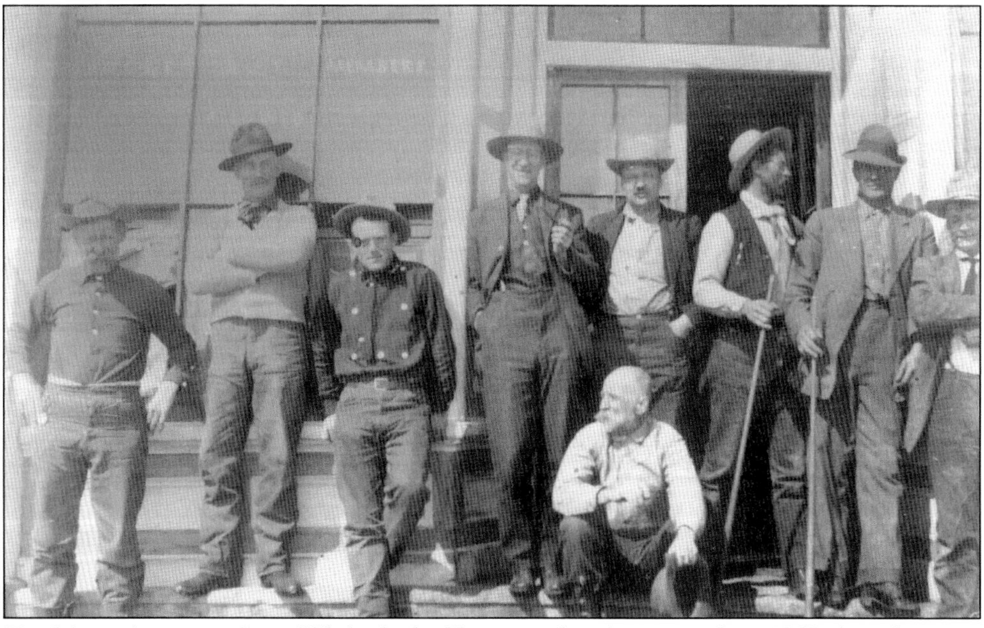

THE MINT, ATLANTIC CITY. While the building may date from as early as 1868, the saloon was undeniably a focal point in Atlantic City during the early 20th century. Pool cues indicate that a game was interrupted to call the men outside. The inscription on the windows to the left reads, "None But Members Allowed." The Bengston family used the building as a residence while they worked on the E.T. Fisher Dredge in the 1930s.

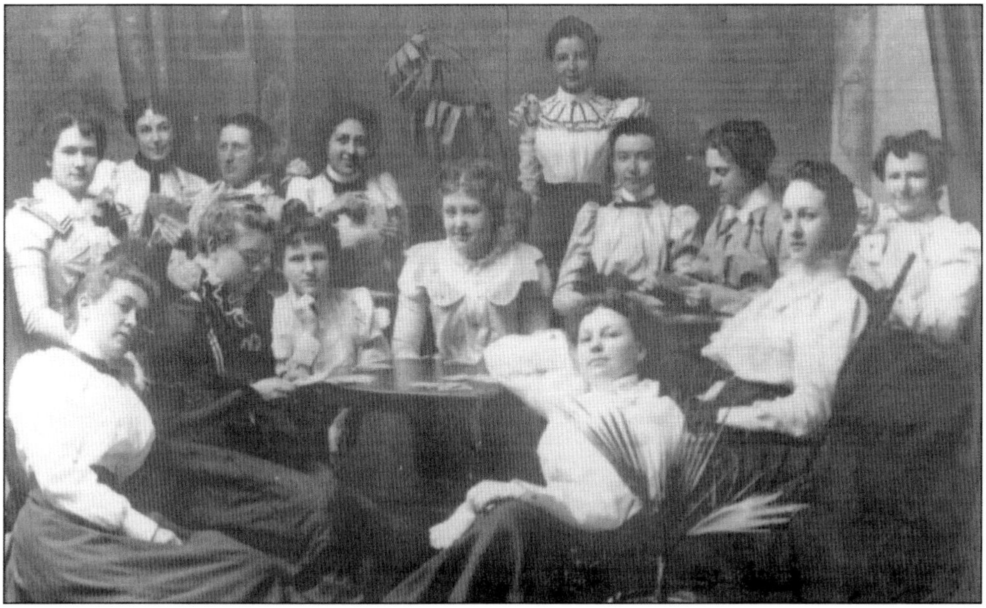

MAME CROWLEY AND FRIENDS. Mame (seated to the right of standing woman at center) took pride in making the most of every social opportunity. Attention to current fashion, popular culture, and style are exemplified in all of these young women's dress, hair, and posture.

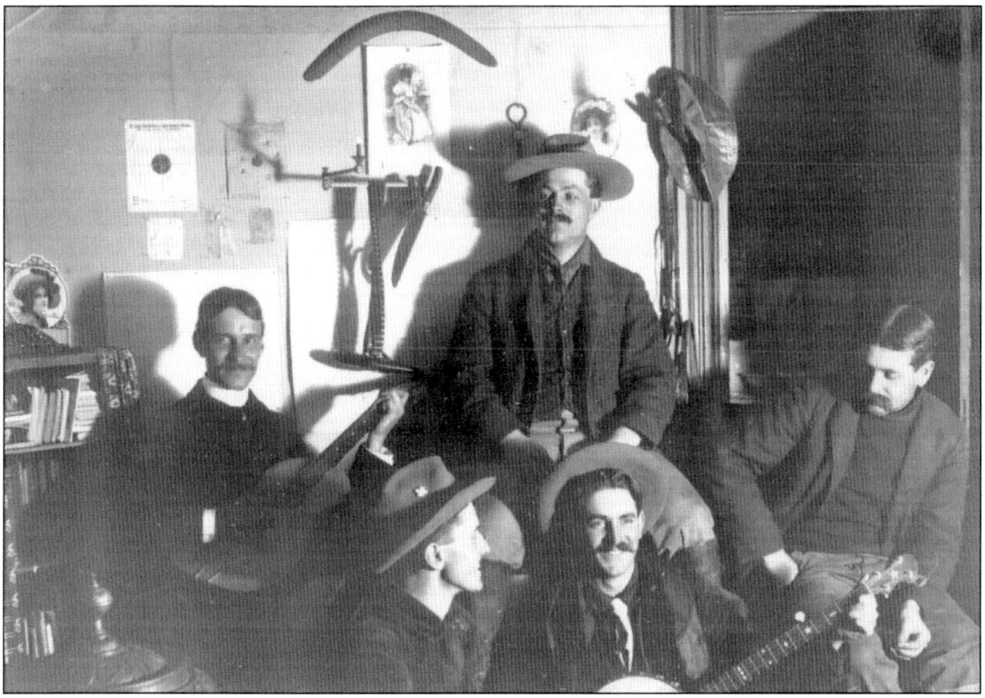

HAROLD A. TITCOMB AND FRIENDS. Titcomb (seated in profile) was the assistant manager at the Carissa Mine in 1900. Taken at the Carissa's bunkhouse, the image reveals much about Titcomb and other male miners outside of work. The men are immersed in musical instruments, pistols, knives, paper targets, illustrations of women, and a rain hat worn in the wet workings of the Carissa Mine. They even have a boomerang hanging on the wall!

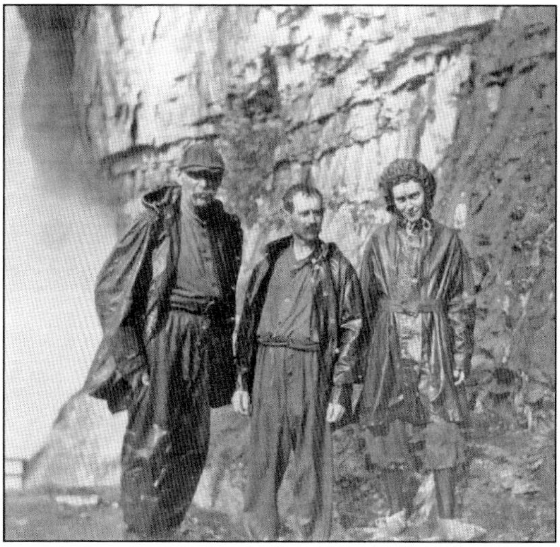

HONEYMOON AT NIAGARA FALLS, 1900. Pictured here are, from left to right, an unidentified guide, Barney Tibbals, and Anna Smith-Tibbals. Popular with newlyweds nationwide, Niagara Falls provided a spectacular backdrop for the South Pass City honeymooners who appear to be thoroughly drenched.

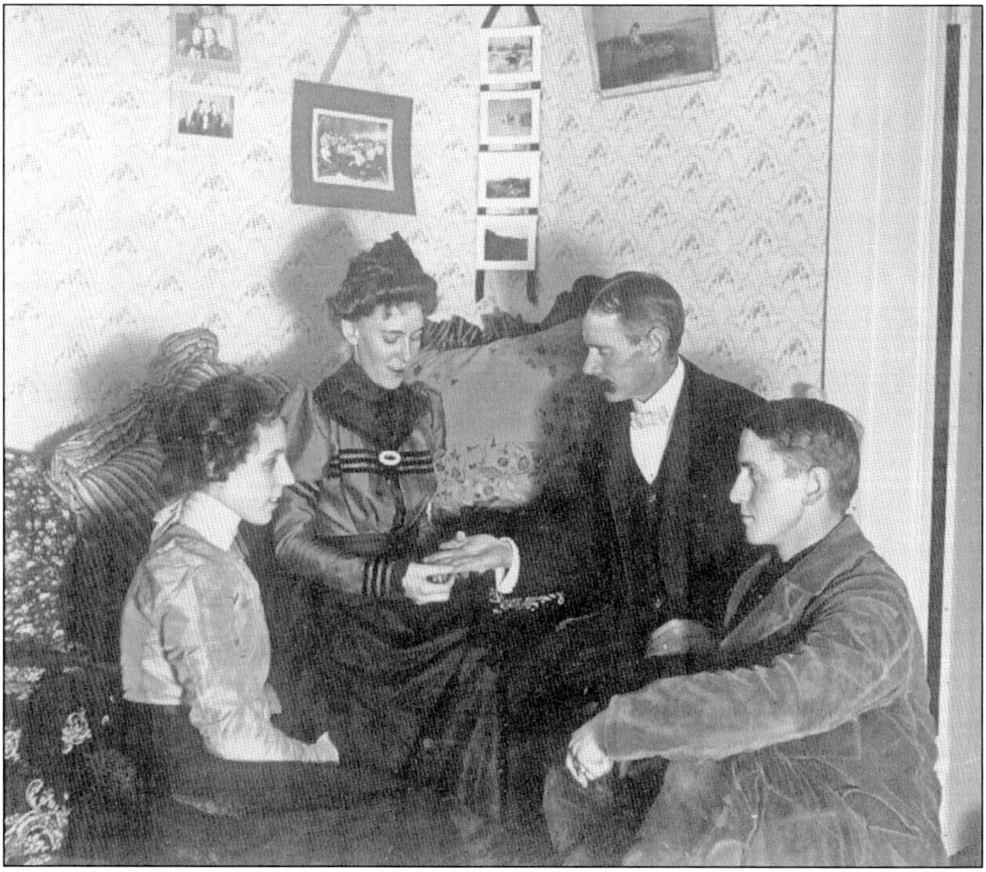

FORTUNE-TELLING, 1900. From left to right are Mrs. Dan Duggan, Anna Smith-Tibbals, Barney Tibbals, and Harold Abbot Titcomb relaxing at the mine manager's residence at the Carissa. Palm reading was one of the supernatural entertainments that enjoyed widespread acceptance at the time. It was simple, required no sophisticated technology, and maintained modesty with a sense of intimacy and adventure.

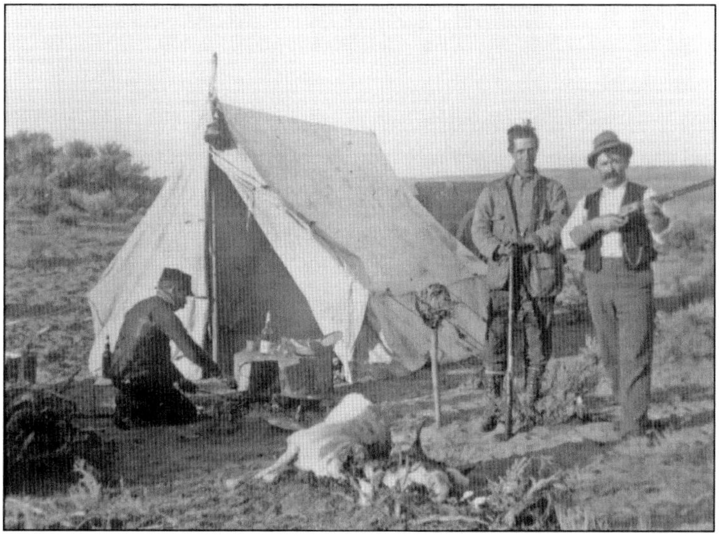

MAKING HUNTING CAMP, 1900. From left to right are Barney Tibbals, Harold Abbot Titcomb, and J.J. Marrin settling into camp with a fresh antelope for the pot. Outdoorsmen from Michigan and Maine respectively, Tibbals and Titcomb hunted Wyoming together for nearly 30 more years, even after both men had left the South Pass area to start families and put down roots.

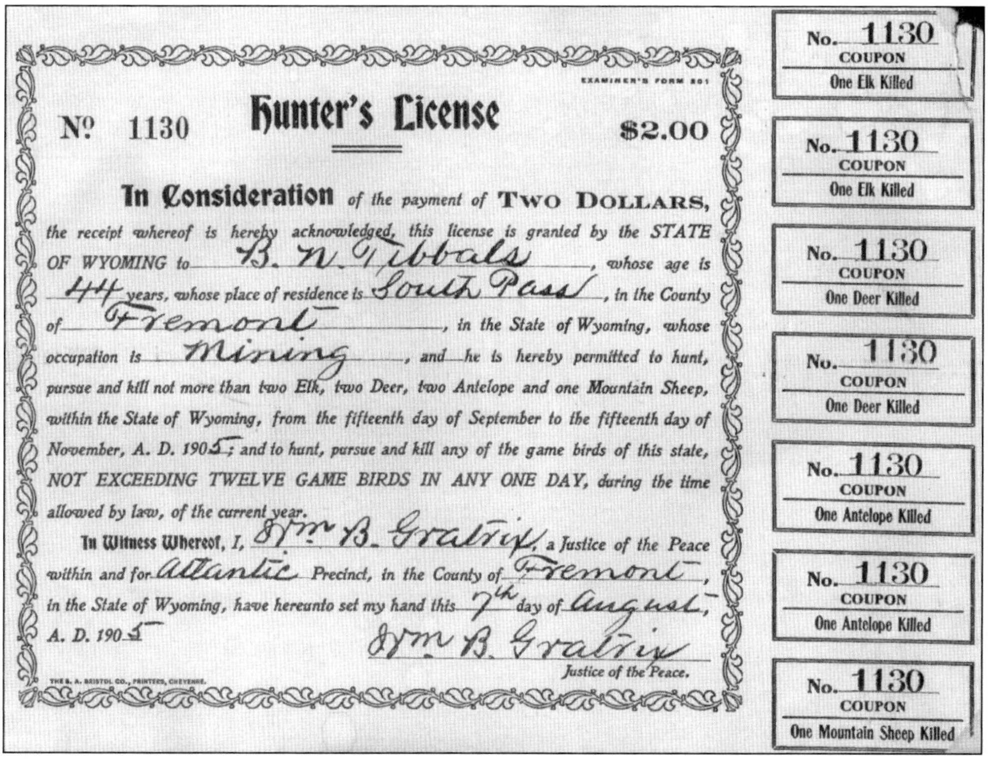

EXAMINER'S FORM 801

No 1130 **Hunter's License** $2.00

In Consideration *of the payment of* TWO DOLLARS, *the receipt whereof is hereby acknowledged, this license is granted by the STATE OF WYOMING to* B. N. Tibbals*, whose age is* 44 *years, whose place of residence is* South Pass*, in the County of* Fremont*, in the State of Wyoming, whose occupation is* Mining*, and he is hereby permitted to hunt, pursue and kill not more than two Elk, two Deer, two Antelope and one Mountain Sheep, within the State of Wyoming, from the fifteenth day of September to the fifteenth day of November, A. D. 1905; and to hunt, pursue and kill any of the game birds of this state, NOT EXCEEDING TWELVE GAME BIRDS IN ANY ONE DAY, during the time allowed by law, of the current year.*

In Witness Whereof, *I,* Wm B. Gratrix*, a Justice of the Peace within and for* Atlantic *Precinct, in the County of* Fremont*, in the State of Wyoming, have hereunto set my hand this* 7th *day of* August*, A. D. 1905*

Wm B. Gratrix
Justice of the Peace.

THE S. A. BRISTOL CO., PRINTERS, CHEYENNE.

No. 1130 COUPON One Elk Killed

No. 1130 COUPON One Elk Killed

No. 1130 COUPON One Deer Killed

No. 1130 COUPON One Deer Killed

No. 1130 COUPON One Antelope Killed

No. 1130 COUPON One Antelope Killed

No. 1130 COUPON One Mountain Sheep Killed

1905 WYOMING HUNTING LICENSE. Barney Tibbals purchased this license through William "Buck" Gratrix, a Civil War veteran and gold rusher to Atlantic City in 1869. Gratrix once commented about his Atlantic City cabin that, "I've lived in three counties, two territories, and one state and have never moved from one place." In his later years, Gratrix, like many other locals, moved permanently to Southern California.

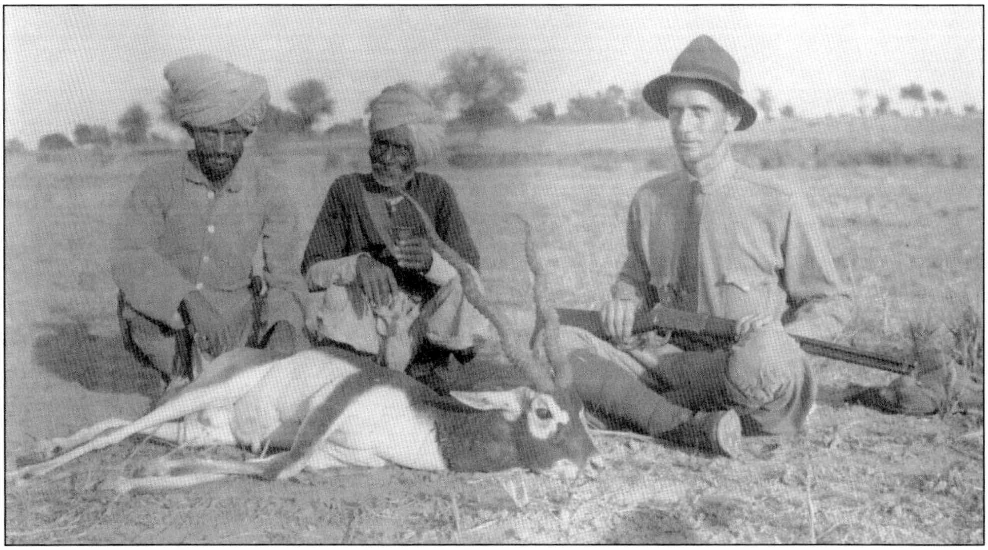

INDIA, 1909. Within a handful of years following his tenure at the Carissa Mine, Harold Abbot Titcomb had become a bit of a world traveler in pursuing his mining assignments. Here, he poses with a blackbuck taken with what is probably the same Winchester that he hunted with extensively in Wyoming.

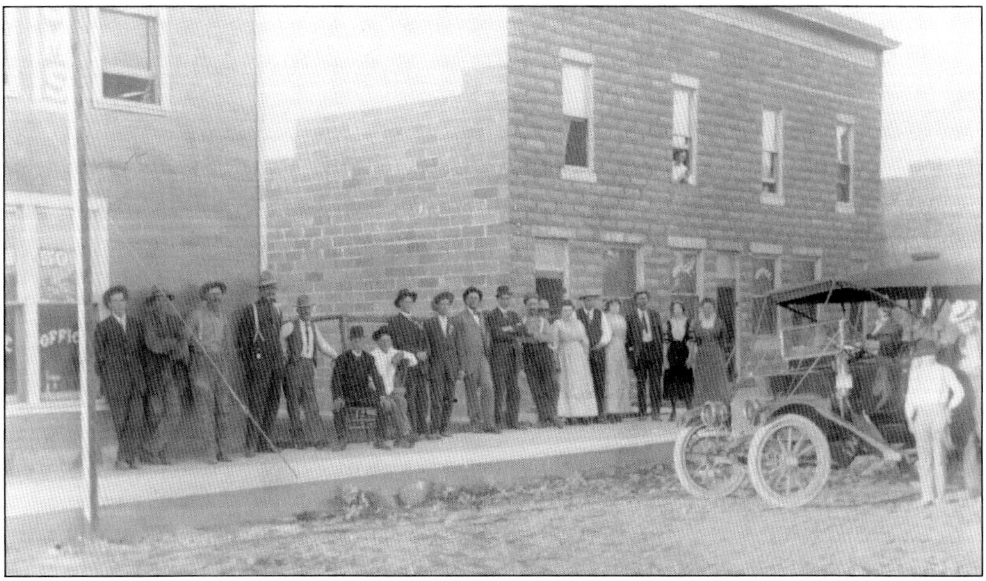

FIRST AUTOMOBILE IN LANDER, WYOMING, 1910. After he left the Carissa around 1906, Barney Tibbals established the life he had written about since leaving Michigan in 1876—that of a ranchman. His new ranch just northwest of South Pass City was then still in Fremont County, but the 80-mile trek to conduct business at the county seat in Lander proved no obstacle, particularly when he acquired a new Overland automobile. Folks gathered to see Tibbals in his horseless carriage.

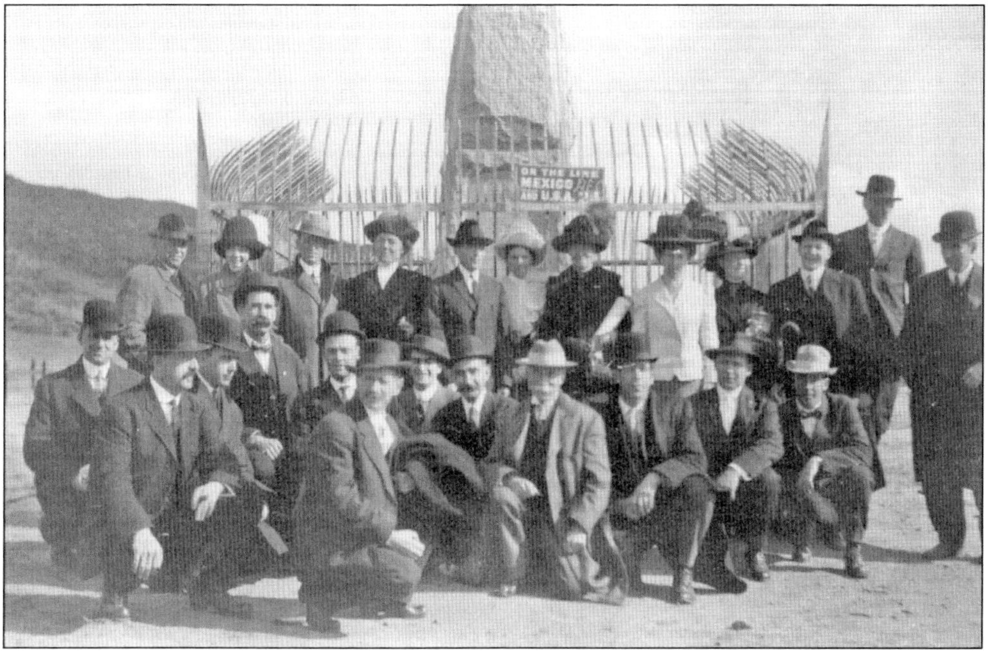

AMERICAN AND MEXICAN BORDER, 1911. Barney Tibbals is seen crouching sideways in the foreground facing the camera. Taken just two days after Christmas between San Diego, California, and Tijuana, Mexico, the occasion for the trip is unknown, but verifies the fact that local residents often took extended travel to visit family, attend to business, or for recreation. This monument was erected between 1891 and 1894 during a resurvey of the entire border from El Paso, Texas, to San Diego, California.

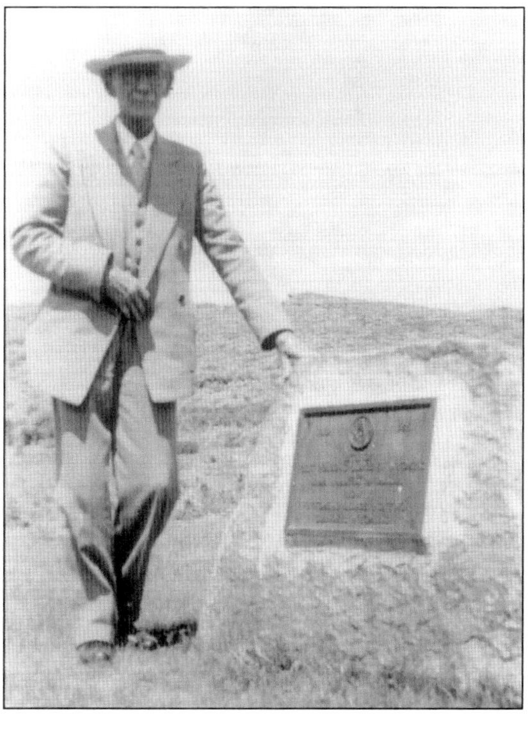

BARNEY N. TIBBALS, 1934. Business and family interests kept Tibbals in constant contact with his old stomping grounds in South Pass City, even some three decades after he left the Carissa as manager. Here, Tibbals inspects a marker that commemorates the location of the first Mason's Lodge in Wyoming, erected during the gold rush. The monument was joined in the 1970s by a replica structure that hosts Masonic assemblies at least once every year.

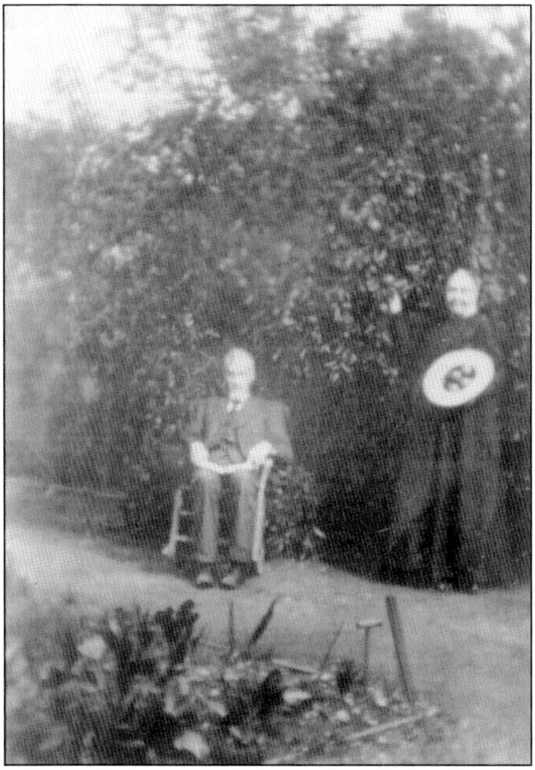

Los Angeles, 1909. The lure of California proved strong for many residents of the area. John Thompson and Janet Sherlock were no exception, as they took time in a lush garden complete with an orange tree heavy with fresh fruit. Unlike many other Sweetwater gold rushers, Janet resisted the urge to remain in the Golden State, living in South Pass City until her death in 1923.

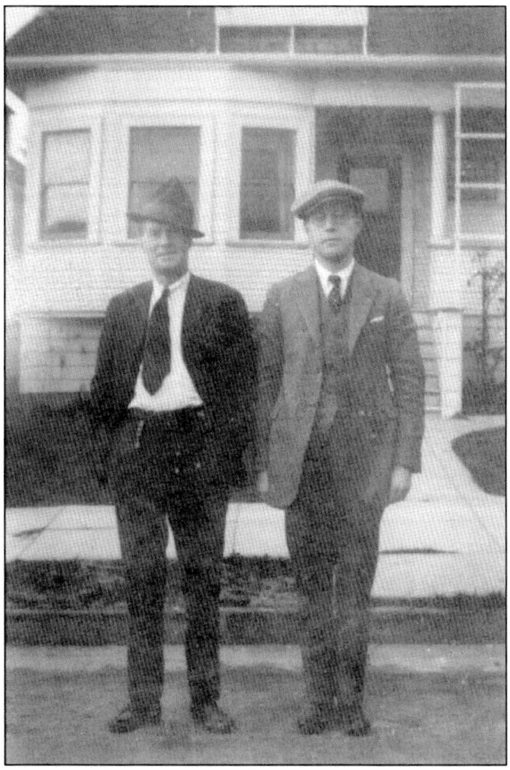

Berkeley, California, 1922. Pictured here are Dan Carmody (left) and an unidentified man. Carmody was a longtime South Pass area local who called himself everything from a gold miner to a sheepherder. Eventually, he, too, answered the call of the Golden State, moving in with his sister Anna Ivens near San Francisco Bay. Here he met a grim fate. Local historian Jim Sherlock recounted how, when he was yet in the South Pass area, Carmody would engage in an occasional drinking binge. At the local saloon, he often reveled in showing off a flashy $500 diamond ring to onlookers. After serving for a time as watchman at the closed Carissa Mine around 1920, Carmody moved to California. While he had regular work, Carmody still observed some of the old habits he demonstrated in Wyoming. Unexpectedly, he went missing and, some time later, his remains were pulled from the waters of San Francisco Bay. Doubtless, both his lapse of judgment and his prized ring were factors in his mysterious disappearance and untimely death.

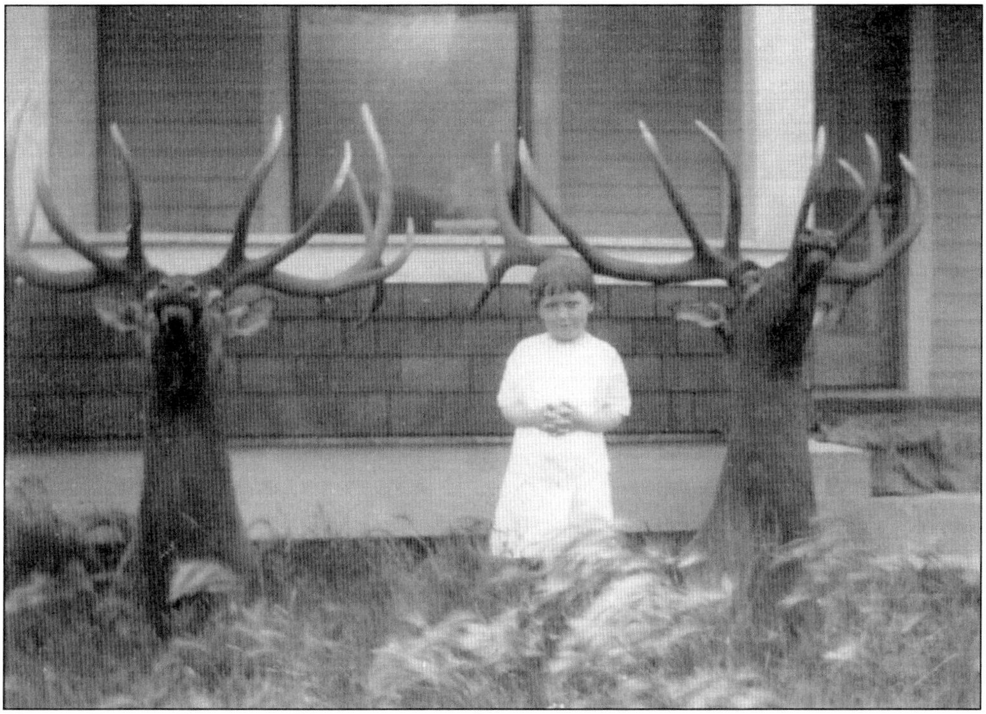

TIBBALS RANCH, BOULDER, WYOMING, 1920. Janet Tibbals, the daughter of Barney and Anna Tibbals, is pictured with two bull elk trophies taken in the immediate area. While known for its registered Hereford cattle, the ranch also served as a base camp for the Titcomb family during their visits to the area. Horses from the Tibbals Ranch were shipped to the Titcombs' Greenacre estate in Farmington, Maine, for their three children to practice their saddle skills.

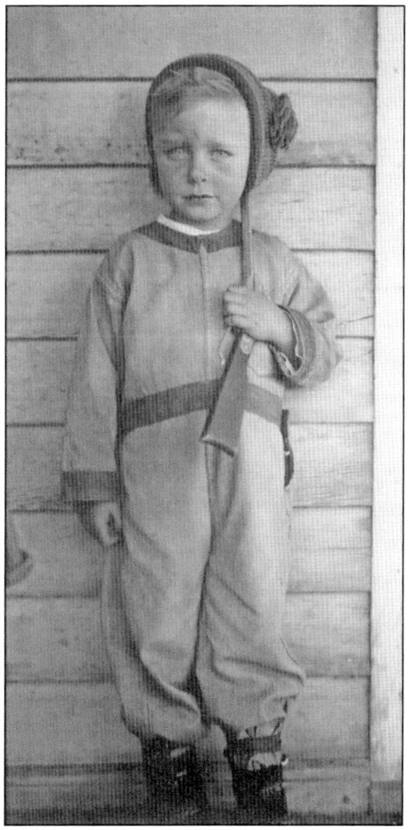

JAMES TIBBALS, 1920. Anna and Barney's only son, James, had no shortage of opportunity or energy to explore the ranch surroundings. He is seen here with his coyote gun. Following his local schooling, James attended the Colorado School of Mines in Golden, Colorado.

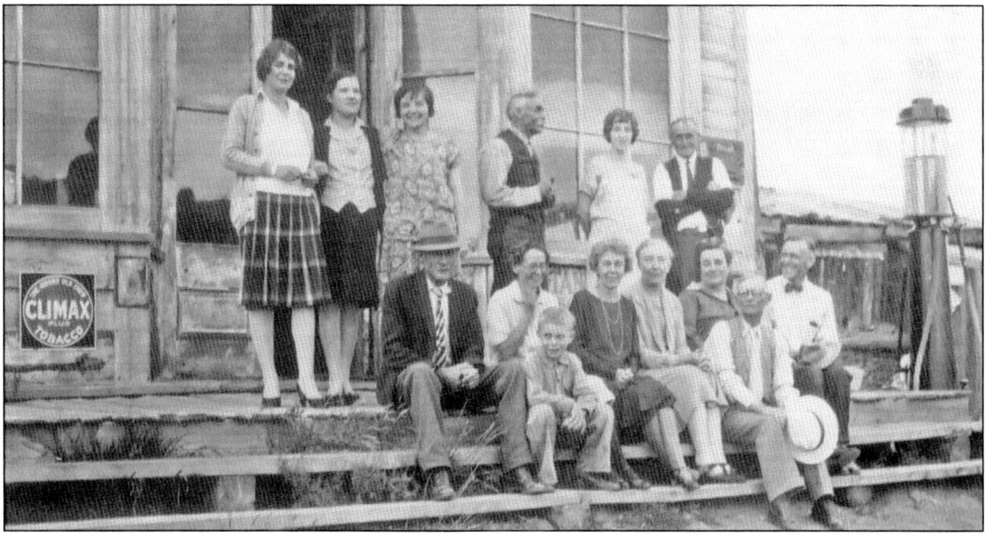

SMITH-SHERLOCK COMPANY STORE, 1928. The main automobile route from the Sweetwater and Red Desert country in the south to the Lander and Wind River country in the north passed directly through South Pass City and past the Sherlock family's store. Motorists and locals alike could top off their gas tank, buy a pack of cigarettes, or get a cold drink from either the ice chest inside or the crystal clear water in a spring across the street. Thousands of store records survive and tell the story of South Pass City's premier merchants.

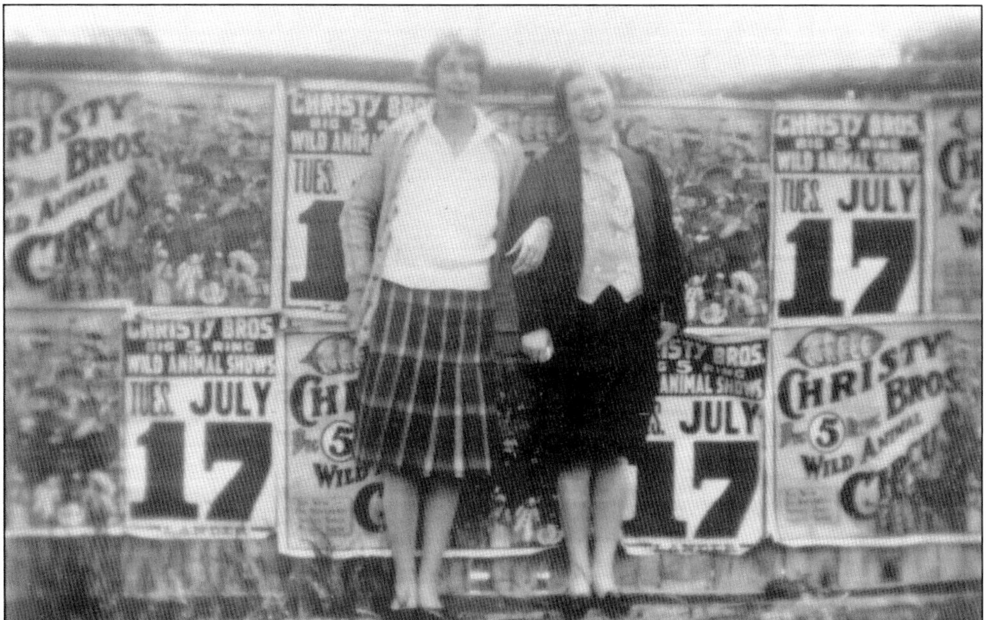

JANET SMITH AND MARIE SHERLOCK, 1928. The daughter of James Ernest Smith joins the adopted daughter of Will and Mame Sherlock for a photograph in front of posters left pasted along South Pass City's main street by a passing circus troupe. The vivid ads bear witness to the fact that locals had access to a great many exotic and colorful experiences, even in rural Wyoming of the 1920s.

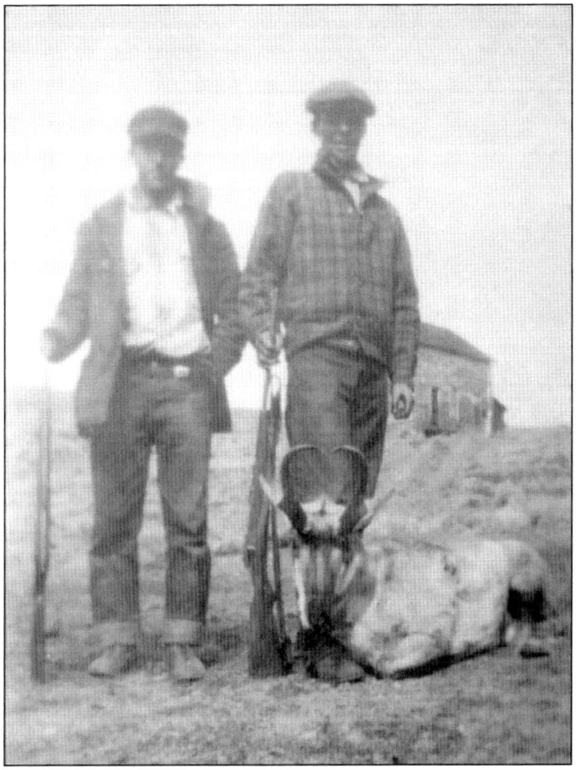

BILLY GREEN AND JACK DAVISON, 1929. The two local sportsmen obviously took great pride in a trophy buck antelope by showing it off in Atlantic City. Davison's rifle with open sights verifies the fact that he was a crack shot. Davison carried mail in the area, sometime wading chest-deep through snowdrifts in the winter. He kept a place in South Pass City as a layover on his route.

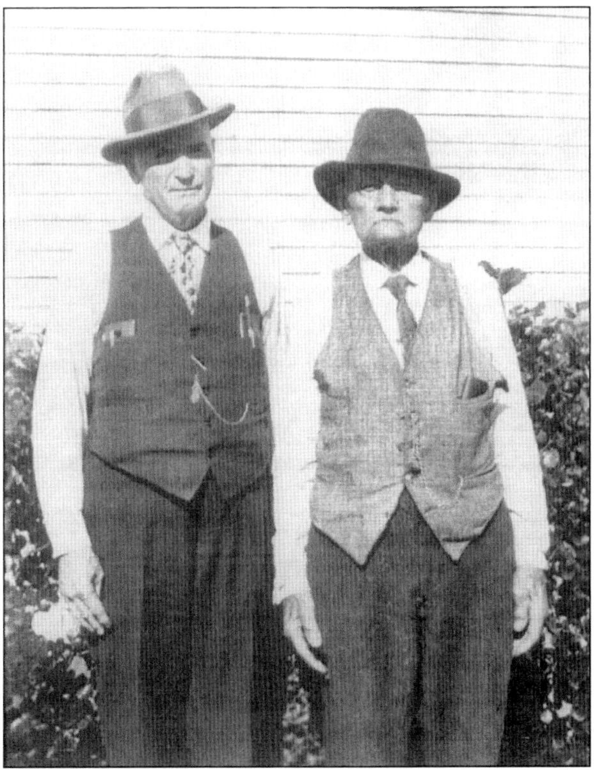

FRED LOVEJOY AND JACK HUFF, MAY 9, 1930. The image was taken at the Soldiers' Home in Sawtelle, California, where Huff spent his final years. Lovejoy was a contributor to the second gold boom at the Sweetwater Mines. Lovejoy and his brother helped to rekindle forgotten properties in the district, most prominently portions of the Mohamet Group on the west end of the Carissa property. Huff was an original gold-rusher to the boomtown of Atlantic City and following his death on January 4, 1931, was buried at the Los Angeles National Cemetery.

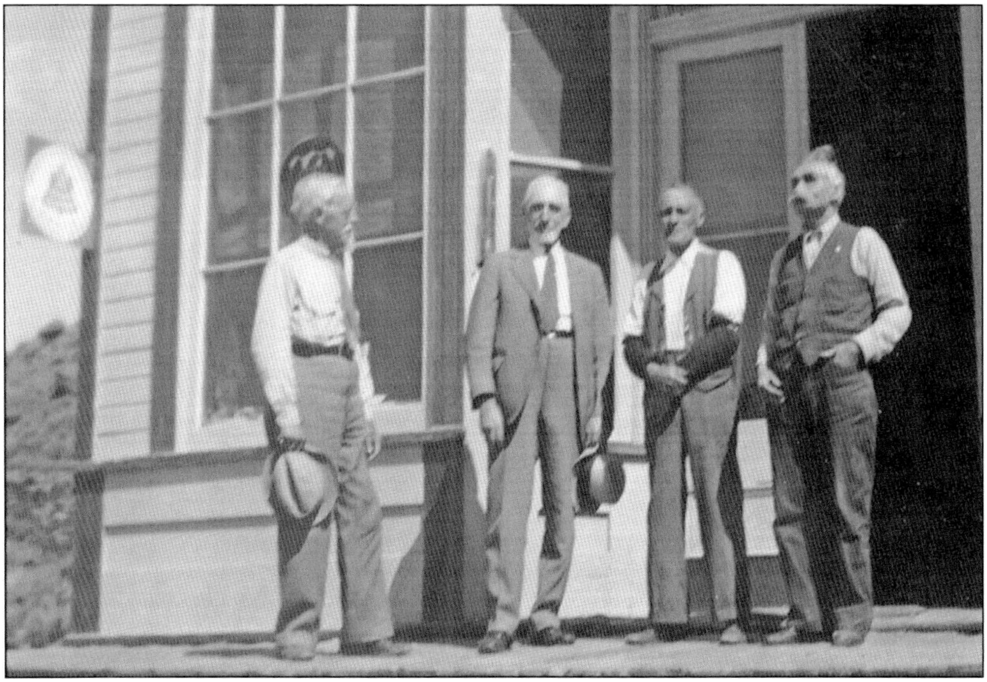

SMITH-SHERLOCK CO. STORE, AUGUST 17, 1934. Pictured here are, from left to right, Frontier photographer William Henry Jackson, Wyoming Gov. B.B. Brooks, John Sherlock, and Peter Sherlock.

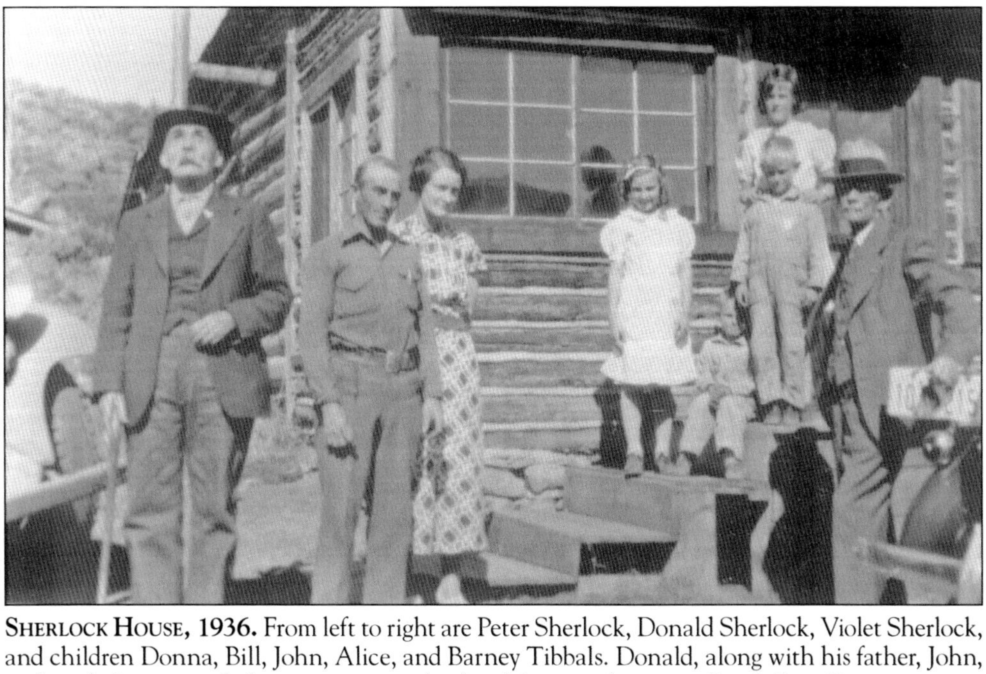

SHERLOCK HOUSE, 1936. From left to right are Peter Sherlock, Donald Sherlock, Violet Sherlock, and children Donna, Bill, John, Alice, and Barney Tibbals. Donald, along with his father, John, and uncle Peter were helping to operate the family's general store in South Pass City.

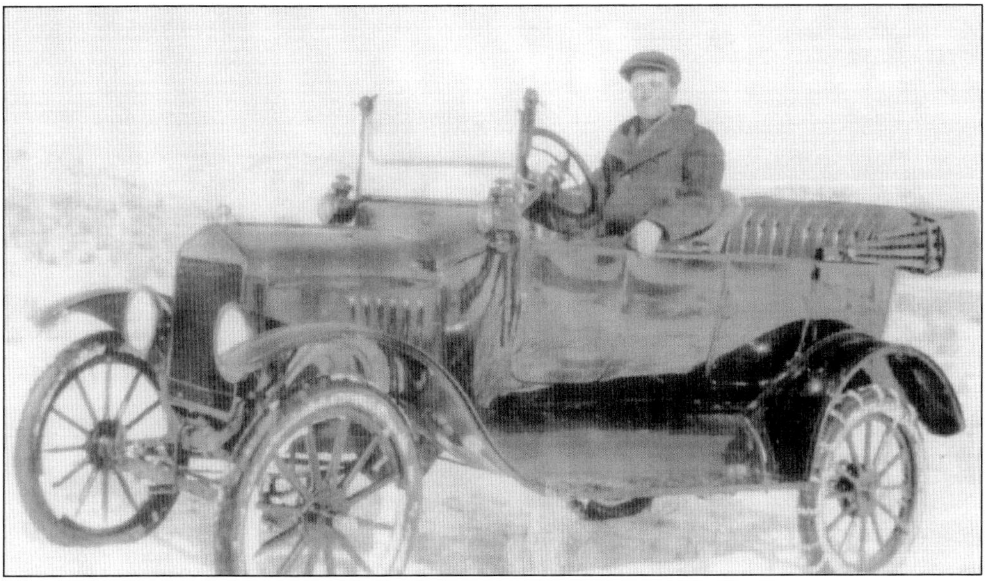

Link to the Outside World. Mail carriers and freighters face tough conditions in the area, even today. Historically, these occupations represented access to the world beyond the immediate area. Around 1910, Ralph Faler moved his family to the crossroads community of South Pass City in order to be in the middle of the area's growing motorized freighting business. In April 1921, he perished only five miles from South Pass City near Slaughterhouse Gulch during a spring snowstorm. Today, a simple monument marks the spot of his death.

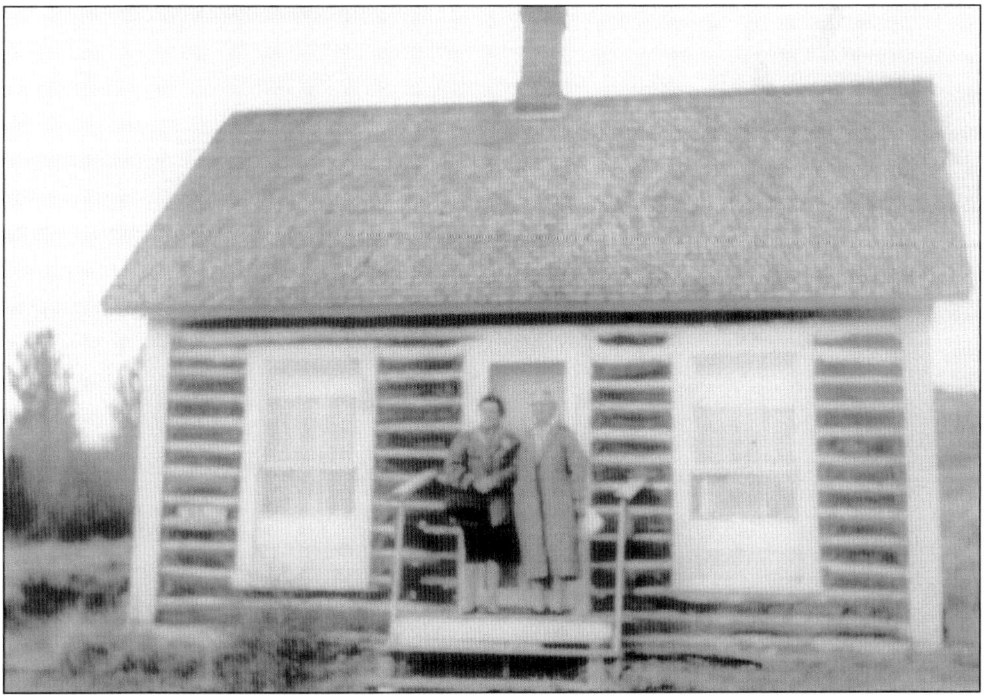

Libby Cabin, 1958. Harry Libby, a mining man from Silverton, Colorado, built this cabin in 1899 after he was dismissed from his position as foreman at the Carissa mine. Pictured here are Elsie Faler (left) and Theresa Ritchie. Ralph and Elsie lived in this cabin in the early 1900s.

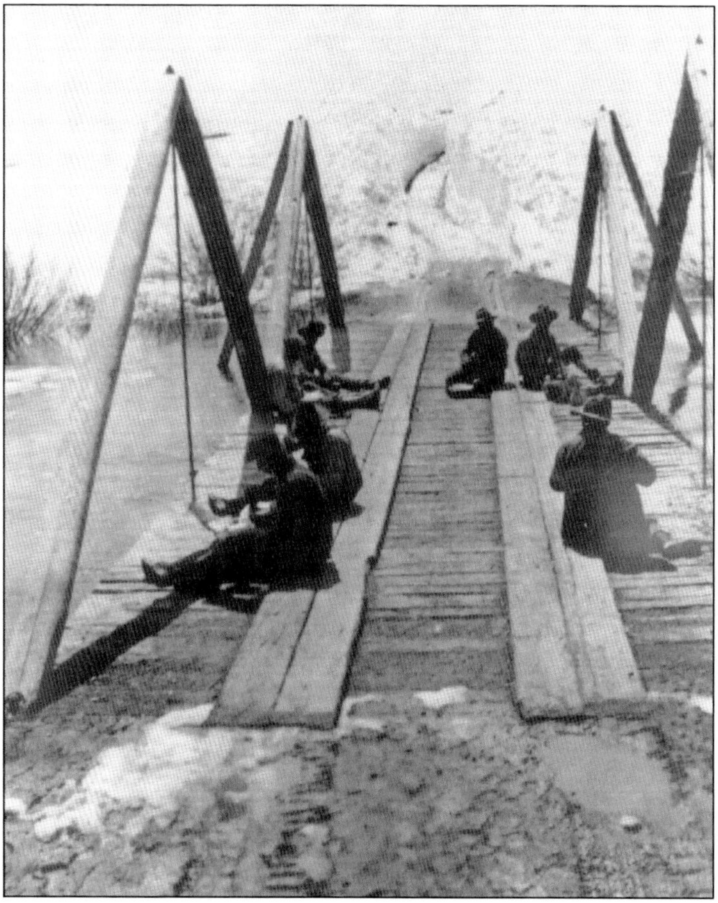

Lunch Break, May 28, 1939. Springtime clearing of snow from local roads was an event for residents who had been snowbound for perhaps six months. This image of the Sweetwater Bridge south of Atlantic City combines elements familiar even to today's residents; snow, mud, and a river brimming with spring runoff.

Winter Fun in South Pass. The Davison and Hart families and friends along with the local third-grade teacher prepare to enjoy some cross-country skiing around South Pass in the 1940s.

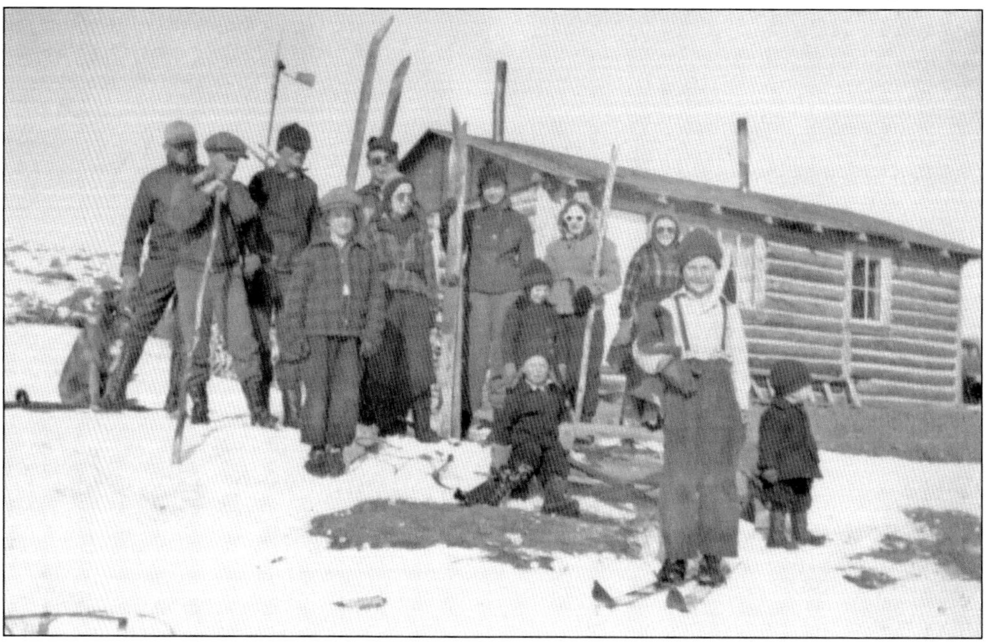

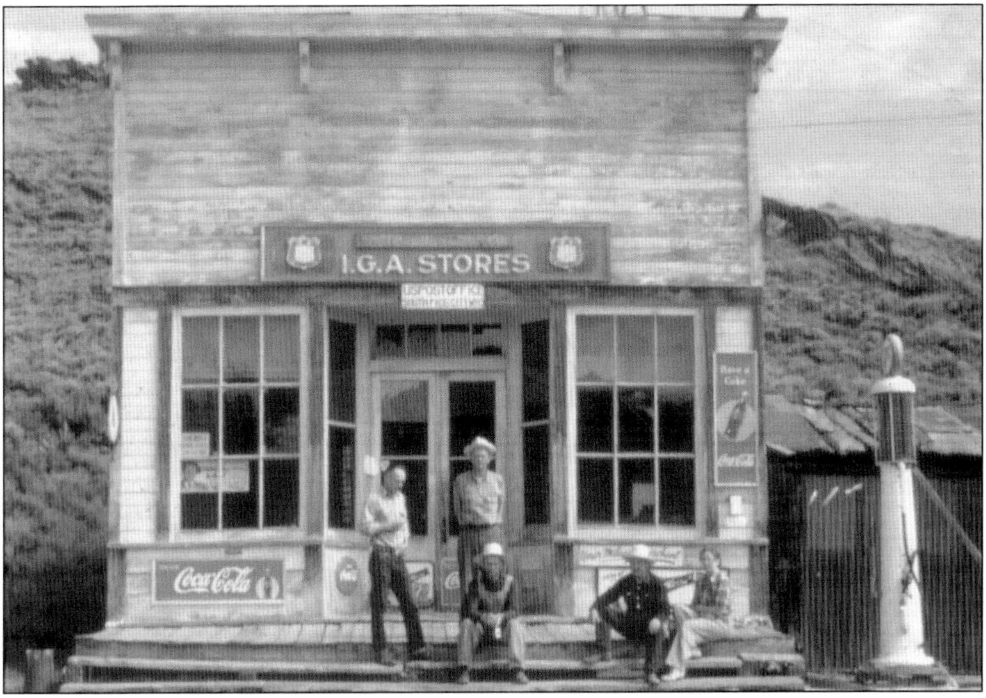

SMITH-SHERLOCK CO. STORE, JULY 1951. From left to right are Fred Stratton Jr., Jack Leermakers, Art Burnett, Peter Decker, and Helen Henderson. Stratton bought the Sherlock family's holdings in South Pass City in 1949. He intended to use the charm of the crumbling town to capitalize on the growing sense of Western history and nostalgia then taking hold across the nation. Noted Oregon Trail researchers and enthusiasts Paul and Helen Henderson were among those who made repeated visits to the area.

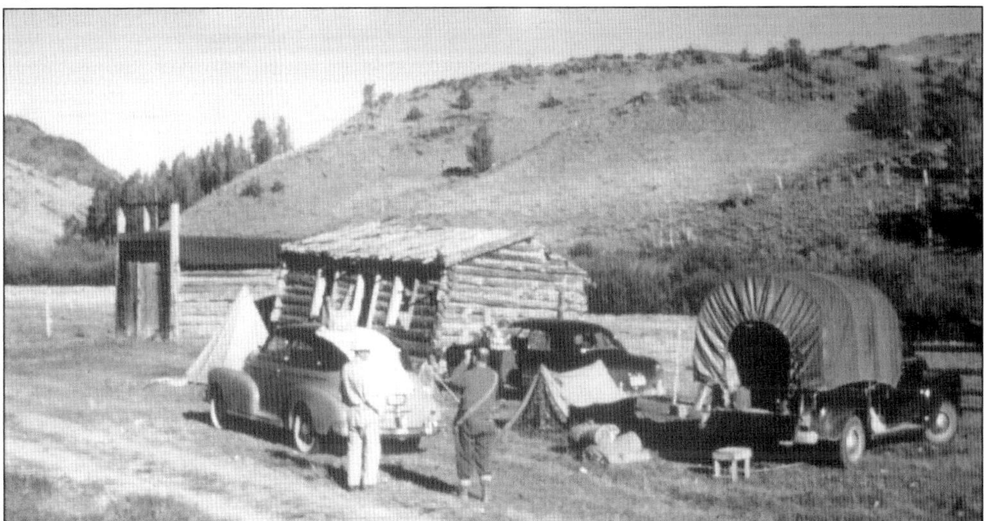

PAUL AND HELEN HENDERSON'S CAMP, 1951. On perhaps their first Oregon Trail research trip to western Wyoming, the Hendersons pitched a well-equipped camp alongside South Pass City's eastern main street. In later years, the couple based out of Atlantic City's Carpenter Hotel and benefited from the extensive knowledge of Jim Carpenter.

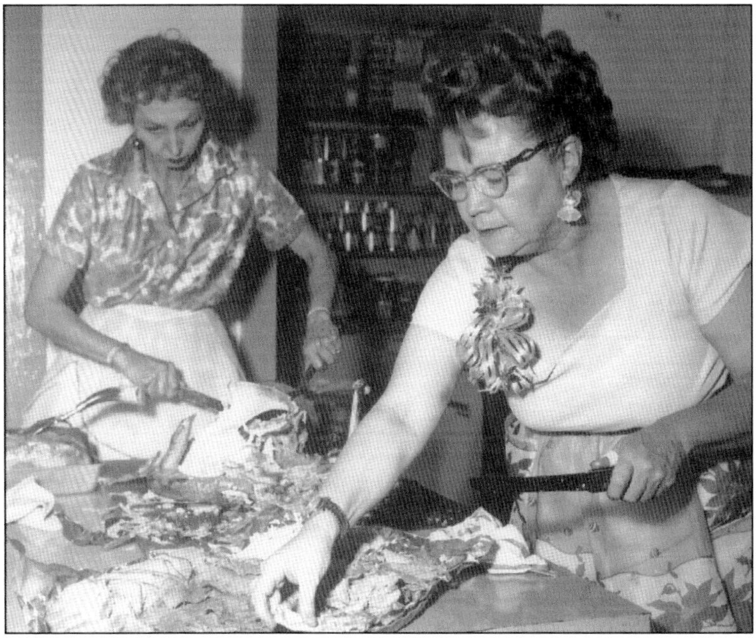

"Christmas in July," 1959. Above, sisters-in-law Virginia and Minnie Woodring carve turkey for their unusual celebration. South Pass City's new proprietors couldn't be deterred from observing Christmas. They just did so in July, when weather conditions were more favorable for their guests who had to travel.

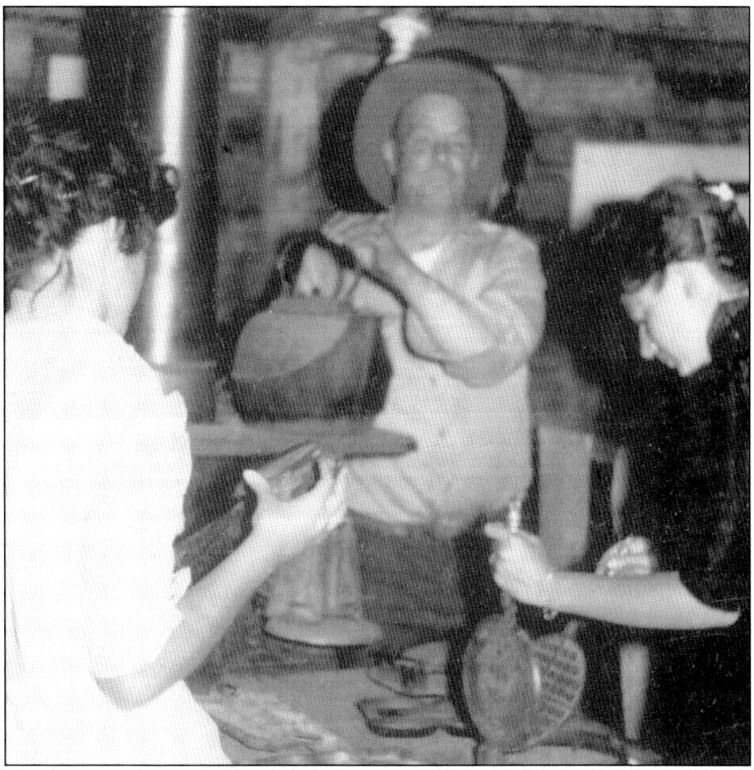

John Woodring. Two unidentified helpers and John Woodring (center) prepare traditional cookware for use. For a decade, John and Minnie Woodring were the faces that greeted visitors to what was fast becoming Wyoming's most famous and authentic ghost town.

Seven

A Historic Site

Even before the boom at the Sweetwater Mines ended, buildings sat vacant along the streets of South Pass City. Some were constructed, but never occupied. The few dozen residents who remained in town even in the depths of the bust took up residences and businesses in the abandoned buildings. Others like James Smith and Janet Sherlock-Smith sought out the legal owner and purchased the structure, remodeling it for their own use. The town shrank as structures disappeared through a combination of neglect, fire, and natural causes.

By around 1905, the town site had taken its present appearance. Matriarch Janet Sherlock-Smith died in 1923, signaling the end of an era in town. Her adult children's haying and stock raising took them farther from South Pass City more often, although Peter Sherlock remained a stalwart at the family's store into the 1940s. Following his death, the surviving gold rush descendants decided to move away from South Pass City entirely.

The post–World War II era was dominated by the first real effort to promote the aging town as a tourist destination by entrepreneurs. First Fred Stratton Jr., and then John and Minnie Woodring actively promoted and preserved the town. But the task of stabilizing some of the hurriedly built gold rush–era buildings was too great. In 1967, the Wyoming 75th Anniversary Commission acquired the town for the public benefit as a time capsule of Wyoming's first days. Some considerable criticism ensued at their perceived folly. However, with the acquisition of the Carissa Mine in 2003, Wyoming could boast of having the best examples of a frontier town and a gold mine preserved side by side for the public benefit.

Today, South Pass City and its surroundings constitute a rare opportunity for visitors to experience an authentic sense of participating in history itself.

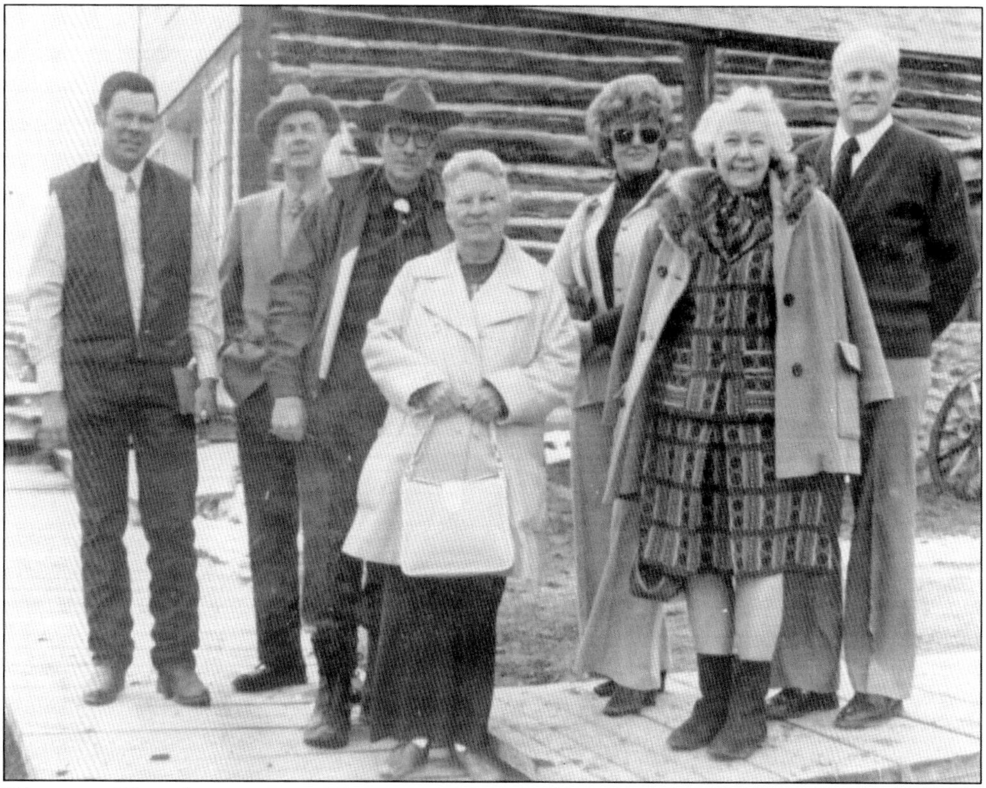

WYOMING 75TH ANNIVERSARY COMMISSION. Pictured here are, from left to right, Tom Shaffer of the Wyoming Recreation Commission, Ed Billie, Dr. Don MacLeod, Alice Messick, Dorothy Cable, Edness Kimball Wilkins, and Judge Jack Nicholas. With creativity and forward thinking, the group of Wyoming citizens built upon their original mission to commemorate Wyoming's 75th year of statehood with parades and parties, and presented the people of Wyoming with the state's second oldest incorporated town, South Pass City.

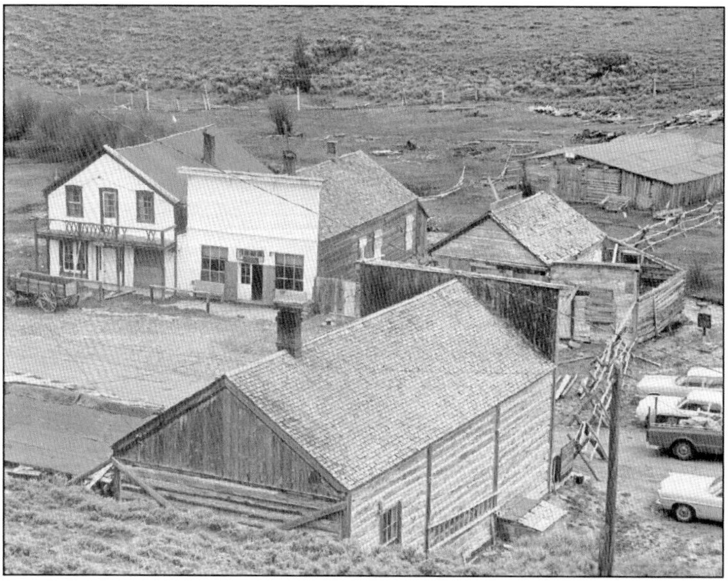

BEGINNINGS OF A STATE HISTORIC SITE. The commission's purchase of the crumbling town was not greeted with universal praise, and public funding for stabilization and conservation was initially slow in coming. Early efforts to responsibly manage the property resulted in a spotty record of successes and shortfalls, often highlighted in local newspapers.

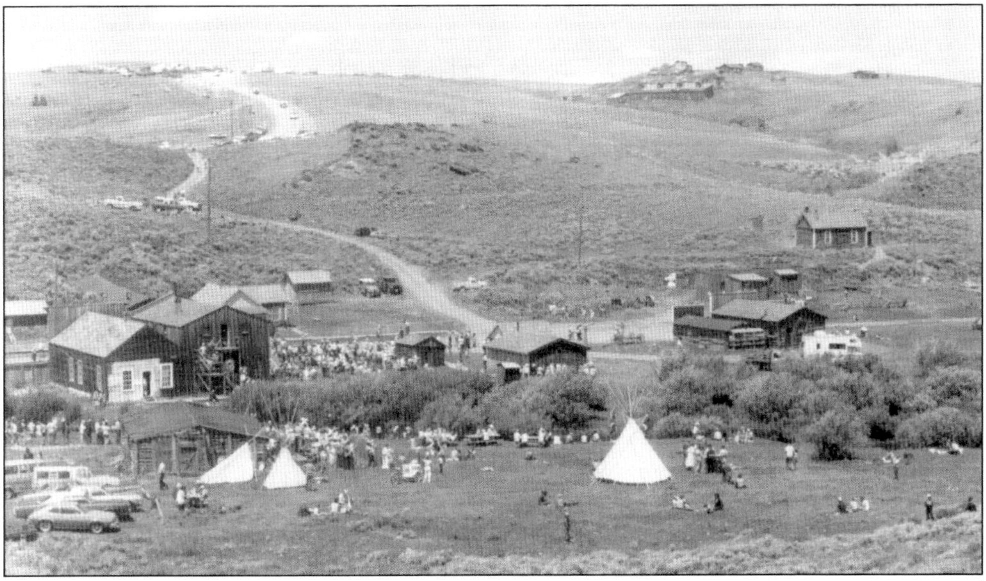

Fourth of July, Late 1970s. Since it first was opened to the public, people have eagerly accepted the opportunity to both learn and play in the historic surroundings. Much of the initial public investment in the town site consisted of establishing basic visitor services.

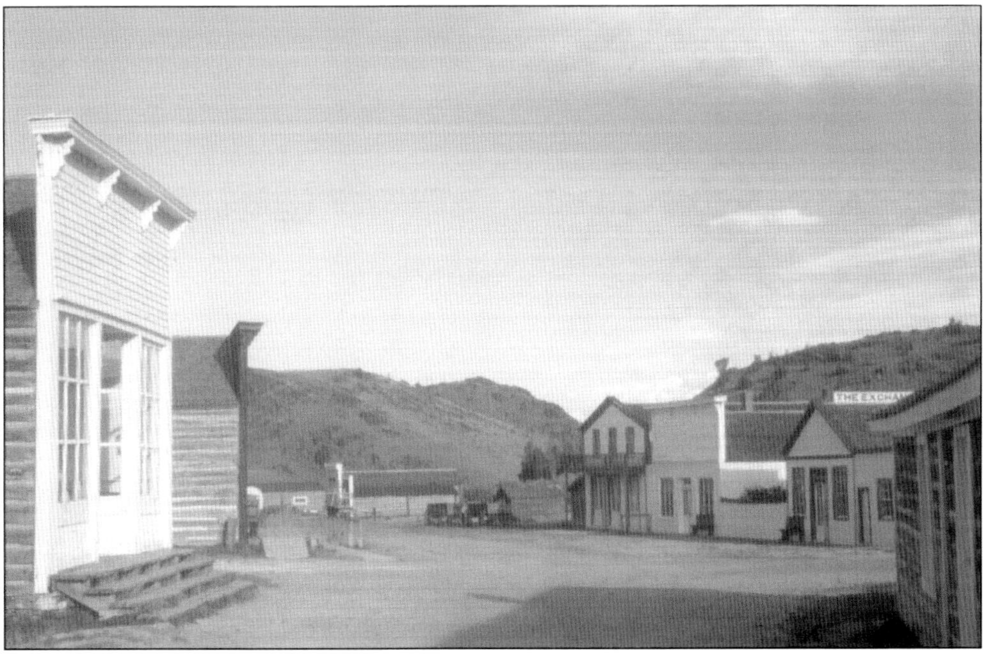

Main Street, Early 1980s. With the initial crush of preservation work past, the focus turned to exhibiting historic structures for the purpose of better acquainting visitors with the reality of frontier life of a century before.

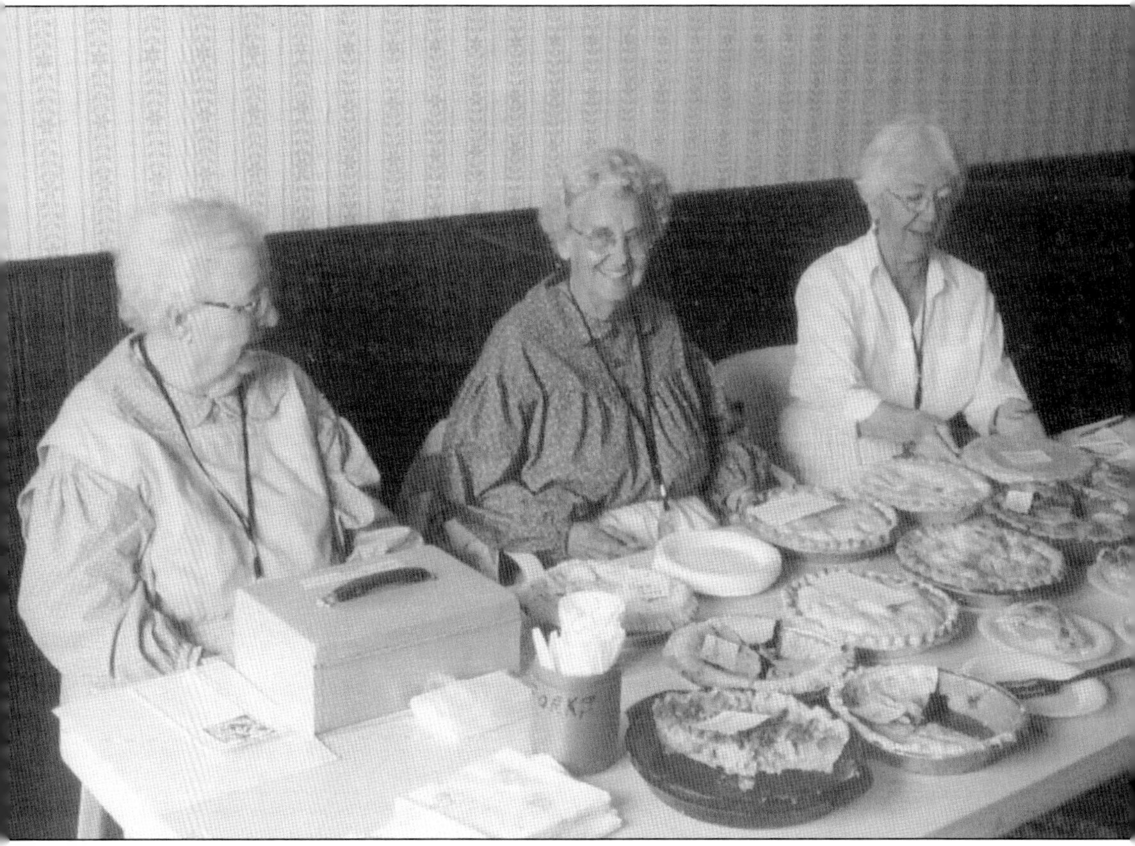

Friends of South Pass. From left to right are Ginger Norton, Pres. Donna Sherlock-Robeson, and Clydene Allen. The Friends are a nonprofit support group for the historic site. At Gold Rush Days every year in July, the Friends hold a bake sale. They also volunteer for school tours and special events at the site.

Baseball in South Pass City, 2001. Baseball has been a favorite local pastime since 1870, when the *South Pass News* reported that the South Pass City team was defeated by Atlantic City. Beginning in 2001, an annual tournament featuring 1900-era equipment and rules has been enjoyed by players and spectators alike. Teams representing South Pass City, Hudson, Lander, and Riverton compete.

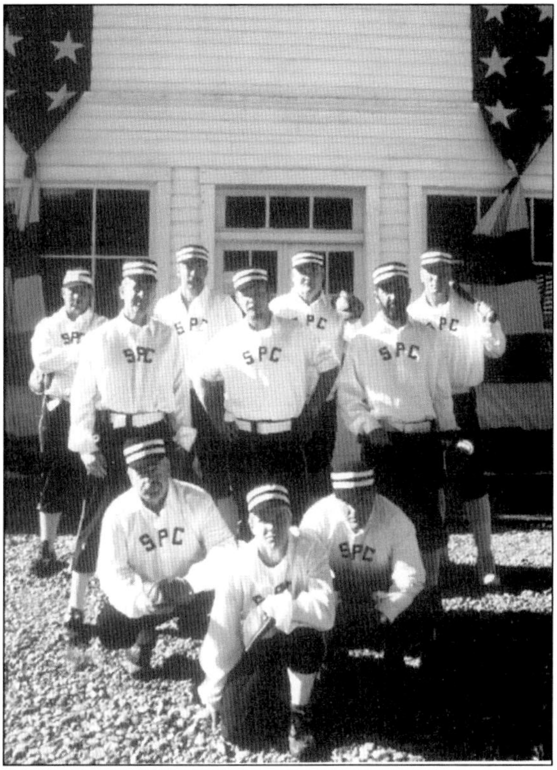

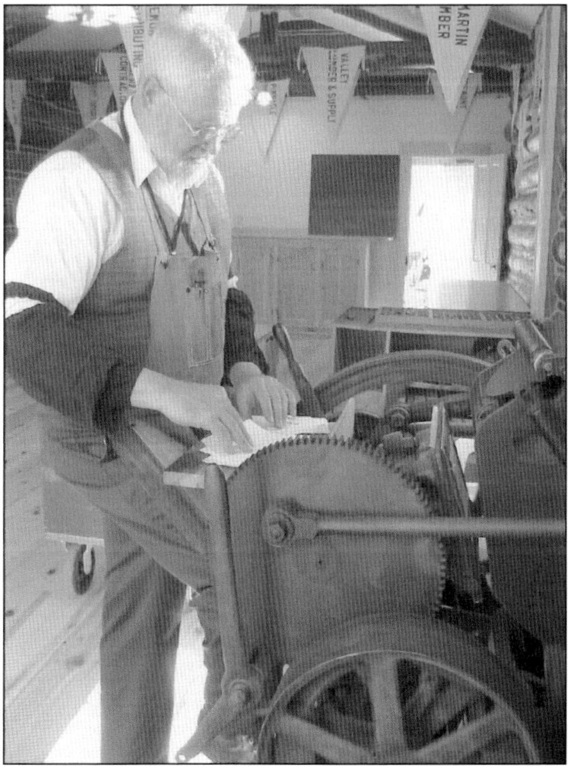

Historic Printing. Mike Parker demonstrates the function of a century-old printing press. Considerable skill is required to mount type, properly ink it, and maintain a press like those used in the early days by printers like "Archy" Slack.

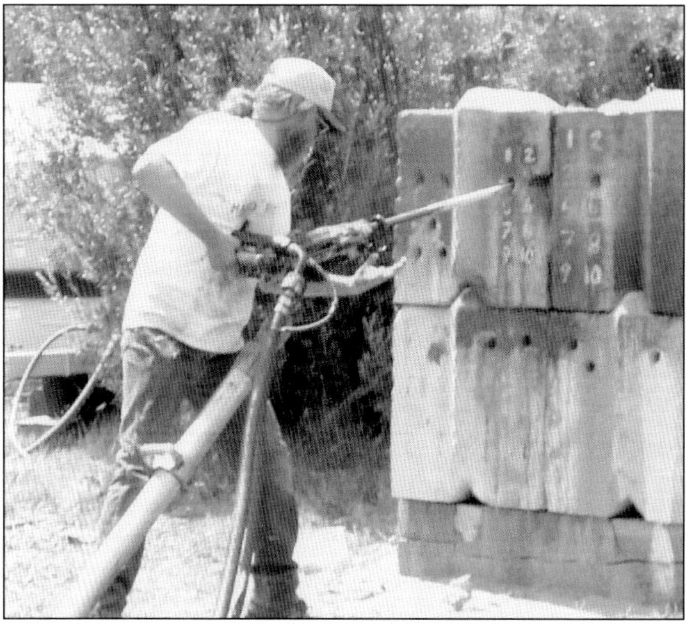

Jack Leg Drilling. Steve Gyorvary displays the function of a modern pneumatic drill. The Carissa Mine pioneered the use of early compressed air-driven models in the district around 1900. Gyorvary is a mine owner, mill operator, and historian.

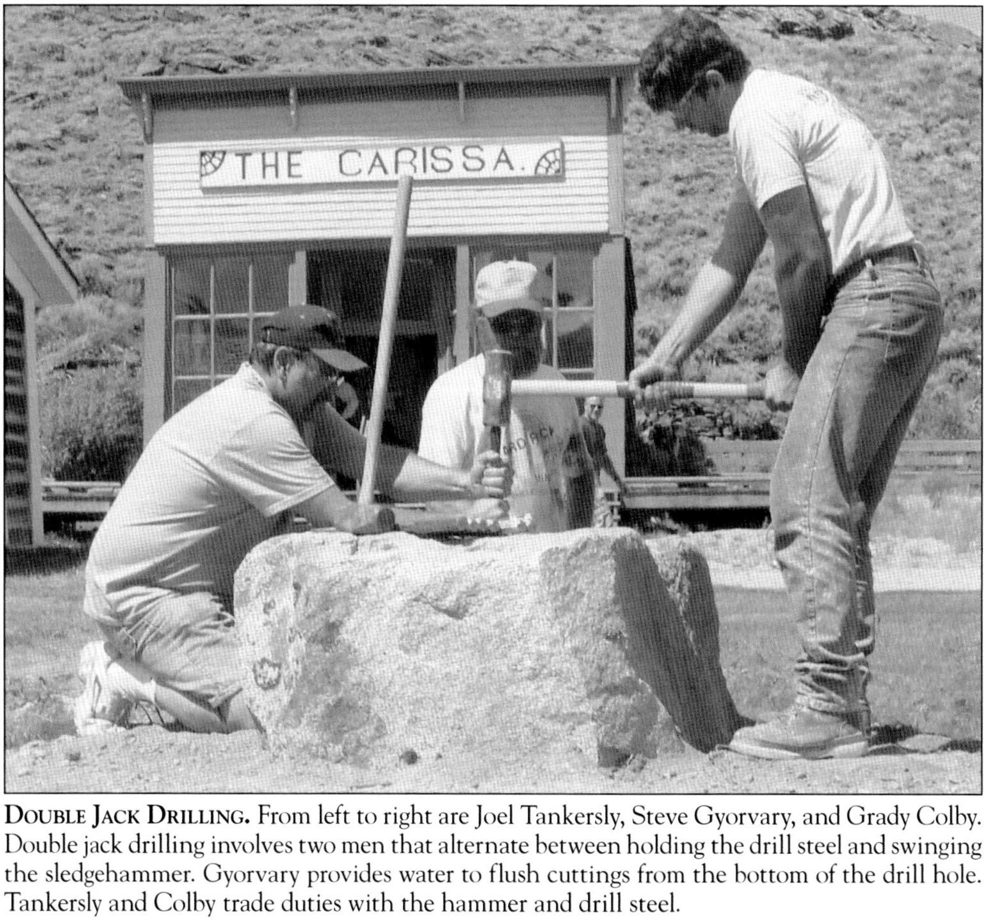

Double Jack Drilling. From left to right are Joel Tankersly, Steve Gyorvary, and Grady Colby. Double jack drilling involves two men that alternate between holding the drill steel and swinging the sledgehammer. Gyorvary provides water to flush cuttings from the bottom of the drill hole. Tankersly and Colby trade duties with the hammer and drill steel.

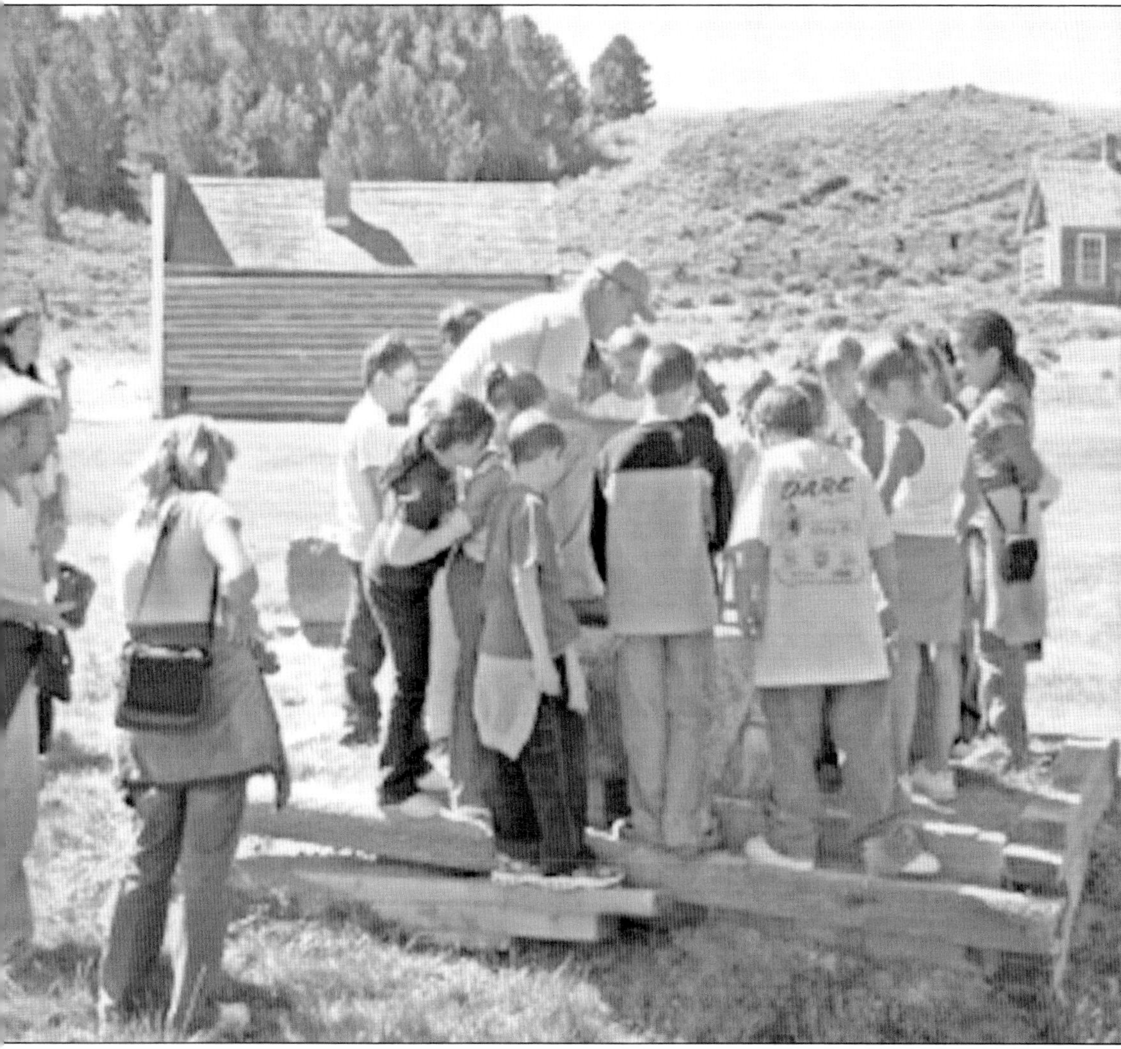

SCHOOL TOURS. Curator Jon Lane (center) demonstrates hand drilling to a group of schoolchildren. Spring and fall months bring daily school groups from all over the state to South Pass City. The groups learn about geology, mining, commerce, and social life of the town.

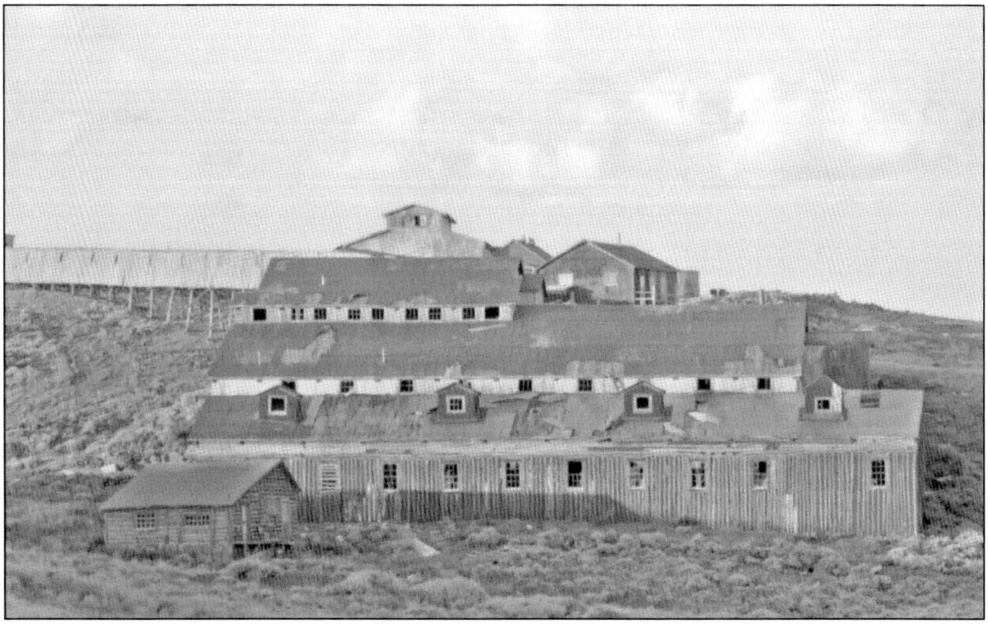

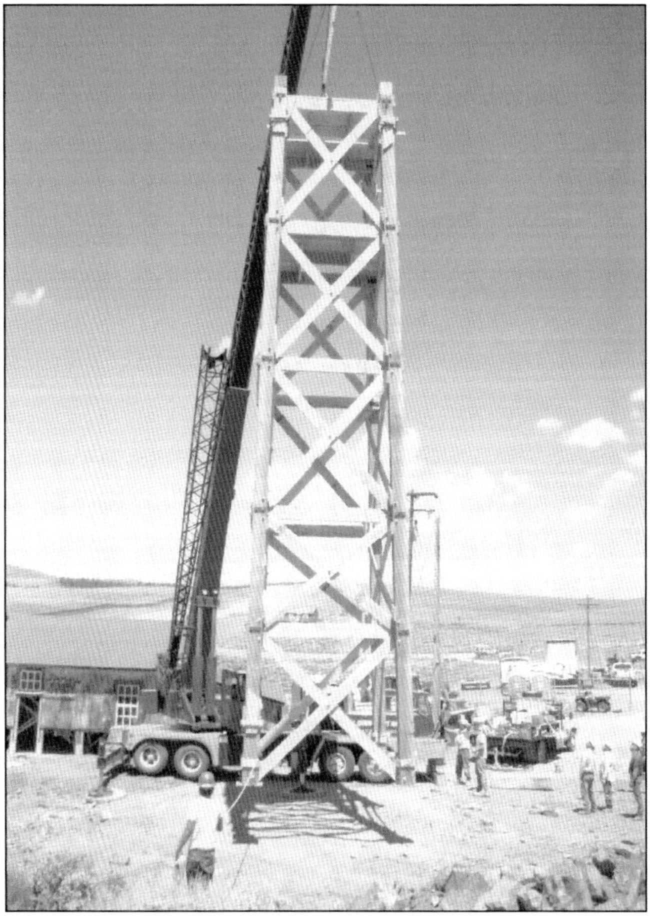

CARISSA MILL. State legislators realized the opportunity for the public when the Carissa was offered for sale in 2003. Prior to final state approval of the purchase, the Department of Environmental Quality's Abandoned Mine Lands Division examined the property for potential hazards that might jeopardize responsible stabilization and reclamation efforts. Since the purchase, Abandoned Mine Lands have worked to ensure public safety and protect historic resources and structures.

HEADFRAME, 2008. As a means of stabilizing and interpreting the Hoist House area, a replica of the original 1929 headframe was constructed. Providing safe public access to authentic experiences at the Carissa is the goal of a series of projects funded by public sources.

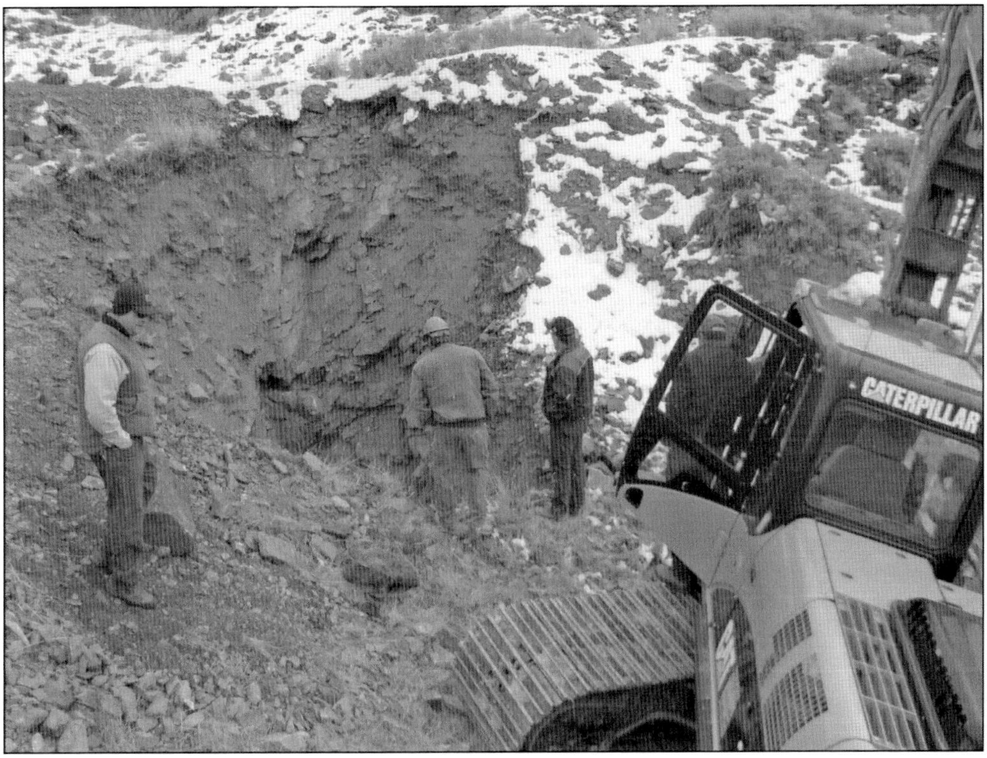

SUBSIDENCE STABILIZATION, 2010. The Carissa was an active mine site for nearly 90 years. As a result, the property was pocked with potentially hazardous features like old shafts, open pits, and caved-in underground workings. Abandoned Mine Lands evaluated these features, proposed remedies sensitive to the historic nature of the property, and implemented reasoned solutions.

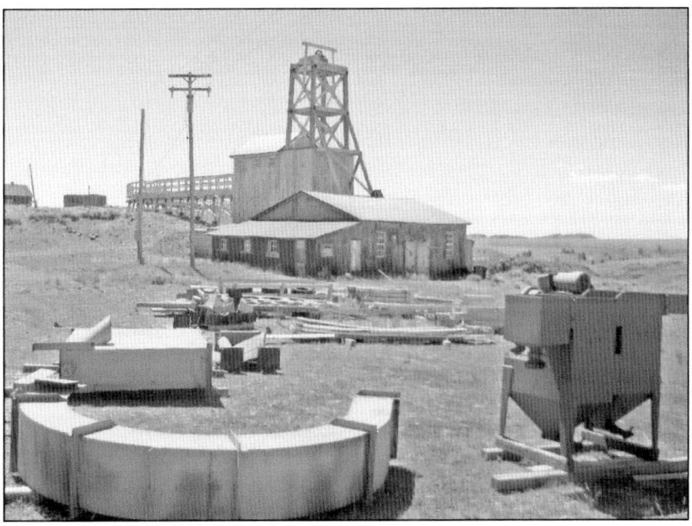

MILL EQUIPMENT, 2010. In the late 1950s, following the most recent gold production, a handful of key pieces of equipment was removed from the Carissa property. Crucial concepts in the recovery of gold from host rock hinge on the limited demonstration of functioning equipment for public tours. In 2008, the state legislature permitted limited funding for reequipping the mill.

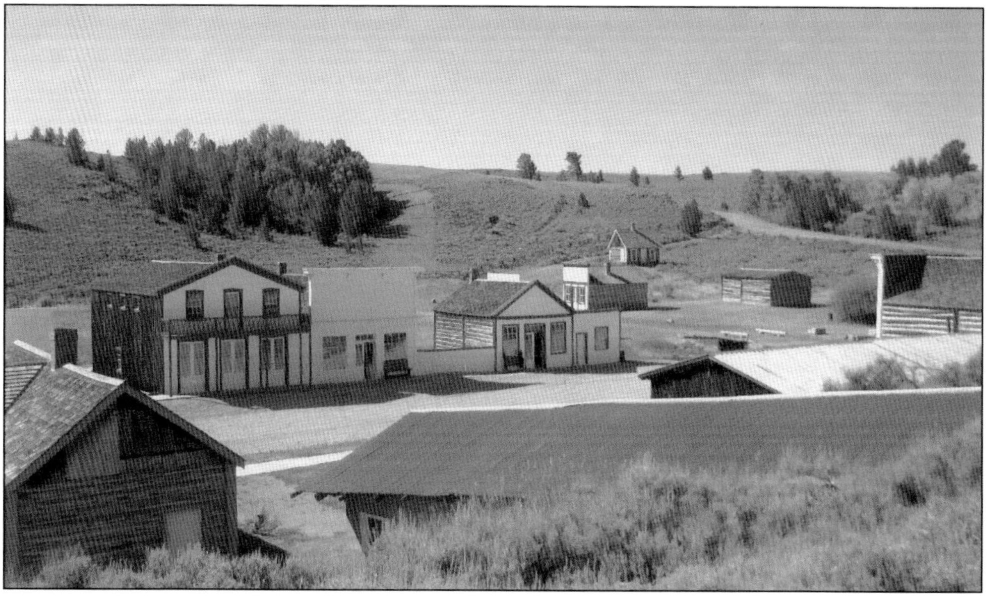

Main Street, 2010. Fresh paint, watertight roofs, and solid foundations help to ensure that the buildings and their stories will endure to inform future visitors to Wyoming's city of gold. The nearby geographic South Pass on the Continental Divide and the California, Oregon, Mormon, and Pony Express Trails provide visitors an opportunity to view the Old West.

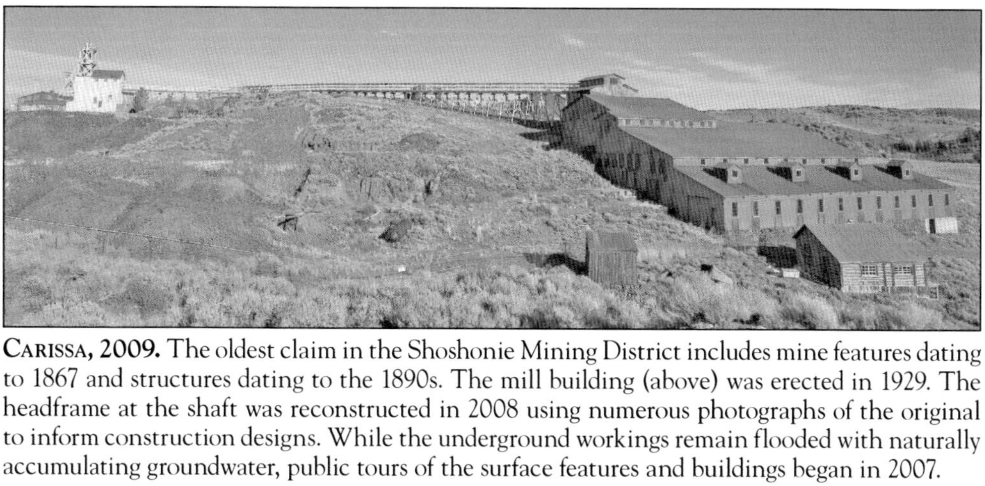

Carissa, 2009. The oldest claim in the Shoshonie Mining District includes mine features dating to 1867 and structures dating to the 1890s. The mill building (above) was erected in 1929. The headframe at the shaft was reconstructed in 2008 using numerous photographs of the original to inform construction designs. While the underground workings remain flooded with naturally accumulating groundwater, public tours of the surface features and buildings began in 2007.

Bibliography

Armstrong, F.C. *Preliminary Report on the Geology of Atlantic City–South Pass Mining District, Wyoming.* United States Geological Survey, 1948.

Bane, J.R. *Report on the B&H Mining Company.* Wyoming Geological Mineral Report, unpublished, 1929.

Coutant, C.G. *The History of Wyoming.* Laramie, WY: Chaplin, Spafford and Mathison Printers, 1899.

Hausel, W. Dan. *Economic Geology of the South Pass Granite-Greenstone Belt, Southern Wind River Range, Western Wyoming.* Laramie, WY: Wyoming State Geological Survey, 1991.

Homsher, Lola M. *South Pass, 1868.* Lincoln, NE: University of Nebraska Press, 1960.

Huseas, Marion McMillan. *Sweetwater Gold.* Cheyenne, WY: Cheyenne Corral of Westerners International Publishers, 1991.

Jamison, C.E. *The Geology and Mineral Resources of a Portion Fremont County, Wyoming.* Geological Survey of Wyoming, Bulletin 2, 1911.

Larson, T.A. *History of Wyoming.* Lincoln, NE: University of Nebraska Press, 1965.

McDermott, John D. *Dangerous Duty.* Fremont County, WY: The Fremont County Historic Preservation Commission, 1993.

Raymond, Rossiter Worthington. *Statistics of Mines and Mining in the States and Territories West of the Rocky Mountains*, Document 207, 41st Congress, Second Session, 1870.

Pfaff, Betty Carpenter. *Atlantic City Nuggets.* Kemmerer, WY: 1978.

———. *Fine Gold*, Kemmerer, WY: 1997.

Sherlock, James L. *South Pass and Its Tales.* New York, NY: Vantage Press, Inc., 1978.

Wyoming State Archives and Historical Department, *Wyoming Blue Book, Volumes I–V.* Cheyenne, WY: Unicover Graphics Corporation, 1974.

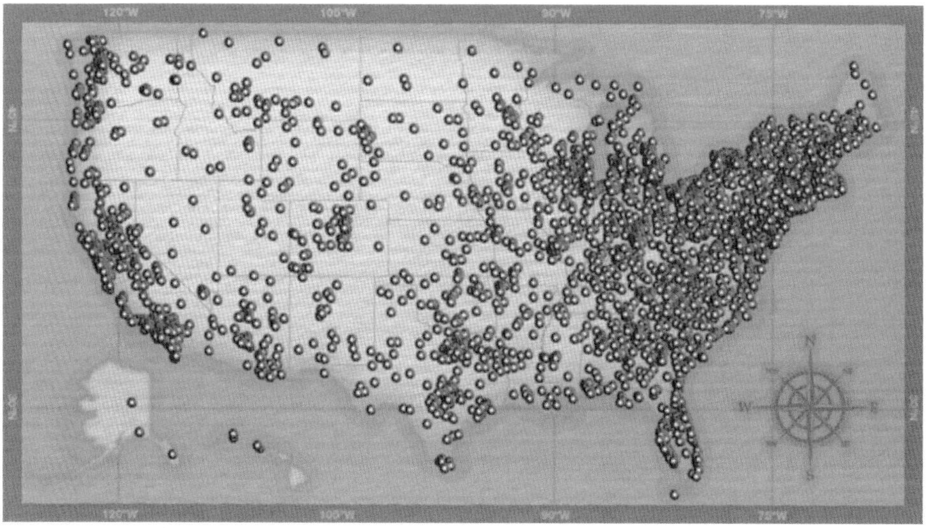